DYNASTY
The Oral History of
the New York Islanders
1972-1984

DYNASTY
The Oral History of
the New York Islanders
1972-1984

Greg Prato

Printed and distributed by Greg Prato
Published by Greg Prato
Front cover photo by Kurt Christensen [kurtchristensen.com]
Back cover photo by Steve Donnelly
Copyright © 2012, Greg Prato. All rights reserved.
First Edition, September 2012

ISBN 978-0-615-86706-9

Introduction

I can remember the very first New York Islanders game I ever watched quite clearly. On the afternoon of May 24th, 1980, my father was going over to our next door neighbor's house in North Merrick, New York, and I followed him along. I wasn't the biggest fan of sports at that point (I was only eight years old), but what I watched that afternoon was pretty darn exciting - game six of the Stanley Cup Finals, between the New York Islanders and the Philadelphia Flyers. I recall everything was going pretty smoothly for the first two periods, but by the third period, the jolly mood in the room turned sour, as the game was all tied and headed for overtime. And then, when Bob Nystrom scored the game winner, I joined everyone in the room jumping up out of their chair in celebration.

I wish I could say that I was a loyal Islanders fan from that point on, but following sports hadn't grabbed a hold of yours truly just yet. But I was very impressed one year later, when I heard on the schoolyard that the Islanders had won another Stanley Cup. However, this would all change on the evening of April 13th, 1982. I heard in another room of my house my father sounding not so happy about what he was watching on the television. It turns out it was the deciding game five of the division semi-finals, between the Islanders and the Pittsburgh Penguins, and the Islanders appeared to be blowing it. I took a seat and watched the Islanders dramatic comeback and victory, and from that point on, I was hooked - I rarely missed watching an Islanders game on TV over the next few years, and thoroughly studied the team's history.

What transpired over the next couple of years was total dominance by the Islanders in the NHL. And the stage was set perfectly for what was dubbed "The Drive for Five," as the Islanders took a shot in 1984 at tying the Montreal Canadiens record of winning five consecutive Stanley Cups. But for reasons you'll read all about in chapters 32 and 33, sadly, it was not meant to be.

Even sadder was that the Islanders were unable to sustain their regular Stanley Cup Final appearances throughout the '80s. And except for a blip here and there (1993, 2002), the Islanders haven't recreated the magic and buzz of their 1980-1983 dynasty. Whenever I talk to people nowadays about the Islanders of the early '80s, I compare them to the New York Yankees of the late '90s/early 21st century, insomuch that the Islanders spoiled their fans - no lead by their opponent was insurmountable and no foe was too intimidating. And in the process, the Islanders created a true *dynasty*.

It's impossible to express the great memories I have of watching the Islanders dominate their opponents on a nightly basis, and what seemed like the inevitable Stanley Cup Finals win at the end of the year. Looking back, the Islanders' Stanley Cup wins remain some of the great memories of my childhood. Hence, I could not think of a better way of paying tribute to one of my favorite all-time teams than by interviewing nearly 30 people that were associated with the Islanders from 1972-1984, and have them tell their true story - straight from the source.

Lets Go Islanders!
Greg Prato

p.s. Comments/questions? Email me at gregprato@yahoo.com.

p.p.s. I'd like to thank the following people, who proved to be a great help in putting this book together - Terry Goldstein (Islanders' Director of Retail Operations), Kimber Auerbach (Islanders' Director of Communications), Brian Fisher (MSG Network), Jimmy Devellano, Eddie Westfall, Bob Nystrom, Clark Gillies, Gary Dell'Abate, and photographers Steve Donnelly and Kurt Christensen. Thanks guys!

Cast of Characters

AL ARBOUR - The Islanders' head coach from 1973-1986 and 1988-1994

CLAIRE ARBOUR - Wife of Al Arbour

BRUCE BENNETT - NHL photographer

BOB BOURNE - The Islanders' center from 1974-1988

GARY "BABA BOOEY" DELL'ABATE - Islanders fan, SportsChannel intern from 1980-81, 'Howard Stern Show' producer

JIMMY DEVELLANO - The Islanders' Eastern Canada Scout from 1972-1974, Director of Scouting from 1974-1982, and Assistant General Manager from 1981-1982

NELSON DOUBLEDAY, JR. - Partial shareholder of the Islanders

STAN FISCHLER - The Islanders' television broadcaster

PAT FLATLEY - The Islanders' right winger from 1984-1996

CLARK GILLIES - The Islanders' left winger from 1974-1986

BILLY HARRIS - The Islanders' right winger from 1972-1980

LORNE HENNING - The Islanders' center from 1972-1981, Islanders assistant coach from 1981-1984, 1989-1995, 2000-2001, Islanders head coach 1994-1995

GORD LANE - The Islanders' defenseman from 1979-1985

DAVE LANGEVIN - The Islanders' defenseman from 1979-1985

BOB LORIMER - The Islanders' defenseman from 1976-1981

JIGGS McDONALD - The Islanders' television broadcaster

MIKE McEWEN - The Islanders' defenseman from 1981-1984

KEN MORROW - The Islanders' defenseman from 1980-1989

BOB NYSTROM - The Islanders' right winger from 1972-1986, father of Dallas Stars left winger Eric Nystrom

JP PARISÉ - The Islanders' left winger from 1975-1978, father of Minnesota Wild left winger Zach Parisé

JIM PICKARD - The Islanders' assistant trainer and equipment manager from 1972-1973, 1974-1990

JEAN POTVIN - The Islanders' defenseman from 1973-1978, 1979-1981

GLENN "CHICO" RESCH - The Islanders' goaltender from 1973-1981

DUANE SUTTER - The Islanders' right winger from 1979-1987

BILL TORREY - The Islanders' general manager from 1972-1992

BRYAN TROTTIER - The Islanders' center from 1975-1990

RON WASKE - The Islanders' head trainer from 1975-1984

EDDIE WESTFALL - The Islanders' right winger from 1972-1979, captain from 1972-1978, television broadcaster

Contents

CHAPTER 1:

WELCOME TO THE ISLAND

Up until 1972, if you were a hockey fan in Long Island, New York, you only had one real choice when it came to rooting for a local team - the New York Rangers, who occupied Madison Square Garden. But that all changed when it was announced that the Long Island-based New York Islanders would join the NHL for the 1972-73 season, and would call Nassau Coliseum their home.

BILL TORREY [The Islanders' general manager from 1972-1992]: I was born and raised in Montreal, and went to school there. I started playing hockey in an outdoor rink one block away from my house. We lived on Atwater Avenue, about four blocks away from the Montreal Forum. I spent an awful lot of time in my youth in that building. Got chased out of there I don't know how many times. You have to understand, back in those days, the Forum not only had the Montreal Canadiens, but they had the Montreal Royals, which were a top-flight amateur team. Many of the Canadiens started with that team, and then went up. There were four Junior A teams, that also played in the Forum, and they had doubleheader junior games. So I used to go to all those games. The Montreal Junior Canadiens, the Verdun Maple Leafs, the Montreal Nationals, and the Montreal Royals. There was lots of hockey in the building. So I just started playing in the house leagues at that rink and played on the school teams.

See, there was no draft in those days - anybody that signed up to play in any of the city or the provincial leagues, when they turned 18 had to sign a "C-form," and they were all property of the Montreal Canadiens. Montreal had all of the province of Quebec; the Maple

Leafs had most of Ontario - other than Kitchener and a few other cities. The Rangers had all of Manitoba and part of Saskatchewan, and Detroit had Edmonton, Alberta, and most of that province. It was totally different than the draft and the organization that you have today. So I played school and junior in Montreal, and then I went to St. Lawrence University and played college hockey at St. Lawrence for three years.

After I left St. Lawrence, I got a job as the business manager and PR man for the Pittsburgh Hornets, because that was before the expansion of 1967. I was with the Hornets for six years, until expansion came in '67/'68. Then I became the vice president and GM of the Oakland Seals. I was with the Oakland Seals for three years. And then I got into a disagreement with the owner, Charles Finley, and left there. I had been told that there was going to be an expansion in 1972 in Atlanta, and probably, Long Island. I was interested in the general manager's job, and interviewed both, and decided to come to Long Island.

The expansion decision was made in January, and my hiring didn't come until late February. So the amount of time we had to prepare for the coming season was not like the previous expansions, where the teams had over a year to prepare. So that made things a little bit difficult. And of course, in 1972, the WHA [World Hockey Association] all of a sudden decided that this was the right time for them to start their league. So we had to contend with the fact that there was a whole new league starting up, in the signing of players.

STAN FISCHLER [The Islanders' television broadcaster]: I got involved with hockey when I was seven. My father took me to a Rovers game - the Rangers had a farm team called the Rovers. They played at the old Garden on Sunday afternoons, and I fell in love with the game instantly. I was very fortunate that he took me to games. And then when I was old enough to go alone, I went alone. My first NHL game was in '42, when I was ten, Rangers/Blackhawks. And I never stopped going.

This was at a time when NHL expansion was flowering. I was covering when it went from six to twelve teams in 1967, and there was some doubt about whether it would work. Of course, teams like Oakland did go under. But others, like Philly and Minnesota, did OK. Then it was Buffalo and Vancouver. But what was interesting was hockey had become so popular that the second league, the World Hockey Association, challenged the NHL, and they declared their first season in '72-'73, which was when the Islanders and Atlanta got into the NHL. So it was a very a fascinating, turbulent time. And the Islanders were challenged, because guys that they would have wanted were also being signed by the WHA.

JIMMY DEVELLANO [The Islanders' Eastern Canada Scout from 1972-1974, Director of Scouting from 1974-1982, and Assistant General Manager from 1981-1982]: I'm from Toronto, Canada. When I was 24 years of age in 1966, I wrote a letter to the general manager of a new expansion team, the St. Louis Blues, wanting to be a scout. He hired me. I was with the St. Louis Blues for five years - their first five years in expansion - and got fired. I got fired mainly due to a personality clash with the head scout at the time. That summer, two new expansion teams were coming in - the New York Islanders and the Atlanta Flames. The general manager for the Islanders was Bill Torrey. I met him and he hired me to be their Eastern Canada scout.

BILL TORREY: Roy Boe was the general partner of the Islanders - he was the general partner of the Nets [a basketball team that was part of ABA/American Basketball Association], and he had a great number of limited partners. Part of the deal that was made to get the building in Nassau is that the colors had to be the same as the county's colors, which are blue and orange. So, the color scheme was set and agreed to by Mr. Boe, when he secured a lease on the Nassau Coliseum [located in Uniondale]. As to the logo, that was designed by an advertising agency in Garden City. Again, the idea was to tie in the Island and where the Islanders were located, to separate it from the New York Rangers.

STAN FISCHLER: Roy Boe was one of the most flamboyant characters in sports. There were guys over the years, like Larry MacPhail with the Brooklyn Dodgers, George Steinbrenner more recently with the Yankees. Boe was a sportsman - liked to take big gambles, like what he did with the team.

JIMMY DEVELLANO: My impressions of Roy Boe was he was a terrific guy. A good guy, a well-meaning guy, who got over-extended. He had too many balls in the air. I don't know if you know the history of the Nets - his ABA team. Going into the NBA merger, and the kind of money that the indemnification cost him to do that. Plus, he had to indemnify the Rangers with the Islanders for their "invasion" of their territory. He couldn't handle it financially.

BILL TORREY: I liked Roy personally very much. He loved sports. He and his family were very much involved in the team when he was running it. But he was basically "a basketball man." He had the Nets already, and the Nets were already in the Coliseum when we started play in the fall. He wasn't terribly knowledgeable about hockey, but he was a big time fan, and really liked the players and liked to be around the team. Unfortunately, our financial situation was such that running both teams put a great strain on him. He eventually had to give up the Islanders and sell the Nets, because he could not financially support them. But he was a very personable man.

JIMMY DEVELLANO: We looked for big, strong guys, that had ability and talent. And lots of character. And we had loads of them on the Islanders.

CHAPTER 2:

LET'S BUILD A TEAM

With the fledgling World Hockey Association snatching both young talent and veterans from the National Hockey League, the pickings were slim for the fledgling Islanders to construct a strong team. But several names that would eventually become major contributors are welcomed on board.

BILL TORREY: All of a sudden, it was a go. I wasn't "on the job" so to speak, until February. Needless to say, there was no office. There wasn't even a pencil, as far as the Islanders were concerned. We started from scratch, literally. I hired Estelle Ellery as my secretary. I knew her from the American Hockey League - her husband had been the public relations director for the American Hockey League. She lived in Long Island, and was working in the ticket office for the Nets. She was the only person that knew what a puck, a stick, and ice were about! So she was my first hire, and one of my most important, because I had to get on the road and start scouting, and looking for personnel and staff. I didn't spend a lot of time on Long Island in the office - I was on the road for the next three months.

STAN FISCHLER: I covered the Islanders' very first press conference, when they drafted Billy Harris as their first pick. I got to know Bill Torrey. Bill Torrey and I didn't get along at the beginning, because I was critical - I didn't think Harris was that good a choice. And I guess I was a little bit over-critical. Later on, we became very, very good friends, and still are. Once they started to play, I covered them, because I was writing for The Hockey News.

BILLY HARRIS [The Islanders' right winger from 1972-1980]: I grew up in the suburbs of Toronto, started out basically in public school here in Canada. We had teams, so I was on the school team in grade four. And then I went into a house league, and from there I went into the Marlie system [the Toronto Marlboros] - which was owned by the Toronto Maple Leafs - at twelve years old. We practiced at Maple Leaf Gardens and I had to take the bus, the subway, and a streetcar - because my dad was a cop, he couldn't take me to a lot of the practices. Or we'd have other parents that would drive to the games. Playing in the Marlie system at that age was quite an accomplishment, and the beauty of it was they supplied all the equipment. When you're a young kid at twelve years old and you're getting all your gear supplied - skates, sticks - it was pretty nice to have good equipment. Even though it was second-hand, it was all top-notch. I think I was wearing George Armstrong skates, and we had gloves that were handed down from other Marlies teams. It was quite a unique system.

I just barely made the team as a twelve-year-old in the Pee Wee League. I got bigger, stronger, and quicker, and started playing Junior A, which is still in the Toronto Marlboro system. We'd play all our junior games at Maple Leaf Gardens, and they kept calling me up to play Junior A, and I was playing Junior B. I finally said to them, "Listen, am I doing to play Junior A or Junior B?" I didn't want to play on both teams, because you play full-time Junior A when you're 15 years old, you get $45 a week, plus about $30 a month they give you for gas money. And they paid for all your school books and supplies. And if you were going to university, they paid for that, as well. It was a big jump. So at 15, I started playing Junior A, and I ended up having four years of Junior A, which most people don't play four years. But it was quite an experience playing with 20-year-old guys. Because they didn't draft 18-year-olds back then - you were drafted at 19 or 20.

So we were playing against some pretty good hockey players. The Montreal Junior Canadiens, their first line was Gilbert Perreault, Réjean Houle, and Marc Tardif. I mean, that's an all-star line. And then their second line was Richard Martin - they could have played in the NHL, that team. It was quite a learning experience for me. It got me so I was able to be drafted. I sort of had thoughts on going to college, because my three older sisters all got university degrees, and my father wanted all the kids to go to college. So I thought, "That's a good way to go - a hockey scholarship." I didn't get one college scholarship offer, because all the scouts figured, "There's no chance of him coming to college - he's going to be drafted pretty high." That extra year in junior, I won the scoring championship, so I knew I was going to be drafted, but I didn't know I was going to be drafted number one. That was probably the biggest surprise.

Cliff Fletcher [the GM for the Atlanta Flames] talked quite a bit to the scouts, and said they were going to try and draft me because the WHA was just starting to come into existence, and there was talk of it, and Bobby Hull had signed with Winnipeg. So it gave me a little bit of leverage. Not as much as the guys coming up the next year had, because the league was already up and running. But anyway, he and Bill Torrey were going to get together and flip a coin, and decide who was going to get the first pick, because then they could start planning around who they were going to draft second, third, and fourth.

So about a month and a half before the draft, I get a call on a Sunday night. I'll never forget it - my dad answers the phone, it's 10:00 at night. He says, "Hey, there's a call for you." "What do you mean there's a call for me at 10:00 at night? Who's calling me on a Sunday night?" And my dad's got his hand over the receiver, and says, "He says he's Bill Torrey from the New York Islanders." And I go, *"Oh shit.* Guess that means I'm going to New York - they must have flipped the coin." [Laughs] I'd never met Bill at that point in time, but I'd met Cliff quite a few times, and he was really building up Atlanta, as far as a city to play in, the climate, and the whole deal. So I ended up coming to New York, and I couldn't tell anybody that I was drafted number one, because we were still in the playoffs - we were still playing Junior A and I'm still in school.

Bill is a great guy, and Ed Chadwick - the head scout at the time, he's the one who scouted me. I still see Ed Chadwick to this day. In fact, he lives in Fort Erie - he's 78, I think. He was a class act and Bill was a class act. I think a lot of people are misled about Long Island, because they figure, "New York" Islanders. They have no idea. I had lots of friends and family come down to New York, I'd pick them up at the airport, and we'd start driving east, and they're going, "Holy shit, this is beautiful!" It's not the image you have of New York, of the concrete jungle, the high-rises, and all the craziness. There are beautiful little towns, there's no high-rises, and it's residential. That was a pleasant surprise to see all that.

LORNE HENNING [The Islanders' center from 1972-1981, Islanders assistant coach from 1981-1984, 1989-1995, 2000-2001, Islanders head coach 1994-1995]: I'm from Melfort, Saskatchewan. I played Junior B in North Battleford, Saskatchewan, and then Junior A in Estevan. My last year of junior, I went to New Westminster - Ernie McLean was my coach. From there, I got drafted 17th overall by the Islanders. And I was there from their inception in 1972.

BOB NYSTROM [The Islanders' right winger from 1972-1986]: I was drafted in the third round, after Billy Harris and Lorne Henning. I was born in Sweden, and then I moved to a small town in Western Canada, called Hinton, Alberta. Pretty much everyone played hockey. My friends really introduced me to hockey. I originally started off playing youth hockey, and then I was recruited. Somebody had seen me play in the small town of Jasper, which was about 45 miles from where I lived. They asked me to come down and try out for the Kamloops Rockets. So I left home when I was 16. I tried out for the team and made the team. I actually lived with a family in Kamloops, until the next year, I moved out to what's called "Tier I," or the Western Canada Hockey League, and started playing in Calgary. I played there for two years, and then was drafted by the Islanders when I was 19. It was the year that they were coming into existence. They built the building, and this was their first draft.

 The first thought that I had was…I didn't know where the heck Long Island was. And the second thought I had was it was like a city. The only thing that I had read about New York was crime and shootings. I was a little tentative. But I came down in July of that year to sign my contract, and I stayed with my agent over in Freeport. I was absolutely dumbfounded by the beauty of Long Island - the beaches, everything. It was truly a great experience. From that point on, I pretty much stayed down here.

BILL TORREY: Ed Westfall was probably the best player that was available in the draft. He was our first pick as an expansion player. First of all, he was coming from the Boston Bruins, who the previous year had won the Stanley Cup. So he was fully aware of what it took to win a Stanley Cup, which is obviously your ultimate goal. He was a very, very versatile player. He wasn't a high scorer, but he was a great penalty killer. He could play left wing, right wing, center. Actually, when he started in the NHL, he came in the league in Boston as a defenseman. So he was very versatile. When you're short in many areas like we were that year, he was very valuable. And we made him the captain.

EDDIE WESTFALL [The Islanders' right winger from 1972-1979, captain from 1972-1978, television broadcaster]: Like all the guys from my era, we grew up across Canada and just played street hockey, pond hockey, and minor hockey. And then I suppose it was a process of as you got more recognition, you wanted more of it. So you worked harder at it and you got a trophy, which was a big deal back then, because they didn't give out trophies to everybody. My love of the game - like everybody my age, we all tried hard. Mine seemed to progress maybe a little quicker than some of the other kids. I suppose it would be similar to an academic student, where they move them along. Years ago, they didn't just move them along by age. They moved them along by ability. So I was playing in the leagues a little more advanced than my age. I was suited for the ability, which is what happens to most guys when they're starting to become recognized and may have potential for the next level.

So I went through all that, and that was in Oshawa, Ontario. Then I went to junior hockey. I went for a tryout when I was 15 and I joined the Barrie Flyers at 16 and played for four years. Actually, three years in Barrie, and they moved the team. Hap Emms was the owner, coach, and the general manager. They moved the team to Niagara Falls, and it became the Niagara Falls Flyers. Then my first year out of junior hockey, I made the Boston Bruins. And that was the next eleven years of my life, until '72, and ended up being taken by Bill Torrey in the NHL Expansion Draft - the first player out of there was me. I had to leave what I thought was security in Boston for the unknown of New York, in Long Island.

The first reaction is that [Westfall's family] wanted to see what my reaction was. In and of themselves, they were disappointed. My kids were old enough to understand all that. They actually found out before I did! I was on a trip to England, Scotland, and Ireland with my parents, and it was announced while we over there. Of course, I didn't know it until I came through customs and immigration in Boston, and my kids were standing outside the glass with tears in their eyes. I was like, "Boy, there's a 'welcome home'." I actually found out from a customs and immigration officer in Boston, that I was no longer a Bruin. The reaction was mixed emotions. "Glad you're home, mom and dad. But dad, *you're out of work.*" [Laughs]

I knew of Bill Torrey, and I probably had met him when he was with the Golden Seals in California. He worked with some people that I happened to meet later - the original owners of the Golden Seals. And Torrey happened to be the general manager. Barry Van Gerbig was one of them. He was a fairly well known college goaltender. Torrey had come out of the ice skating business and into the hockey business. He was in Pittsburgh in the Ice Capades, I believe. Anyway, he was the general manager, and then Charlie Finley bought that team. I knew who Torrey was, so when he drafted me, I came down to Long Island to meet with him. There was a World Hockey Association start-up too, so I was negotiating with the New England Whalers, and with Bill Torrey and Roy Boe. But after I met with Torrey and Roy Boe, I had a different feeling about coming to Long Island.

JIM PICKARD [The Islanders' assistant trainer and equipment manager from 1972-1973, 1974-1990]: At the beginning, we were called assistant trainers. I'm originally from a small town near Niagara Falls, Ontario, called Queenston. It's a town of 500 people. I was interested in hockey forever, and didn't really play much, because my little village wouldn't accept kids from my little town or outside of Niagara Falls area to go up and play and take spots in their deal. So we couldn't play really. It was always outdoors, pretty much. I was interested in golf, and I got a job at a golf course after school and in the summers. And my boss turned out to be Kenny Carson, who at the time was the trainer for the Rochester Americans - previously with the Niagara Falls Flyers of the Junior A. He ended up being the first trainer with the Pittsburgh Penguins.

And the second year of expansion, which would have been '68/'69, his pal, who was also a trainer with Niagara Falls, got the job in Oakland, with the Seals. And they were looking for an assistant trainer. Back in those days, there wasn't a whole lot involved, and Kenny liked me and asked if I would be interested. I said, "Are you kidding? Of course!" So I went there - I was in Oakland for four years. Mr. Torrey was there. When he got the job with the Islanders, he asked if I would come. I did - I was there the first year. I was 22 years old then. I had a brand new daughter, she was born when I was at training camp in Peterborough in '72.

BILL TORREY: Since we had no prior development other than the amateur draft, our team was made up of players that we were able to draft in the expansion draft that year. And having been involved in a number of expansion drafts since, without question that was the toughest expansion draft - as far as getting quality players or NHL-type players. Of that expansion draft, we really only got four players that had any real NHL experience. All the rest were basically minor league players. And then on top of that, we had to contend with the fact that the WHA wanted to sign as many of the players that we drafted, because they were putting a WHA team in New York City, and they were out obviously to embarrass or make the appearance that they were a stronger franchise than we were. But I wasn't too concerned. I looked at the drafts that we had, I looked at the experience of the players we were given, and it was pretty evident that we weren't going to get very much youth out of those players. And basically, I told the ownership that in all probability, the Rangers at that time were one or two in the league as far as being a Stanley Cup contender. They had a very powerful line-up, and for us to try and compete with them right off the bat didn't make any sense. But I was going to concentrate on future and amateur drafts, because I knew that in the next two or three years, those drafts were going to produce some of the best prospects that the NHL had had since the draft was started.

JIMMY DEVELLANO: Well, we had an expansion team. We drafted 20 players in the expansion draft, of which we lost nine of them to the new World Hockey Association. So, we had a very, very bad team.

CHAPTER 3:

1972-73

Picture a hockey version of the Kelly Leak-less Bad News Bears, and you have an idea of what the Islanders' first-ever season was like.

EDDIE WESTFALL: Training camp wasn't even organized confusion…it was just *confusion*. Phil Goyette was our first coach, and I believe he didn't have any coaching experience. I felt a little tough for him, because he was kind of "hands on learning," as far as how to run a training camp in Peterborough, Ontario. That part was fine - it was close to where I grew up. But a lot of players didn't know each other. There weren't very many NHL players on that first team. And eleven of the drafted players jumped to the World Hockey Association. Now, whether they ever played - some of them did, some of them didn't - but they lost *eleven* of their draft picks that first year. It was slim pickings as far as getting any kind of competitive team together. When I look back at it, I probably come to the conclusion that the first two years, they didn't care, because they'd already drafted Billy Harris, and of course, Denis Potvin was the coveted draft pick coming up. We'd have messed them up big if we had finished a little higher up in the standings!

JIM PICKARD: We didn't have a regular practice facility, with our own locker room. So we'd dress at the Coliseum, and bus all the way out to Suffolk, up on the north shore. Probably a good 40/45 minutes. And after practice, they'd be all sweaty, and have to come back to the Coliseum on the bus. That wasn't a good set-up. On occasion, we practiced in New Hyde Park. One day we were there, and three teams were practicing, one right after the other - the Rangers, Montreal, and us. And I remember back in the day, they had "initiations." I remember Montreal was initiating somebody - I can't remember what player - and it wasn't a pleasant sight. Our then-trainer, a guy named Nick Garen, was from the Bronx and he had been with the Chicago Blackhawks for like 25 years. He would suit your guys up, and he always smoked a cigar. I remember him stitching up Terry Crisp - he had a cut up by his eye, and he stitched him up right in the lobby! Once again, in full gear. Right in the lobby, he's stitching him up with his cigar in his mouth.

BILLY HARRIS: We'd share basically two locker rooms. The New York Nets and ours were right next door to each other. We'd share a shower between us, so it was pretty lame. We could never practice at Nassau Coliseum, because they wouldn't pay the unions.

EDDIE WESTFALL: Once you've made up your mind that that's what you're going to do - and then they had selected me to be the captain of the team - you can't do anything other than try and carry a positive attitude into practices and games. The reason that they picked you was because you had leadership qualities, so you don't want to let everybody down. And I suppose having the most NHL experience when they drafted me, once I committed to that, I just wanted to be as good as I could be, as far as the captain, and trying to lead the team a little bit in all of the categories. I often said that with that crew, the "C" didn't stand for "captain," it stood for "cash" - I was forever lending money. [Laughs] But it was difficult for a professional athlete - I was coming from the best team in the NHL to *no* team. To the worst team. There were bumps in the road, but most of the guys, there was never a time I felt that they didn't try hard. They were all trying to earn a permanent job, and that was really the bottom line. Everybody was working hard at whatever level they were, as far as hockey players were concerned.

JIM PICKARD: Fantastic [in response to "How was Westfall as the Islanders' captain?"]. He included us in everything. He thought of everything that a captain should think of. He'd organize parties, and he was a good spokesman for the team. Always a gentleman. To this day I speak to Eddie.

BILLY HARRIS: Phil was out of his league as far as a coach. It didn't seem to make any sense - practices, the coaching. We didn't have a good team, but there were some practices where we just skated around the rink one way, and an hour the other way, and we'd be cutting through the ice to the concrete. That seemed a little extreme. We're not going to get any better just skating in a circle. The first season, I always said to some of my friends, "I wish I kept a journal." I could have written a book myself. It was just one comical thing happening after another. There were times when the bus driver...I think we were going over the Throgs Neck Bridge, we're going up to the Bronx. And I'm going, *"I'm sure the airport's not this way."* We'd get lost going to the airport! And then another time, Eastern Airlines had that shuttle service to Boston, and half the team got on one flight, and half the team got on another flight. We're taking off, and half the team is missing! And then there were the road trips - there was always stuff happening and going on.

It was such a cast of characters. Brian Spencer - that's one of the all-time lunatics. Nice guy, I knew him from Toronto. But he was whacked. He always carried guns in the trunk of his car - he carried *an arsenal*. We were at Kings Park, all the way out by Commack there, and he'd come over, and say, "Harry, Harry" - for some reason, my nickname changed from "Hinky" to "Harry." He calls me over to the trunk of his car, and he drove this old Valiant, and he goes, "Take a look at this!" And he opens up his jacket, and he's got this brand new revolver hanging under his armpit. I go, "Spencer, you can't take that in the locker room. Leave it in the trunk of your car." So he opens up the trunk, and I look in there. How many guys in New York or in the NHL carry a .458 Weatherby? I don't know if you know what that is - that will knock down an elephant. [Laughs] And the thing was, I think it might have been sort of legal for him to have them, because his first wife was from Oklahoma City, and I think he owned a piece of a sporting goods store there. So I think he could actually legally buy guns. But not too many people carry that big of an arsenal around. That was just one guy, then Ronnie Stewart.

Here's a guy, Ronnie Stewart, who played 20 years in the league - he's the guy that got into a fight with Terry Sawchuk, and ended up [allegedly] killing him. There were a lot of guys that were at the end of their career and then a lot of younger guys from the minor leagues. They were just characters, like Brian Lavender, and practical jokers.

You never knew what they were going to do. Terry Crisp's kids were real terrors. They were ripping around the locker room, so I think Brian had to come off the ice for some reason. So we come in after practice, and here's Terry Crisp's kids, all taped up to the pole in the middle of the locker room! [Laughs] He took rolls and rolls of tape and taped them to the pole.

There was one time that Eddie Westfall, Craig Cameron, and I were in Oakland - the Oakland Seals were in the league, and we're going up into the wine country to go to dinner. There's a place up there that was an old brothel, and it's famous for its prime rib - it's a restaurant, it wasn't operating as a brothel. This big old fat broad, Juanita, was running it. So we get out of the car, we've got some cans of Budweiser. And all of a sudden, "You can't bring those goddamn beers in here! You've got to buy them in here!" So we get rid of those, we go in there, we have a great meal. Well, this was when they had that gas shortage. We've got a rental car, and we go, "Holy shit...we're not going to make it home." Here I am, my first year in the league, and we're going to be stuck in Northern California somewhere. My life was flashing in front of me. We had to knock on some farmers' doors - we already missed curfew, curfew was out the window. So now, we're stuck - we've got no gas. We finally buy some gas off of some farmer up in the middle of nowhere in North San Francisco, and we got back to Oakland. Road trips were always an adventure...

JIM PICKARD: There were a lot of characters. There was Craig Cameron, he was funny. We had Germain Gagnon, Spinner Spencer. Back in those days, guys would even smoke right in the locker room when they were getting dressed. Germain sat right next to Spinner Spencer, and Spencer didn't like the smoking. I guess he told him, and Germain must have said, *"Whatever."* So I remember Spinner getting tape, and putting up "LA PA FUMAR," or words to that effect - "no smoking."

EDDIE WESTFALL: The goaltending wasn't significant, only because the team was so lousy [the goaltending duties for the Islanders' first year were split between Gerry Desjardins and Billy Smith, who were obtained by the expansion draft via the Chicago Blackhawks and the Los Angeles Kings, respectively]. They were just trying to figure out who they might have going forward, that might turn into something they could use in the short-term. And as it turned out, Billy Smith turned out to be long-term. So that was a bonus.

BILLY HARRIS: Gerry Desjardins was a pretty nice guy, a good guy. He was probably one of the more normal goalies, because most goalies have a tendency to be a little bit whacky. But his wife was whacky - so that sort of made up for it. He ended up getting traded to Buffalo, and I think they [allegedly] ended up switching wives - him and one other [player]. She was that nuts. I forget which player it was, but they wound up switching. I don't think Gerry ended up staying with the wife he ended up with, but his ex-wife stayed with the [other] player. [Laughs]

EDDIE WESTFALL: I don't think we really knew [if Smith was going to be a good goaltender]. He was like everybody on that team at the time - particularly the younger guys. They were trying to establish themselves, one, in the NHL, and two, with the team, that hopefully was going to go somewhere. Billy wasn't anything special - he didn't start out being a real good goalie, because you couldn't tell! Most of the goalies that we had, they were like target practice. We were so weak, and we played most of the nights in our own end of the ice. So those are elements that you could pontificate, and say, "Looking back, he was this or he was that." But he was just another player that they were going to find out whether or not he could play. And he had a personality that worked for them. He was a contrarian. Most goaltenders have all been kind of different, and Billy turned out to be that way. He was contentious, and you have to be a little bit like that when you're a goalie.

STAN FISCHLER: I was impressed with the attendance. Nobody knew what kind of team they would have, nor how they would draw. And there was already a following. Of course, a lot of people were Ranger fans who couldn't get into the Garden, and lived on the Island and grew up as Ranger fans. But this was a closer rink and they were part of that crowd. The attendance was good - there was an enthusiastic bunch of guys, even though they weren't winning much.

BILLY HARRIS: You know what the headlines in the Post said [after the then 5-37-4 Islanders beat the then-reigning Stanley Cup champion Boston Bruins, on January 18, 1973]? "BREAK UP THE ISLANDERS!" [Laughs] It was either the Post or Newsday. We were joking about that the next day. I think I scored a couple of goals in that game. Eddie Johnson was in goal, I think Bobby [Orr] was playing too, I don't know if he was injured or not. To play against Bucyk and Espo - they had a pretty good team. It was 9-7.

STAN FISCHLER: They were so bad, that Bill Torrey said that he thought the middle name of his team was "Hapless," because everybody was calling them "the Hapless Islanders." That's why Bill Torrey went out of his way to trade for Jean Potvin, to ensure that Denis Potvin - who he was planning to draft - would come to the Island.

JEAN POTVIN [The Islanders' defenseman from 1973-1978, 1979-1981]: Growing up as a French-Canadian kid in Canada, the winters at that time were quite a bit colder than they are now, and they lasted a good six, seven, maybe seven-and-a-half months. Denis' and my father [Armand Potvin] played some very good hockey as well, as a junior hockey player. Went to the Memorial Cup twice, and both years were beaten by a team that I believe was called the Verdun Maple Leafs. And on that team, there was a guy by the name of Rocket Richard. When my dad got married shortly thereafter, he had three boys - we have an older brother, Bob, myself, and Denis is last. My dad naturally wanted to introduce his boys to the sport that he loved, and he made a rink in the backyard. We would have that as soon as possible - whether that was the end of October or early November, whenever he thought it was cold enough for the snow to stick. He would go and spray the hose out there, and we would have a rink in a matter of three or four days. And it would usually last until late March/early April.

And the routine was simple - back in those days, you didn't have a lot of channels on TV. We were not allowed to watch TV during the week, at all. So we'd get home from school, do our homework, have dinner, and then go and play outside on the rink, until it was bedtime. Then we'd come in, take a bath, and go to bed, and then the next day, the routine would start all over again. So that's where we learned initially where to play hockey. And when I was about 15 years old, my first organized hockey team was a midget team in Ottawa - an all-star midget team. And from there, played with the Ottawa 67's for I believe three years. Then I turned pro. Even though my rights had belonged to the Montreal Canadiens, my rights were eventually sold to the LA Kings. This was in 1969. So I went to the LA Kings' training camp, and made the team. I was there for about a year and a half, before being traded to the Philadelphia Flyers. I was one of I believe four or five players that were traded from LA to Philadelphia. It was like a "four for four trade" - it was a pretty big trade back in those days.

I was in Philadelphia until March 5th of 1973, at which time I was traded to the New York Islanders for Terry Crisp. And that was at the end of the very first season. I think it was a pretty good move on Bill Torrey's part - I'm sure he wanted my services, but he also knew that there was a young player in Canada who was unanimously the choice to be drafted number one overall. And it happened to be Denis, my brother. So by bringing me to the New York Islanders in March, before the June draft, was a pretty good move, because Bill had done his homework and knew that Denis and I were quite close, because we had played junior hockey together. So by drafting me, it was obviously even more attractive for Denis to come here, as opposed to going to the World Hockey Association.

[The Islanders] were terrible. [Laughs] Up until that point, they had the worst record in the history of the NHL. I remember when I went to see Keith Allen, who was the general manager of the Philadelphia Flyers, and asked him if they would trade me, he said, "Do you have a preference of where you want to go? I'll see if I can make a trade happen." So I said, "Well, I'd like to be traded to the New York Islanders." Keith Allen is a very reserved man - always wore a work suit, shirt, and tie. Very dapper, and laid back in his chair. And when I said, "I'd like to be traded to the New York Islanders," he shot up in his chair, and he said, *"Are you out of your mind?* They've got the worst team in the history of the NHL! Why on earth would you want to go there?" And there were two reasons. They were so bad that I would get a chance to play a lot, and the other thing was that their general manager - who I didn't know - is Bill Torrey. And Bill's been very public about the fact that they will draft Denis Potvin, because they had last place sewn up at that point.

And he said, "I'm not trading my draft choice." Everybody knew that at that time, a number of teams were trying to get that number one pick. So they were making offers, and the ones that were the most aggressive were the Montreal Canadiens. But Bill Torrey was adamant that he was going to keep it and build his franchise around that number one pick. He felt that confident that Denis would become the leader that he would eventually become.

LORNE HENNING: When you pull an expansion draft, you pull players from every which team, so it took us a while to get any chemistry.

JEAN POTVIN: The Islanders, at the end of the first year, at the same time I was traded, that was also the deadline that Bill Torrey could bring up any minor league players. And he decided to bring up Dave Pulkkinen's line. So on March 5th of 1973, I was traded to the Islanders from Philadelphia, and Bill Torrey brought up Dave Pulkkinen's entire line from the minor league team, which at that time was playing in New Haven. Dave Pulkkinen was the center iceman, and on the right side, you had a guy that was known as Bobby Nystrom, and on the left side, you had a feisty guy by the name of Garry Howatt.

LORNE HENNING: Once Bobby and Garry came, we started getting a bit of an identity - we were tougher and harder to play against.

BOB NYSTROM: The first year I didn't play the entire year with the team. I was in New Haven for most of the year, and I came up for eleven games. But certainly, when you're in the minors, you pay a lot of attention to what's going on with the parent team. So we watched most of the games that we could. It was a struggle. I think we set a record that year for the most losses. But I got my first opportunity to go up somewhere around Christmas - I went up for three games. And then I went up for the last eight games.

BILLY HARRIS: They played in New Haven most of the year - they didn't play much that first year [with the Islanders]. I think the big thing was how bad a skater Bobby Nystrom was. And with Barbara Williams - the power skater - he worked hard that first year [to improve his skating]. He wasn't a *bad* skater, but he had no balance. And he worked his ass off, to become a really good player and really good skater. The same with Garry Howatt - they both worked with that girl in the summertime. And the thing about Garry Howatt, I'd have to rate him - pound for pound - one of the strongest, toughest little pricks in the league. He was an old farm boy from out west - he had wrists and hands on him. He'd grab you, and no one was getting out of his grasp once he grabbed your sweater or grabbed your hair. I remember he made that rule change - about grabbing guys' hair in fights. He loved it. He always joked about how he loved grabbing Dave Schultz's afro. He said, *"You could get a really good grip."* [Laughs]

JEAN POTVIN: I believe there were twelve games remaining in the regular season [after Potvin joined the Islanders]. We had a coach, Earl Ingarfield, who had replaced Phil Goyette. Earl was really a good guy. He was one of their lead scouts, and he had been asked if he would take the interim position of coaching the Islanders until the end of the season. And Earl had made it quite clear to Bill Torrey at the time, "Once the season's over, find yourself another coach, because I don't want to be a coach. I'm happy to remain a scout." Earl was from out west, and he just wanted to go back home to his family. So I got to know Earl the last month and a half of the season - very nice guy, very good guy. And Bill Torrey, I was very impressed with him, as well.

BILL TORREY: It was very evident to me that we were going to make a change [with head coaches]. Phil Goyette, who was hired initially, was a very popular player in New York, that I thought would be good with a young team. But Phil had difficulty in communicating with the players, and the losing got to him. So I made a change at the end of the year - I brought Earl Ingarfield, our western scout, to come in and finish the year.

EDDIE WESTFALL: Phil Goyette was a wonderful person. I played against him, and he was a wonderful hockey player and a classy guy. He was brand new at coaching. He had never really coached before. I never asked Bill Torrey why he had somebody come in that had never coached before. But I guess it wasn't important at the time. Phil

Goyette, I felt really bad for him, because even training camp, it was evident he was brand new at it. You're trying to do your best to help him, and he struggled. Hell, you win only won twelve games, you can't blame the coach - I don't care, you could have put Al Arbour in his heyday behind that bench, and it wouldn't have really made a whole lot of difference. And when they let him go…what did they expect, really, when you think about it? You have somebody who has no experience at all, and so the expectations weren't very high for him. You knew that they had to go find somebody.

BILLY HARRIS: Earl was a great guy. He said, "Hey guys, you're not going to make the playoffs. But you've got to put a show on." He was a good coach - I think he was actually offered the job, but he wanted to go back to Lethbridge. He could relate to the players and he knew a little bit more about the game and dealing with the issues with the players. He did a good job - we had a good little run at the end of the season there.

It was a relief [when the season ended]. Our last game was in Atlanta, and we were flying back on an Eastern Airlines flight that night, so we had some time to kill. Just sitting down in the locker room with Earl Ingarfield, and Bill Torrey came in, and they brought in a bunch of beer. We were able to sit there, and go, "Holy shit, we survived!" It was a real sort of relief. Thank god that's over with, and let's move on.

LORNE HENNING: I think we only won twelve games, regrettably.

JIMMY DEVELLANO: We finished with 30 points that first year. We went through two coaches. Because we finished last in the league, we had a plum of a franchise player waiting for us in our second draft, Denis Potvin. We drafted Denis, and he was an immediate superstar. That summer, I recommended to general manager Bill Torrey that we hire a fellow that I was associated with when I was with St. Louis, to be the coach. His name was Al Arbour.

EAST DIVISION STANDINGS: 1972-73

TEAMS	W	L	T	POINTS
Montreal Canadiens	52	10	16	120
Boston Bruins	51	22	5	107
New York Rangers	47	23	8	102
Buffalo Sabres	37	27	14	88
Detroit Red Wings	37	29	12	86
Toronto Maple Leafs	27	41	10	64
Vancouver Canucks	22	47	9	53
New York Islanders	12	60	6	30

CHAPTER 4:

AL ARBOUR AND DENIS POTVIN TO THE RESCUE

The futility of the '72 Islanders was too much to bear for most. Thankfully, it didn't take long before two figures emerged, that would help turn the team around.

AL ARBOUR [The Islanders' head coach from 1973-1986 and 1988-1994]: I started when I was young, in Sudbury, Ontario, in Canada. I started playing on outdoor ice, outdoor rinks - there were no indoor rinks in those days. Everything was outdoors. I went to St. George, and when I was 15, I went to Windsor, Ontario, to play junior hockey for the Spitfires.

CLAIRE ARBOUR [Wife of Al Arbour]: We grew up in the same neighborhood. He literally was on the other side of the track, in the creek. [Laughs] There was a creek and railroad tracks that ran between our street and his street. He went to the same school - I'm a little younger than he is, but not much. He was in my older sister's class. But he left home at 15 - I just saw him in the summertime. We dated one summer, and got married the next [1955].

AL ARBOUR: I turned pro with the Detroit Red Wings, then I went to the Chicago Blackhawks. From Chicago to Toronto, from Toronto to Rochester, and from Rochester to St. Louis.

CLAIRE ARBOUR: You learn very quickly to be self-sufficient. And the drawback with me is I didn't drive. I didn't learn to drive until I had my second child, so I was dependent on other wives, when [the players] were away. But you become very close to one another. It's the friends you have for the winter, but the NHL seasons weren't that long then. By April 15th, everything was over. If you made it to April 15th, you had won the Cup or you were in the Finals. They played Semi-Finals and Finals then. That was it. I knew it was just for the winter, and we did this for 14 years - we would head right back to Sudbury right after the season was over. When the kids started school, we were in St. Louis then, so we had to stay for the school year, because it just got to be too difficult for them. But like I said, you have to become self-sufficient, and you become friends with all the other wives. And usually, we're all in the same place, so we just all support one another.

He was really the kind of player that a goalie depended on. Because we were always friends with the goalie - some of our best friends in hockey were Glenn Hall and Johnny Bower. The thing is, Al was really depended on by them, but he was not the big name on the team. So that was fine. I know that he worked very hard - everything was geared toward preparation for the game. Our whole life centered around his schedule and his needs. The timing of our meals, the whole thing. And our social life was going to the hockey games. That was it.

That was like overnight [Arbour's transition from player to coach]. We were in St. Louis. Mr. [Sid] Salomon was the first to install "a wives' room" in their building, so we would have a place to go and wait for the players. They even served us food and the whole thing. And they had an area where they would have the coaches' wives, and the manager's wife and the doctor's wife would come in. One year, Al's a player, and all of a sudden, overnight, he's a coach. I remember going in, and thinking, "Where do I sit now? Where do I belong?" God rest his soul, his roommate was Barclay Plager. They were very close friends, and Barclay said, "Does that mean we don't room together anymore?" All those little things that change in one's life. As a coach, they're part of the team, but you can't hang out with the players. It's kind of different. So all of a sudden, "What should I do?" With them, I was still the same, so that was fine. When I arrived on Long Island, I was definitely "the coach's wife," and that was it. Although I must say, these gals, whenever they had any kind of a function, they invited me, and I was always included. They never thought of me as any different. That was kind of neat. They're a neat bunch of kids on Long Island - we grew as a family.

The sad part - when all was said and done - was that Mr. Salomon's son [Sidney Salomon III] ran the team. He let him run the team, and he really was not a well person. As it turns out, he died a couple of years after, he had a brain tumor. In hindsight, when you know now why he was behaving like that. But he was impetuous - he would call Al and say, "Change that player, put in the goalie, and do this and do that." Well, Al just ignored it. He was the owner's son, so thirteen games into the [1972-73] season…I still remember, we came home, and Al said, "I have to stay up. They're putting Noel Picard on waiver." And no one called, so we finally went to bed. But we got an early call from Sid Abel, saying, "Put the coffee on, I'm coming over." And we thought, "Holy cow, why is he coming over?" I said to Al, "Is your job in jeopardy?" And he said, *"Who knows?"* And that's what it was - Mr. Salomon didn't want him to coach. It was only thirteen games into the season, so that was kind of hard to believe.

I remember poor Sid Abel, it was a really difficult job for him to tell Al. He said, "You're better off not coaching anyways, that's a tough job, blah blah blah." So anyways, Mr. Salomon wanted Al to stay with the organization. The only time in the hockey season that we ever went up to Sudbury for Christmas. We came back, and he met with Mr. Salomon, and he said, "No, I cannot stay with the organization. I will move on." So that left us high and dry. "Where are we going?"

BILL TORREY: [Earl Ingarfield] was a very valuable scout. He was a great evaluator of talent, and I didn't want to keep him there [as head coach]. I wanted to find another coach, and the thing that I was looking for more than anything else was someone who could get us going as far as scoring goals. We weren't good at that. But our defense was *atrocious.* I think we gave up more than a hundred goals than any other team in the league. So I was looking for someone that I thought could come in and give our team the foundation for good, solid defense, and then work from there. Having known Al Arbour as a player and then seeing him as a short-time coach in St. Louis, and then in Rochester - and being as a player one of the soundest defensive defenseman you could ever want - he was in the age bracket that I wanted. Someone relatively young, that could grow with the team.

CLAIRE ARBOUR: Al got several phone calls right away, but Cliff Fletcher was the first one to call him, and he asked him to join his scouting staff [for the Atlanta Flames], which he did. Al even went to Russia that year, to scout out there. And Cliff organized the whole Atlanta group to go to Florida for a gathering after the season, and insisted that we join them. Boom Boom Geoffrion was the coach then, and I had befriended Arlene, his wife - a lovely gal. It was actually there that I said to Al, "Bill Torrey offered you a job. Maybe you should consider that place, too. Because I think you're making Geoffrion very nervous by going on their staff!" Cliff was just protecting himself. That was my feeling. So we ended up accepting Bill Torrey's invitation. Which was not an easy move, but one that was very beneficial in his career.

AL ARBOUR: Bill Torrey got in touch with me. I told him I wasn't interested at all, because it was New York. [Bill said] "It's Long Island, it's not New York. Come on down to see us." I said, "Oh no, no, no. I'm not going down." He coaxed me, and I said, "OK." I visited Bill on the Island, and I said, "Well, the Island is not like what I thought it was. It's not like the big city. This is a different thing." He showed me all the places, and he called the house. I had an offer from Vancouver, also. They thought I had agreed. They called me and I said I wasn't going to go to Vancouver. I was going to go to the Islanders.

BILL TORREY: So, I approached him at the draft and told him what our plans were. We had already drafted Denis Potvin, we had drafted Dave Lewis. I had signed Bert Marshall, who was a very good defensive defenseman for me in Oakland, and also in Detroit. So I was starting to make over the personnel of the defense.

JEAN POTVIN: It was not exactly a surprise [when the Islanders drafted Denis Potvin]. Everybody in the world of hockey certainly knew that Denis was going to be drafted. And I remember the Islanders organization flying my mother, my father, and myself to Long Island, to take that famous picture after you're drafted - with him holding his jersey up with his name on it, and me holding mine. And I believe at that time we were sporting what was very much in style, the old Fu Manchu. So that's what happened that summer. We were very excited about the fact that we would be playing together again, because we had played two years together with the Ottawa 67's. But now, we could do it in the National Hockey League, as a brother act, which was very exciting.

BILLY HARRIS: I played against Denis in junior - for three or four years. He was a great player in junior. We always had a great rivalry there, because he played for the Ottawa 67's and I was with the leading scorer with the Marlies and the leading scorer in the league. So he was on the ice most of the time I was ever on the ice, so I kind of knew him. I didn't know him from playing with him, but I knew him from playing against him as much as I had over the years. There's no doubt that he wasn't the best defenseman and the best person to draft. Now we had somebody who could get the puck out of our own zone.

BILL TORREY: I first heard about Denis when he was 15 years of age, and started playing junior hockey. You have to understand, the draft in those days, you couldn't be drafted into the NHL until you were 20 years of age. And yet, he was - as a 15-year-old - strong enough, big enough, and good enough to play for the Ottawa 67's in the Ontario Hockey League. And not only was he good enough to play there, but he very quickly became the best player in the league. So, he played basically four years of junior hockey before he was eligible for the draft. I saw him play lots as a junior, and I knew his coach, Leo Boivin, a former Bruins defenseman. I knew Leo very well, so I had a very good book on Denis. Because of our record the year before as the worst team in the league, we had the first pick in the draft. I knew that he was going to my pick. Even though Tommy Lysiak and Lanny McDonald [were also available], and there were a number of other players that were very good, none of them had all the ingredients that Denis brought.

CHAPTER 5:

1973-74

Although they managed only several more wins than their nightmarish inaugural season, the Islanders' second year sees improvements in other areas.

LORNE HENNING: When Al came along, he gave us some discipline. Then we became certainly a lot better, and it got to be a lot more fun.

BOB NYSTROM: From that point on, things changed. The interesting thing was the first year of training camp with Al, it was certainly a whole lot different than anything that we had experienced, because you usually do an introductory skate, where you just get your equipment on - your brand new equipment - and go out for a light skate. Two and a half hours later, we were still out there! I think Al in general really turned the team around that first year. He brought in a game plan, and basically said he wanted to cut the goals against by a hundred goals, and this was the type of system that he wanted to play. So he started the whole process. The second year was a major improvement on the first year.

EDDIE WESTFALL: Al was much more organized. But also, he didn't have a lot of coaching experience either. Even in the second year, we weren't sure what we were practicing half the time. All of that stuff was trial and error, when you think of the practice rinks and the places we practiced - just trying to get ice time. It was very unsettling in some ways, but it was also comical in others. So when Al got there, one thing that he had was he had a program for practice. We used to joke with him, "We can do this practice with our eyes closed, just by listening to the whistles." We were like trained dogs! And then he started to learn a little bit more about each one of the players. He did his homework - he was very diligent about handling the players. And there was no favoritism. Some players wanted to be coddled, but he would have none of it. Denis Potvin was often at loggerheads with Al about what he thought was not the treatment he deserved.

BILLY HARRIS: He was a great motivator. He knew certain guys he could go after, and certain guys he just couldn't go near. I mean, I thought Denis Potvin was going to kill him at some point in his career. And he was quite a motivator. We'd have "breakout systems," and he'd make the guys go home at night, and we'd have to hand in reports the next day on all our different systems. And they were brilliant - forechecking systems and our breakout, y'know, where the guys all had to be at certain times. The puck's here, you go here, and da da da. That part of it was brilliant, but there was also this other side - the psychological side. He was quite a unique guy.

LORNE HENNING: He instilled discipline in us. And work ethic. All the things teams are doing now, Al was on the forefront back in the day. Certainly, he was a strong personality, and he just molded the team in his personality. He knew system-wise what it took to win. Leadership was probably the biggest thing. But he did instill discipline. It wasn't like we were "rag tag" before that, we certainly came to play. It was team chemistry - he knew what it took team-wise to win and individually to win. It became *a team,* instead of a bunch of individuals.

CLAIRE ARBOUR: He started [using videotape as a coach] when he was in St. Louis. He had some very good workers there that helped him out on that. When we arrived on Long Island, he purchased a video machine, and I taped his games. I was stuck in the basement, taping those games. And trust me, it wasn't with a remote control, where you sat there and didn't do very much and push a button. No, this was reel-to-reel, and I had to put down when there was a goal scored. So I didn't get to sit very much. [Laughs] And I sometimes had to tape our game and we'd be getting the Rangers game, and he'd say, "Tape that too, because I'll need to watch that."

BILLY HARRIS: We just wanted to keep games close and not get blown out, and we'd get a power play, and we might score a late goal and get a tie or win. We were all defensive-minded - right off the bat. That was our fallback, that was our safety net. And we were able to score more goals as we got more maturity and more experience. One thing about Torrey, we did have a cast of characters on the team, so he was able to weed them out over time. And a team is not just your physical or your playing ability, you also have to be in the locker room. You spend so much time together. You can't have...we picked up this one guy from Washington, and he was a complete goof. All he wanted to do was smoke dope - it was just nuts. Got rid of him real quick.

AL ARBOUR: We got rid of a lot of players the first year.

EDDIE WESTFALL: Immediately, the expectations were greater from somebody like Denis. When he was younger, his aggressive play, he was a physical player as well as a finesse player. He had a lot of tools in his bag to use. It wasn't even a hiccup for him to come from junior into the NHL, and particularly, with the team that he joined. He was probably immediately *the* best player on the team - if not close.

JEAN POTVIN: Denis went on to have just a superb first year and won the Rookie if the Year Award [the Calder Memorial Trophy], which I think was one heck of an accomplishment, because we still had a pretty terrible team. We only had two or three good players. We had a great captain, which was Eddie Westfall. Eddie brought a winning attitude and he was just really a good guy, a really good leader. And we had Billy Harris, who had been the number one draft choice the previous year. And in his rookie year, he had scored 28 goals. The team was quite a bit better the second year with Denis, and I'll say myself.

I think throughout our first year [with Arbour as head coach], we never knew this guy could smile! But the improvement was there to be seen. We literally shaved a hundred goals against from the first year. From the first year, the Islanders had given up a total of 347 goals. Under Al Arbour, we gave up 247 goals. We lost a lot of games by one goal. So the bottom line is, even though we didn't have a great team by any means, there was significant improvement, and Denis played a big role in that. And we had a couple of goalies that were pretty good, in Billy Smith and Chico Resch.

GLENN "CHICO" RESCH [The Islanders' goaltender from 1973-1981]: Born in Moose Jaw, but really raised in Regina. I played my first year of goal in my rubber boots, because I couldn't skate. And back then, rubber boots were *big* - they were actually snow boots. I thought, "Hockey. I can't skate…it would be pretty hard to run up and down the ice as a winger. I guess it's better to be a goalie - they've got to come to *you.*" So that's what I did, I just started playing. I was OK, I played all through minor hockey and got a scholarship to the University of Minnesota Duluth. I was fortunate to be a captain my last year, when goalies could still be captains in pro hockey. Then at the end of that year, I had a teaching degree, and I was a mailman. I went to Montreal Canadiens training camp. Scotty Bowman was a rookie coach, and I lasted only five days - they shipped me off to Muskegon. Which was a frightening word at the time. You just felt, you're not totally buried, but you're buried up to your chest. And you think, "How am I going to get out of that?" But it was a great year. I met a lot of good people - Moose Lallo was my coach, he taught me a lot about being a pro. We had a really good team, I had a terrific year.

Quite honestly, it was a turning point year in that I went to training camp in Montreal and had a chance to watch Rogie Vachon for five days, and he had just won the Stanley Cup with the Canadiens. So I figured, 'If I can just imitate what he's doing, I have a shot." And that's all I worked on that year in Muskegon. Then that summer, again, it didn't look very promising, because in Montreal's organization, no matter how well you're doing on the lowest level, you're still a long way from getting to the big team, because they had great teams. I was a mailman in Regina that summer, and then I got a call from a guy who was an agent. At that time, there weren't a lot of college players in the NHL. His name was Harry Ottenbreit, and he said, "Hey, I represent a lot of the agents, and I just got a call from Bill Torrey, who said that the Islanders had made a trade." The Islanders were just forming, and Denis DeJordy got shipped off to Montreal, and I was kind of "a throw in" on this deal. I got a $12,500 signing bonus, $12,500 to play the first year, and $13,500 the next year. So that was the beginning of my pro career with the Islanders. I signed that contract - I've got a picture of it - in my mailman uniform. Then I went to their training camp, and the rest is history.

I played there and it wasn't looking very good. And then Gerry Desjardins, he and his wife decided they needed to get out of New York City and get a new environment. The World Hockey Association had just started, and he signed with the Michigan Stags, playing out of Detroit. That was after a very lucrative offer by Bill Torrey. I heard the rumor that they offered him like a three-year, $100,000 deal, which was a lot of money. But he wanted to go to Michigan and get a new lease on life. So that opened up a chance for me. Bill Torrey was there, and Bill was great. He said, "I want to break you in easy, kid. I'll play you in some easier games, I'll let you get your feet wet." Billy Smith had already played there for two years. Then it just started to unfold from there.

I played two games that second year [1973-74]. I got called up just to see what I had. I lost in Oakland - we played the Seals [on February 3rd]. I was really disappointed, we lost 4-2. But they told me, "We'll take you back to Long Island. You'll get a chance to play another game." I got to play against the North Stars [on February 5th] and we won, 6-2. That was my first win in the NHL. I did get sent back to the Central League. The Islanders organization was in New Haven the first year, but I didn't get called up. Then the next year, they moved to Fort Worth, Texas, of the Central League, and that's where I was playing when I had my first two game call up, and then they sent me back. There, we had a really good coach in Ed Chadwick, who was a former goalie in the NHL, and we had a pretty good team. I won some awards that year, too. I think they just felt that when Gerry Desjardins decided he wanted to move on, they could trust me. And the next season, I started the season. I played regularly from that point on.

STAN FISCHLER: There was a very popular television program, 'Chico and the Man.' And the feeling was that Resch looked like the Chico in the television series [played by the late Freddie Prinze].

EDDIE WESTFALL: They made the deal to get Chico Resch, when we got rolling along pretty good. They still weren't sure where Billy Smith was going to fall in the big picture. They might not have been happy about splitting the goaltending duties, but they certainly didn't create an issue about it. The personality part about it was good that way. I think the fact that they both knew what losing was about, and neither one of them wanted to be losers anymore. We'd all had enough of that. So the interest of the team then came first. As long as you can keep that element, then you're way ahead. If you've got that kind of dual goaltending, when you can rely on both of them. And sure, you're going to have a bad game or a few bad games, and then you get somebody out. And if somebody is struggling for whatever reason or they're just getting more ice time than they can handle, then you've got the next guy coming in, who is just as good. It was a perfect situation.

GLENN "CHICO" RESCH: I never had a problem with Smitty. I'd seen Smitty in New Haven - he had come to our training camp, we had connected then. I have to tell you, Smitty and I - and I'm not just saying this - we never had one little disagreement. I mean, it's an old cliché - he totally respected the way I was, and I respected the way he was. We just appreciated each other. Even the competition among us, I mean, goalies *know* - they know that if the other guy plays unbelievable, you're not going to play. So you're hoping that the other guy is good, but not great every night. And as long as you know he's thinking the same thing when you're playing, it's not like backstabbing or behind the back deals. We just knew it would revolve around. And Al was really good. Again, Al really tried to keep the goalie that wasn't playing fired up, involved, and "going to get a chance." Honestly, there was not one issue - and I'm saying that truthfully - that ever caused any kind of friction. The reputation of Smitty, unless you know him and you know each situation, it's hard to blanketly say, "Smitty's this" or "Smitty's that." I know there's things said about him and he has a certain kind of reputation, but in most instances, if we talked about it…and if I told you the situation, you'd say, "Oh, I can see that a little bit." That was why Smitty and I got along so well.

EDDIE WESTFALL: [Resch and Smith] created the competition, which is good. It's healthy for a team to have competition throughout all the positions, but particularly in goal. When you find that you've got two guys that are all of a sudden starting goaltenders and are pretty good, then you've got a big plus there. The competition was good, and in that '75 year, Glenn Resch was "the guy." That situation was created, and it turned out to be very good, because it probably made Billy Smith a better goalie.

JIMMY DEVELLANO: We improved the team from 30 points to 56 points, from one year to the next.

BILL TORREY: Instead of being a pushover team, we became at least a relatively competitive team. We started to get a nucleus of a future team.

JIMMY DEVELLANO: I was with the Islanders for two years as their Eastern Canada scout, and by year three, [Torrey] promoted me to the head scout of the New York Islanders. I was the head scout of the New York Islanders for the next seven years.

EDDIE WESTFALL: We were all excited at the end of the second season. We won twelve games in the first season, and we may have doubled that in the second [19 wins]. But you knew right away that the team, game after game, we were much more competitive. We weren't successful by any means, but we were growing, and we were getting better. And management was starting to get a much better feel for what they wanted to keep and what they didn't want to keep. So Jimmy Devellano and Bill Torrey were "piecing together." Not only waiting for the next good draft pick that Jimmy D could scout out somewhere in eastern or western Canada, but also, the supporting cast. That's one of the things that not too many people recognized between Bill Torrey and Jim Devellano. They started to collect a supporting cast for these young draft picks that they were bringing in, that were hopefully going to be the nucleus of the New York Islanders. And Torrey regularly talked about how he wanted to copy as much as he could the Montreal Canadiens' plan, of building the nucleus, and then surrounding that nucleus with a supporting cast that was as strong as he could get it. He already had me, but then Bert Marshall, JP Parisé, Jude Drouin, and Billy MacMillan [arrived] - these are all quality guys, that had experience in the NHL. But they still had heart, they still had legs that could move, and they were very good with the young players that were coming to the team.

CLAIRE ARBOUR: It was very hard for him to think that he wasn't going to be in the playoffs [the first year Arbour coached the Islanders]. That was always his goal - to make the playoffs. He just didn't have that good of a team to start with, and I remember when the season was over, he was pacing back and forth, and I said, "Well, you knew that was going to happen." You didn't have to wait too long, praise be to god.

EAST DIVISION STANDINGS: 1973-74

TEAMS	W	L	T	POINTS
Boston Bruins	52	17	9	113
Montreal Canadiens	45	24	9	99
New York Rangers	40	24	14	94
Toronto Maple Leafs	35	27	16	86
Buffalo Sabres	32	34	12	76
Detroit Red Wings	29	39	10	68
Vancouver Canucks	24	42	11	59
New York Islanders	19	41	18	56

CHAPTER 6:

1974-75

Suddenly, the Islanders are to be taken seriously, as they post their first-ever regular season winning record, and even earn a playoff spot.

GLENN "CHICO" RESCH: It was an amazing transformation from "year two" to "year three." Year three, Denis had a year under his belt, Billy Harris had a couple, there was Smitty. We had gotten Bobby Bourne and Clark Gillies out of that draft. Nystrom was up, Garry Howatt was up. Gerry Hart was a good, solid player, Bert Marshall was there. Dave Lewis came in that year. But, the thing for me, Bert Marshall *really* helped all of us. Bert was an interesting guy, because he was an "accountability guy." He was competitive, and he would say little things - and he wasn't the only one. JP Parisé would say to me some nights that year, if I had a bad night, "Chico, it seems you're very difficult to hit tonight!" And Bert was the same way - he'd give you little digs. They were just a reminder of, "Hey, this is the reality."

But they weren't cutting, they weren't mean-spirited veterans. Billy MacMillan was there, and Ralph Stewart was there. It had everything, but mostly, it had Al Arbour. And Torrey too, don't get me wrong - they were a great team. But Al, as a coach, gave you a sense of calmness, confidence, and direction. And he was a good teacher. I can't say enough about him. To me, he is the greatest coach that ever coached a hockey team. I don't know Dick Irvin Sr. and some of those old guys, but he just did it all. He was a complete guy. Other coaches were good in certain facets of the game, but Al nailed them all. The personal interaction, understanding the game, when to be upset, when not. He could have fun with us, but he knew how to clamp down. That was one of the big factors too - the calm and direction we were getting from Arbour.

So quite honestly, right off the bat that year, we started to win some games, and we started to think we were a pretty good team. We grew that year, but it wasn't like we were really terrible at the beginning of the year and we turned it on later. Bobby Nystrom, Garry Howatt, these guys in their positions were as good, as intense, and as driven players at that time. I think one of the things that was happening at that time was this whole "fitness" [approach] - looking at the NHL in a different way. The Russians had come in. They had shown that fitness level and different kind of training was positive. So you had young guys that were willing to go into the gym and work out after, and do extra with weights. We were starting to train off-season. But that group was on the front edge of working really, really hard off the ice, as well as on. I think that was one of the first teams to do that, and that gave us a huge edge. Because we had a lot of young guys that were really overachievers. Not Gerry Cheevers, but *overachievers*. [Laughs]

BILL TORREY: We were a physical team, and we were a hard-working team. You could see that the discipline that Al Arbour demanded was taking hold.

JEAN POTVIN: Just like in the second year, we were seeing a significant amount of improvement. We added a couple of guys, by the names of Bobby Bourne and Clark Gillies. And that year, they drafted Bryan Trottier, but sent him back [to the minor league].

CLARK GILLIES [The Islanders' left winger from 1974-1986]: I grew up in Moose Jaw, Saskatchewan. A little town, about 30,000 people, sort of Midwestern part of Canada on the prairies. As every little boy in town, we all played hockey. That was kind of the way we filled our time - strap on your blades, go to the corner outdoor rink, and just have fun all day long. So that's really where my hockey beginnings started. Just getting out there with my friends and doing what everybody did - played hockey all day long. I mean "all day long" too, from sun-up to sundown, basically.

When I was 16, the junior hockey team in Moose Jaw, they failed, and there was no team for me to play junior hockey in my hometown. I was approached by the Regina Pats, who still are in the Western Canada Hockey League. Regina's only 45 minutes from Moose Jaw. I was approached by them to play in Regina, which I did. Actually, my first coach in junior in Regina was Earl Ingarfield, who happened to be affiliated with the Islanders at that time - he was the second coach to coach the team. So Earl, after his initial season with the Islanders, came to Regina to coach the junior team. It was really at that point that Earl was the one that took me aside, and said, "Look, you have the ability, the size, and the strength to be a very good hockey player. And from what I can see, you have a very good shot at playing in the NHL if you apply yourself." So that's really when "the light" got turned on, because up to that point, I really was just playing hockey and having a good time. One, I didn't know if I was good enough to play in the junior league, and two, I certainly didn't know that I was going to be an NHL caliber player. So it all really began when I was about 17, about putting more effort in concentrating on how good a player I could be.

I played three years of junior hockey, and the last year, we attracted the eyes of a lot of scouts, because we went to the Western Final, and ended up winning the Memorial Cup in 1974. I think a lot through Earl's influence…he spoke with Bill Torrey and some of the scouts - he was scouting for the Islanders at that time. They were a team in the early building stages in 1974, and they were looking to fill different parts of the team. I was taken in the first - fourth pick overall - in the third year. I guess to add some size and toughness to the team. It was a good break for me, because I got to come to an expansion team that was really looking to just build through the draft. So I was able to step right in from junior hockey into the NHL.

BOB BOURNE [The Islanders' center from 1974-1988]: I was born in Kindersley, Saskatchewan. Actually, we lived a little bit out of town on a farm, so I was very fortunate - I got to skate every night of the winter. Just progressed from there, and ended up playing for the Saskatoon Blades in junior. It was kind of funny, the year I got drafted, I was drafted by the Kansas City Scouts, and I couldn't come to contract terms with them. I had a friend who was a friend of Billy Torrey's, and they did the deal with him after about 20 minutes on the phone, and I had a contract within an hour. I was going to the University of Saskatchewan when I was 17, and I couldn't decide whether to stay in college or go play hockey, but it turned out pretty good.

JEAN POTVIN: Bobby Bourne had not been a draft choice. He had been drafted by the Kansas City Scouts, and Billy Torrey made a trade for a guy that may have had the best name a hockey player's ever had - Bart Crashley. So we added these two guys, and all of a sudden, we become pretty respectable.

EDDIE WESTFALL: The excitement was in practice, even. We all kidded Al, a lot of us felt strongly about, "These are boring practices, Al." [Laughs] But we knew that he had a game plan. And the redundancy in the game plan probably wasn't any different than watching a golfer who for years and years monotonously works on his game. And that's what it seemed as though Al was trying to get us as a team to do. They were slowly showing up - the power play, the penalty killing. So now, we were probably playing as a unit for the first time. Where lines stayed together for a little bit, and defense partners for a little bit. All of that was part of the game plan that Al Arbour had put together, I'm quite sure.

JIM PICKARD: I lasted one year [with the Islanders], didn't get rehired, and ended up selling life insurance in the Niagara Falls area. And then Mr. Torrey called me up, and said, "Would you like your old job back?" Meanwhile, I had been in contact - Eddie Westfall had helped me out - I was going to go and be with the Washington Capitals for their inaugural year. But Mr. Torrey called me and asked if I'd like to come back, which I did. So I was with the Islanders the first year, missed the second, and then was there from '74/'75 until '89/'90. It was night and day. There was a lot of structure.

RON WASKE [The Islanders' head trainer from 1975-1984]: I was born and raised in Upstate New York, and grew up playing hockey as a youngster. I attended St. Lawrence University, where I played hockey, and wasn't good enough to go on to try and play professionally, so while at St. Lawrence, I became really interested in sports medicine and injury situations. For graduate school, I went to Bowling Green State University, in Ohio. Worked as a graduate assistant athletic trainer, and from there, I taught high school and coached hockey for a couple of years. Then the World Hockey Association came into play. The former Bowling Green coach became the general manager of the Cleveland Crusaders, and he offered me a job in their American League affiliate, the Jacksonville Barons. So I went there for a year, and at that time, Florida wasn't a very popular place for hockey, so we only lasted a year. During that time, I developed [friendships with] a couple of people in the NHL, the athletic trainers. So I asked where positions were opening for that next year, and one of them that I heard about was the New York Islanders. I applied to them, had an interview with Al Arbour, and happened to be in the right place at the right time. They were looking for a young, energetic athletic trainer, and I fit the bill. So I joined them in 1974, and I stayed until 1984.

JIM PICKARD: The first time I met Ron Waske, we were at Racquet and Rink - the year I came back, 1974-75. Ronnie was one of the first college educated trainers in the league. He's from Canton, New York, and he told me that he was going to work for ten years, because the trainer at St. Lawrence University - where he went to school - was of the age that he was going to retire in about ten years, and he was going to end up going back there. Which he did a year earlier, it turns out.

RON WASKE: It was a great situation for us. We complimented each other. I think we did a very good job for the organization. Any time you live and work with somebody for as long as we had to be together, and the hours that we had to put in, I think we did very well not to fight much. I really have a great friendship with Jim.

JIM PICKARD: I remember we had training camp in Peterborough, Ontario, and we were going to play an exhibition game in Minnesota. Back then, the dressing room that we had in Peterborough was like a big barn, attached to the building. The coach's room, he had a little room underneath the stairs where he dressed - Al. So now there was just the two of us - Ronnie Waske and myself - trying to look after all these players. So we get on the bus to go from Peterborough to the Toronto airport, and we're like halfway there. Ronnie and I are nervous as well - it was his first exhibition game with the team. And he said, to me, "Hey, did you get Al's stuff out of the room?" I go,

"Oh no, did you?" "No!" I remember we told Al, and he says, "I should get rid of you guys right now!" [Laughs] He was kidding, and we survived that.

CLARK GILLIES: Obviously, it was a very exciting time for me - being a rookie and playing in the National Hockey League. When I got drafted by the Islanders, just to go back a step, when I left to go to training camp, everybody said, "Well, we'll see you early in April," because the team really hadn't done much the first few years and nobody expected the team to make the playoffs. And I said, *"I wouldn't be so surprised."* Because I looked at the some of the names, and a lot of the guys I had played against on junior, and they were pretty darn good junior players - Lorne Henning, Dave Lewis, Bobby Nystrom, Garry Howatt, Denis Potvin, Billy Harris. When I got here, we had a good mix of very young guys and old guys. And obviously, that year, we traded for JP Parisé and Jude Drouin. And boy, they really gave us an added ingredient that I think we were missing - some experience. But these guys were still able to play. Sometimes, you get some old guys that can't play much anymore, but these guys were in...I wouldn't say the prime of their careers, but certainly had a lot of gas left in the tank.

JP PARISÉ [The Islanders' left winger from 1975-1978]: I'm from a little town in Northern Ontario, called Smooth Rock Falls. I started to play when I was about eight years old, in organized hockey. You had to be dedicated in those days, because we lived probably three-quarters of a mile from the arena, and I had to go to the arena carrying my equipment on a sled. From there, when I was 16 years old, I didn't have a team to play for. So I went and tried out for a men's league - it was an organized men's league, with maybe four or five little towns in Northern Ontario. I made the team. I had a little incident that kind of led me to possible disaster...or not. I was playing in the game before the Finals, a two out of three. We had to win the game. I was 16 and thought I was tough - I was banging this guy around. And about the third time, this 26-year-old guy didn't like it, so he turned around and hit me over the head. It was the funniest feeling - I had my senses, but my knees could not hold me up. I was on my knees, bleeding, so my teammates took me to the bench, and from there they took me to the hospital. I was cut on the side of the head for eight stitches.

So I came back, and we were playing the championship game the following Sunday afternoon, and I am…I don't know if "kill" is the right word, but I'm just going to knock [the player] on his ass. And I am going to be making an ass out of myself. My coach is looking at this, I'm skating around before the game started. The coach came over to me, and said, "JP, I know you want to get this guy. But you seldom have an opportunity to win the championship. I want you to focus on playing hockey. Maybe next year you can 'get him' or whatever." So I went out and got four goals and one assist, and we won 6-5. And the amazing thing is at that time, there had happened to be a scout from the Boston Bruins watching this. After the game, he asked me if I would be interested in playing for the Boston Bruins junior team in Niagara Falls, Ontario.

And so that particular game, I go back and say, "If I had done what I was going to do, I would never have played hockey." So it was a good lesson. At that time, there were only six teams in the National Hockey League - it was really, really difficult to make it. You had to be one *good* player. For five years, I played in the minors for the Boston Bruins, and not quite at the level to play in the National Hockey League. And then the '67 expansion came along, so I was able to stick to the National Hockey League. And from there, I stayed for eleven years.

GLENN "CHICO" RESCH: It started with the incredible trade that Bill Torrey made. He knew that the Minnesota North Stars were struggling; they were in transition in terms of older guys that needed to be moved. And he made a sweetheart deal there. We needed some veteran leadership, and we got it with Jude Drouin and JP Parisé. JP is so underrated as a complete hockey person - not just a person. His professionalism, his drive. Like I said, he would always say things to guys that were funny, but they also drove home a point. Plus, he was tough. You look at the lines we had there - we had Eddie Westfall, JP, Jude, Bourne, Clarkie, Lorne Henning. We were pretty darn good. The guys at your position have to be a little bit better than the same guy on another team at the same position. We always look at the stars, but you go all the way through the roster, and we had a lot of the positions that were as good as anyone. We didn't have the super scorer with Trots coming in, or Bossy. But we had a lot of components.

JP PARISÉ: At the time, the North Stars, I could sense that they were going to make some moves. We were not "doing it." I don't know if it was a financial thing, but they started to get rid of Barry Gibbs and some of those guys who were really good players. I compare that to if you are going to change tires on your car, you've got to put some good tires on there. [Laughs] But the [new] "tires" were not good. One year on our team, I think we had like nine 20 goal scorers - we had a good team. He got rid of three, four, or five of those guys. I'm thinking, "Who's going to replace those guys? You don't come in and replace a guy with 20 goals." So he got rid of Barry Gibbs, Danny Grant - there was a whole bunch - and I went. They never recovered.

I think it was one deal [Parisé and Jude Drouin coming to the Islanders], but they made it separate deals, because there was an injury. I went first, and then it was going to be Jude and I, I think it was Ernie Hicke [and Doug Rombough, who the Islanders sent to the North Stars]. And one of those guys was hurt; so then the deal was not completed until a couple of days later. It turned out to be two individual moves.

The first thing, when I was told I was being traded to the New York Islanders, I did not want to go to New York. I had visions of Long Island being like New York - I was speaking out of ignorance. So I went there, and I wanted to win the Stanley Cup before I retired. And the Islanders had never made the playoffs - never mind the Stanley Cup. So it was total disappointment for me. And then I'm in the locker room, and I'm expressing how I dislike New York and all that. And a wiseass kid starts asking me questions. He says, "What do you like in life? Do you like fishing?" I say, "Yeah." He says, "Great fishing here. Do you like the beach?" "Yeah." "Great beach. Do you like restaurants? The best restaurants in the world here." And this wiseass kid happened to be Denis Potvin! [Laughs] Denis Potvin is the guy who "enlightened" me about the New York area.

BILL TORREY: Jude had speed and was a good playmaker, and JP was good enough to play on the '72 Team Canada team against the Russians, and was one of their best forwards. So, he gave our team experience and toughness along the wing, and good scoring ability.

JEAN POTVIN: We were now scoring more goals, we were winning more games. If you look at our statistics, they were getting better every single year, so it was very encouraging as a player, when you're seeing that improvement year after year. It gives you a lot of confidence in your general manager and your scouting staff, and obviously, in your coach…and by the way, we *still* did not know if he could smile.

LORNE HENNING: The whole year we got better and better. We were a great defensive team, and good goaltending.

EDDIE WESTFALL: It was really, really exciting during the season. We weren't sure we were going to make the playoffs, but there's an old thing in hockey - if we didn't make the playoffs, we might keep some of the people that had been picking our bones for the last two years out of the playoffs. So they better be careful, because now we felt like we were a threat every hockey game. I would never think of it as being cocky, but I could see the confidence level was building in the team.

BRUCE BENNETT [NHL photographer]: I was born in Brooklyn, but grew up and lived on Long Island my whole life. Started taking hockey photos in 1974 - working for the Hockey News, which was based in Montreal. Just a naïve 18 year old kid, sending some photos from the blue seats at a Ranger game and from a photo box that I snuck into at Nassau Coliseum. They offered me three bucks a photo, and that was 37 years ago.

When I started my career, I was a bit of a fan, but I found it was necessary for me to succeed to take "the fan" out of the picture, and concentrate solely on the photography. So I really didn't make any connection in terms of assessing team's talents, [or] getting involved in the Rangers vs. Islanders battles in those days. But the turnaround that I really noticed was when the Islanders were building that small group of superstars.

The early days of when I started, the Islanders games were pretty quiet. Not too many photographers were showing up. The local media guys from the New York papers would populate the photo box each night - the photo positions in the corners. And then as the Islanders got better, it started to get crowded at some of those games.

STAN FISCHLER: Spencer Ross and I did the very first Islanders telecast, in March '75, which was the Flames at Islanders. That game was the playoff clincher for the Islanders.

JP PARISÉ: It didn't take very long - four or five games - before I was into it. I was put in a position to be a leader and help young guys. It was so much fun to go out. And all of a sudden, I started to feel like a young guy again. Things started to fall into place, and we were winning games unexpectedly. We made the playoffs. That was our goal.

GARY "BABA BOOEY" DELL'ABATE [Islanders fan, SportsChannel intern from 1980-81, 'Howard Stern Show' producer]: I grew up on Long Island. I grew up in the town of Uniondale - I lived there as a kid, before the Coliseum was built. The Coliseum was built in the early '70s, I was probably about ten years old or so. My dad was always a big sports fan, my dad was from New York City. We weren't very big hockey fans, although I do have a vague recollection of going to see a Rangers game when I was a kid. But not much more than that. So, when the Islanders first came into being - or being something worth watching - I remember being in junior high school, probably in seventh grade. I remember going to the games, because you could walk from my house to the games. We used to go for the Islanders and the Nets. By the way, the Nets was a much tougher ticket at the time.

I used to go up there with my buddies, and what you'd do is "grub a ticket." What that means is you'd stand out front, going, "Does anybody have an extra ticket?" Inevitably, there would be a Cub Scout troop, who would have 30 tickets, but nobody was taking them. And then, we figured out you could grub tickets, and you could keep grubbing them and grubbing them, and then we would sell them. We'd actually make money, keep one ticket, and then go inside and see the game. I remember doing that through seventh and eighth grade, and I remember I was in the eighth grade that they made the run against the Rangers. I remember taking my father's super 8 camera - because I was able to get right down by the glass - and shot some pretty good footage, but god knows where it is now. My dad was really into the fact that they were playing better, that they came from out of nowhere.

AL ARBOUR: The players [are the reason the Islanders improved in '75] - there's no doubt about it.

BOB BOURNE: We were a pretty good hockey team in '74. I think we got 88 points that year, and ended up playing the Rangers in the first round.

PATRICK DIVISION STANDINGS: 1974-75

TEAMS	W	L	T	POINTS
Philadelphia Flyers	51	18	11	113
New York Rangers	37	29	14	88
New York Islanders	33	25	22	88
Atlanta Flames	34	31	15	83

CHAPTER 7:

RANGERS '75

What better way to kick off the Islanders' first-ever playoff series than against their most hated rival, the New York Rangers, in a short (yet highly memorable) preliminary round series?

GARY "BABA BOOEY" DELL'ABATE: It seemed mostly like a Rangers town. But as a kid from Uniondale, I didn't really care about the Rangers.

JEAN POTVIN: We were *huge* underdogs. We went in there feeling pretty good about the year we had had. We had finished with as many points as the Rangers. But the bottom line is the Rangers, on paper, many of them were on their way to the Hall of Fame. But they were also closer to their retirement than they were to the beginning of their careers. We had a couple of guys that were on their way to the Hall of Fame also, like Denis, Clark, and Billy. But these guys were fairly early in their careers, so at that time, we had no way of knowing for sure if they'd make it. They had the likes of Jean Ratelle, Rod Gilbert, Brad Park, Eddie Giacomin - some very good hockey players. But we went in there and we had no fear. Because Al Arbour had taught us if you play hard and if you play smart, you stay away from stupid penalties, you stay away from making bad, stupid plays, you can compete with these guys. Although I remembered as a kid seeing a lot of these players, like Rod Gilbert, play in the NHL. So at the beginning, when you start playing in the NHL, you're in awe of some of these players, like I was of Jean Béliveau the first time I ever played against him. And Bobby Hull and Stan Mikita. But we went in against the Rangers. It was a "best of three series," which you don't have nowadays.

GLENN "CHICO" RESCH: I felt bad for the Rangers, they got stiffed a little bit. It was a two out of three series, which really isn't fair. It's funny, we won one of the last games of the season in there [at Madison Square Garden], and then we started with the first game of the playoffs [also at Madison Square Garden].

EDDIE WESTFALL: I felt sorry for the Rangers. [Laughs] Because all of the bitterness that had built up in the guys was still around. I mean, the Rangers back in those days had home games at Madison Square Garden and "home games" at the Nassau Coliseum, and a lot of us were very resentful. We had slowly started to gain our own fans. So when we got to the last game that season, we beat the Rangers in order to get into the playoffs. They were supposed to beat us - they had a hell of a team that year. There were still a lot of guys from the '72 Finalist team, when the Bruins beat them for the Stanley Cup. But we remembered how they used to handle us when we were younger. We were growing up - so look out. Like, "Hey dad, that teenager now can probably take you, so be careful." [Laughs] We carried that enthusiasm into the first game.

BILLY HARRIS: I think that series I was playing with a partially separated shoulder.

BILL TORREY: Everybody in and around New York picked the Rangers to beat us very quickly. But we surprised them in the first game in the Garden, and upset them [3-2] - which was a huge surprise.

GLENN "CHICO" RESCH: I had a really good game against them in the Garden, and we won.

JEAN POTVIN: I scored the goal that I believe tied it up at two. And if I remember correctly, we were down two goals to nothing going into the third period, and we scored three straight goals. Billy Harris got the first one, I got the second one, and Gillies got the winning goal - I believe about a minute/a minute and a half after I scored. I got the goal playing as a right wing on the fourth line with Lorne Henning at center, and Billy MacMillan on the left side. Even though I was a defenseman, Al felt that I had a lot of speed and that he wanted to know if I would not mind occasionally...because in a series in the playoffs, you can't just think you're going to go with three lines. You like to go with four lines, at least for a couple of periods, because you keep your players more fresh that way. So he threw us out there in the third period. I ended up getting the goal on a wrap-around. So we won game one.

EDDIE WESTFALL: I think in the second game in that series, all of a sudden "a light" went on, and we started to realize we were in the playoffs, and one up in a short series!

JP PARISÉ: It's kind of like we woke them up. They came back to Long Island and kicked our ass.

GLENN "CHICO" RESCH: Al started me at home, and I got blown away in game two [the Rangers won 8-3].

BILLY HARRIS: I'll always remember this - the second game was at the Coliseum. The visiting team has to submit their starting line-up. So they start Ratelle and Gilbert - the big line. And they've got Park on defense. All good players. Al Arbour starts five defensemen. Five of the toughest guys we got on the team - Dave Fortier, Denis. And as soon as the puck was dropped, they just started pummeling the shit out of Ratelle and Gilbert. [Laughs] *It was a brawl.*

CLARK GILLIES: A brawl broke out. I was actually sitting on the bench, and I got so excited to get out there and get involved with what was going on that I hyperventilated on the bench, and I had to be helped off the ice - which kind of wrecked me for the rest of the night. But it was pretty funny, because we didn't really know what was happening to me. As it turned out, I was fine, and was able to play in the third game.

JEAN POTVIN: Again, you had the momentum switching, and they felt, "Well, the Islanders were lucky to win that first one. There's no way they're going to win the third one. The Rangers really showed them who's boss in the second game. So they're going to come in here, and they know they're going to get more of the same."

CLARK GILLIES: Everybody thought this thing was going to be over. Here we are, going back to the Garden, and that's going to be our last game.

GLENN "CHICO" RESCH: Then Al came back with Billy, and Billy had a really good game.

JP PARISÉ: Al Arbour was such a great, wonderful coach. Just a motivator, smart coach - everything. Just a wonderful person. He had us believing to just basically play one shift at a time - the old slogan. But it worked. We came back against the Rangers at Madison Square Garden - we dominated for two periods. We were going into the third period leading 3-0. And then it's as if we woke them up again, and they came storming at us in the third.

CLARK GILLIES: As that turned out, I didn't realize until I watched some of the replays that the we were leading that third game, 3-0, going into the third period, and the Rangers came back and tied it.

GLENN "CHICO" RESCH: In the third period, I mean, they were all over us. We were just hanging on by the ends of our fingernails.

JEAN POTVIN: I remember the Rangers just throwing *everything* at us in the third period. And Billy Smith played unbelievably well in the third period. I remember looking at the clock, and thinking, "*Please* speed up. Get this period over with!" Because we couldn't get out of our own zone. They had us hemmed in - they were just bombarding us. They tied the game, and naturally, it went into overtime.

BILL TORREY: Billy Smith saved that game for us in the third period. In all the years that he played for me, that third period was as good as any, and was "Stanley Cup caliber," to say the least.

STAN FISCHLER: No [Stan did not attend the deciding game of the series]. I was rooting so hard for them, and when they were leading in the third, I decided to walk my dog - I couldn't handle the tension. I came back, and it was tied.

EDDIE WESTFALL: I had been there before in the playoffs and overtimes. So my thought was, "What did we do when I was a Boston Bruin when we got to the playoffs and overtime?" One thing we always said in the Bruin dressing room was, "When you're going to go to overtime, you've got to win as quickly as possible. You've got to be aggressive, you've got to take a little bit of a chance. You don't want to sit back." So that's what we had drummed up in the dressing room. They put out the oldest line on the team - JP Parisé, Jude Drouin, and Ed Westfall. And that's all we talked about - "Win the face-off, get the puck in, put pressure on them, and we'll take our chances down in their end of the ice. They can't score if the puck's in their backyard."

JP PARISÉ: I think it was Dave Lewis who dumped the puck into the Rangers corner. And at that time, Jude and I had a play, where he would go to the puck, and just kind of bang it behind the net. I would automatically go to the far corner and receive that pass. We bought time so I could make a play - give him a chance to get back in front of the net or follow behind the net. We had different options. And for some reason, I decided to go to the net, instead. And Jude got to the point, first. One of the Rangers didn't pick up the puck, so Jude was right on top. He's the guy that made the whole play - he spotted me going towards the net. All of a sudden, it was right on my stick, and I had a whole open net. I scored, and that's the last I remembered, because after I scored, I got hit from behind. Brad Park hit me, and I fell down on the ice. But we all went nuts, and the game was over. It was just a great, great feeling.

STAN FISCHLER: The overtime happened so fast, it was a blink of an eye. The whole sequence was surreal - so fast and very little replay availability in those days. I watched it on television. I *still* can't believe it.

EDDIE WESTFALL: That was a playoff record at the time [the goal was scored eleven seconds into overtime]. We were surprised. You don't know you're going to score. You can't set it up to say, *"This* is how you're going to score it." You set it up so you give you and your teammates the best opportunity to win the hockey game. And that's really what that whole thing was about - to give yourself a chance to win it.

JEAN POTVIN: I remember sitting on the bench, and watching a lot of the fans still trying to make their way back from the hot dog stand to their seats, when JP scored eleven seconds into overtime. I will never forget with all the cheering we were doing, you couldn't help but when you were skating off the ice, to notice all the fans that were still in their seats - many of them were just there with a blank stare. They could not believe that this had taken place. And you had people who were still coming back from the hot dog stand, rushing to see what the roar was, and they couldn't believe it! People were telling them, "It's over. They scored." It was unbelievable.

GLENN "CHICO" RESCH: To get the early goal in the overtime really helped. I wouldn't have wanted that to go too much further than that.

AL ARBOUR: It really sticks out. Beating the Rangers is really something. We were just starting at the time, and that made our team go. It was a very big win for us.

CLAIRE ARBOUR: I certainly do remember that! Oh my gosh - I was there. I went to very few Rangers games. It wasn't an easy thing for me to do. Our neighbors down in the courtyard, they knew nothing about hockey, but they said, "Claire, if you want to go to the game, we'll take you." So off we go to the game. We're sitting, and we're very politely applauding every time the Islanders scored. So people around us kind of knew we were Islanders fans. They didn't say anything. Then, when they tied it up and we were going into overtime, they tapped us on the shoulder, and said, "Oh, you guys had a great season." They were kissing us goodbye. "We go to the Coliseum, we have season tickets there too, and it's really nice. You can be proud of your team." And of course, the overtime lasted so little - I still don't know how I got the courage to turn around and say, "Well...*see you at the Coliseum!*" I was so excited; it was such an unexpected thing. Poor Al - he was in tremendous pain with his back.

And they all got up at the same time. The bench went flying on his feet, and he's trying to cheer that he's happy, but he's trying to get the bench off his feet. [Laughs]

BILLY HARRIS: We get down the back freight elevator to the bus, and there's a mob scene out in the street. They've got beer bottles; they're throwing shit at us. We had to get a police escort to the Midtown Tunnel.

CLAIRE ARBOUR: We came back home, and sat there in total disbelief, that we had won the series. But that was always what he aimed at - to win the playoffs.

AL ARBOUR: It was really great to beat the Rangers in the first round, the first time we were in the playoffs. I mean, *it was unbelievable.*

BOB NYSTROM: In just the first round with the Rangers, I think it was as if we had grown up. That series really put us on the map, because we beat "the big bad Rangers." From that standpoint, it was a real feather in our cap. We finally got a little bit of recognition.

GARY "BABA BOOEY" DELL'ABATE: With the Rangers series, my dad was really excited about it - he always loved the underdog. So after they beat the Rangers, it was a huge statement.

STAN FISCHLER: That series was without a doubt the turning point for the team. The enormity of the upset - considering the relative talent on the team - cannot be measured. It was one of these hundred-to-one shots, and the way it was done was even more amazing. It was so tremendous in so many ways. First of all, it established that this was an exciting team. There were individuals now who were becoming personalities, like Potvin and Gillies. And of course, the fact that they were young and were underdogs, there was a romance about these guys. It was the key. It was the kind of thing that's missing in teams like the Blue Jackets, for example, or the Thrashers - these guys never won. And the Islanders won. It started with that playoff.

GARY "BABA BOOEY" DELL'ABATE: Everything after the Rangers win was gravy.

GLENN "CHICO" RESCH: It was just sort of our year. It was meant to be our "Cinderella year/coming out year."

JEAN POTVIN: I'll never forget in the paper the next day [after the Islanders eliminated the Rangers], Derek Sanderson was quoted as saying, "This is a terrible hockey team" - the Islanders are. "They were lucky to beat us. I predict they will never win another game this year in the playoffs." And we almost didn't.

Preliminary Round (2-1):

New York Islanders over New York Rangers

Game 1   April 8   New York Islanders 3   New York Rangers 2
Game 2   April 10   New York Rangers 8   New York Islanders 3
Game 3   April 11   New York Islanders 4   New York Rangers 3 (OT)

CHAPTER 8:

PENGUINS '75

The Islanders dig themselves a mighty big hole against the Pittsburgh Penguins in the Quarter-Finals. Their season appears over, until Al Arbour delivers a now-classic speech to the team, and the Islanders rekindle the spirit of the '42 Maple Leafs.

CLARK GILLIES: One of the comments that we didn't want to come true was Derek Sanderson, saying "The Rangers should have beat us, and the Islanders probably won't win another game in the playoffs." He was looking like a pretty smart guy at that point, after we had lost three.

EDDIE WESTFALL: My thought was always we were still basking in the playoffs of one, making the playoffs that year, and then two, upsetting one of the best teams in the league. I think we got off to a slow start against Pittsburgh. But not to take anything away from Pittsburgh - they were a hell of a team too that year. In a seven game series, by the time you tripped and stumbled through the first couple of games, and then you realize, "Geez, we're not doing as well as we should be," they've won another one.

BOB NYSTROM: I think that was something that was so new to most of us, that before we knew it, we went into that series and we were down three games to nothing. I would have to say that I remember a speech that Al made. He said, "If anyone thinks that we're not going to win this series, I want them to go off the ice right now. We've got them exactly where we want them." And he challenged everybody. He said, "If you don't believe that you can just go out there, and win one shift at a time, one period at a time, one game at a time, I don't want you here." That's kind of the attitude that we took. I think that's an attitude that really stuck with the team.

AL ARBOUR: I said to the team, "If anybody here doesn't think we're going to win, the door's open - you just go on out."

JEAN POTVIN: I remember losing game one [5-4], game two [3-1], but especially game three, because game three was the first of two in our rink. They beat us in Pittsburgh, and we said, "That's OK. We just need to win one in Pittsburgh - that's all." So, "OK, they beat us the first two. Big deal, we're a little tired, we had a tough series against the Rangers, we'll get them when they come to our building." Well, they come to our building, and they're leading two games to none, and they beat us [6-4]. I remember we were practicing at Racquet and Rink, the day after that terrible loss. We start practice, and Al is blowing the whistle. When you blow the whistle once, you speed up to start the practice, skating in a circle, counter-clockwise. And when he blows it again, you go full speed, then he blows the whistle, you slow down. You could see there was no life in practice.

He blows the whistle, and says, "OK, everybody here in center ice." So he got us all around him - close to the boards. He was still very much believing that we could come back, and was trying to inject into us this belief. He says, "Let me ask you guys, collectively. You know that we've been matching lines. We've been putting certain players against certain players. When I put you on the ice - whether you're the first, second, third, or fourth line - you're going to play against somebody that you've played against in this series. And you've played against them maybe a couple of years during the regular season. When I put my defensemen out there, I'm going to put my best defensemen against their best lines, which I always do. So there's nobody there that's got any secrets. You know what they have to offer, you know what they do. If I ask each and every one of you, 'Can you be better than the guy you play against for one shift?'" "Yeah, sure!" "OK. How about two shifts?" "Yeah, sure - damn right I can!" "OK, how about doing it one shift at a time. One period at a time. I don't want us to even think about, 'Oh man, we've got a huge mountain to climb - nobody's ever done this except the Toronto

Maple Leafs back in 1942. *One shift at a time.* That's the way I want us to approach it."

And I know for myself, that made me rethink the job ahead significantly, and I know it made others feel the same way. To the extent that we did take it one shift, one period at a time. "Let's win the first period. Let's win the second period, regardless of the score. Let's win the third period. And if we win that game, OK, boom - put it behind us. Let's win the first shift of the next game."

BILLY HARRIS: That was like a normal thing with [Arbour] - he'd have great meetings and great talks. Like, "Where is he going with this?" And then all of a sudden, it would make sense.

GLENN "CHICO" RESCH: Al would tell stories about Sudbury, and he always had some stories about putting things into perspective. You just couldn't not like the guy.

GARY "BABA BOOEY" DELL'ABATE: The funny thing was had they got swept by the Penguins, it probably would have been seen as an unbelievably successful season. They beat the Rangers, they won their first playoff series - it's all good stuff. When they went down 0-3, I remember nobody really giving a shit, or nobody really expecting much from them. Then they won a game. Then they won another game.

CLARK GILLIES: We were having so much fun - just going out and playing every night. Nobody wanted to finish. It was like, "Is this really happening?"

EDDIE WESTFALL: We finally got the wake-up call and started to come around. And once we started to catch some breaks, then of course, the momentum shifts in those kinds of things, where after you've won two games, they're certainly concerned, and teams will naturally start to tighten up if things aren't going the way they were going. They expected to either sweep the series or maybe we'd win one. By the time you get tied, it doesn't matter what building you're in - we're on a real roll by that point.

JEAN POTVIN: The turnaround was unbelievable. And the enthusiasm, the positive vibes that we gained with almost every shift, because I'd get excited when I'd see JP Parisé's line go out there, and not only shut down the line they played against, but to maybe score a goal. Or knock them into their own zone, where they can't even come out, because they're forechecking so aggressively. And JP Parisé, Eddie Westfall, and Jude Drouin were such tremendous influences, a positive influence on us, who were younger than these guys. But they were leading the way - they were like the hardest workers on the team. And we got great goaltending. Chico at that time I think was still playing most of the time as a goaltender, and it was just wonderful. We were picking up steam. And I think on the other side of the aisle, Pittsburgh was starting to lose that enthusiasm that they had after they had us down three games to nothing.

EDDIE WESTFALL: Absolutely [it was the greatest comeback Westfall experienced as a player]. You were feeding on all of the stuff that was going on in the last three games as you go into the final game. But as I remember correctly, the seventh game, *everybody* was tight in that game. No one wanted to lose it. It wasn't like we just sat back and protected our own nets - there was still some wonderful goaltending and some good opportunities. Pittsburgh was still the favorite.

GLENN "CHICO" RESCH: We were winning by [a small margin] every game. I'm playing well, but I'm lucky, and the team is playing well. It was in that seventh game when in one shift, they got two goal posts. It's funny, then you start feeling invincible. Feeling fortunate and getting the lucky bounces in hockey is almost as good as playing well. Because you just know that playing well or not, things are going to bounce your way. Some incredible occurrences. Like, if they score those two goals in the first period, it's over. But they didn't. They hit two goal posts, and a third one hit me right in the "island" on the front of my mask. I just went over and kissed that goal post. At that time, that goal post and I were tied together pretty strongly.

JEAN POTVIN: I remember that seventh game, here's a guy, Bert Marshall, that we would joke around, had the slowest shot on our team - and maybe the NHL. Shot the puck, and I believe it was from the right point, and Eddie Westfall was standing in front of the net, to the left of the goalie, and deflected it in. It was late in the game, 1-0.

EDDIE WESTFALL: There was only five minutes or so left in the game. It's much similar to when you talk on the bench between periods and you come out for the third period - it was like an overtime. You can't sit back. You've got to take it to them. And that was really the conversation - "We've got to be in their end of the ice as much as we can." I think we were doing really well as far as that was concerned. We weren't out-played, but at the time, I remember Bert Marshall, we got the puck back to him. He was playing on the right point and I was down in the corner. I started towards the front of the net, and he kind of slid the puck to me. And as quickly as I could, it was just "get anything I could to the net," and hope for a rebound or maybe it would hit somebody. Just instinctively. He passed me the puck and it was on my forehand when I got it, and I was heading off the right boards towards the middle of the ice. I fired a backhand, and it went right in under the crossbar.

CLARK GILLIES: It was a unique experience, to come back and beat them four straight, with Eddie Westfall [scoring the clinching goal in game seven]. As a matter of fact, I'm going to see Eddie now! We won the game 1-0, and we just kind of looked at each other and laughed, like, *"Is this really happening?"* We had to pinch ourselves to keep going, saying, "Holy shit, we've accomplished a lot. Let's just keep doing this."

BILLY HARRIS: The one thing that I remember the most about that is the Islanders fans that came to Pittsburgh for the games. And then when we knocked them out in the seventh game, we came back to the hotel, and you couldn't get into the hotel! Everybody was out partying all night. It was just nutty. The fans were unbelievable.

JIM PICKARD: My wife was pregnant with our second child. And when Eddie Westfall scored, I remember after, we're in the locker room, and we're all exuberant. I'd known Eddie since I was a kid - I used to deliver his paper, in my little town of 500 - and I said to Eddie, "You just paid for my kid by scoring that goal!"

EDDIE WESTFALL: I remember when the Red Sox came back against the Yankees [in the 2004 American League Championship Series], Tim McCarver - who is quite a hockey fan, he used to come and sit in our broadcast booth with Jiggs and I in Philadelphia occasionally - accurately depicted the last time it was done [that a pro sports team came back from a 3-0 deficit to win a series]. He said, "My friend Eddie Westfall scored the only goal in the seventh game when the Islanders came back." I got a kick out of that - my 15 seconds of fame! [Laughs]

GLENN "CHICO" RESCH: Winning that game I think changed a lot of the fortune of us. Because it gave us - even for years down the road - a feeling of "We could always come back."

CLARK GILLIES: And then as it turned out, we went down in the next series 3-0, to Philly.

Quarter-Finals (4-3):

New York Islanders over Pittsburgh Penguins

Game 1	April 13	New York Islanders 4	Pittsburgh Penguins 5
Game 2	April 15	New York Islanders 1	Pittsburgh Penguins 3
Game 3	April 17	Pittsburgh Penguins 6	New York Islanders 4
Game 4	April 20	Pittsburgh Penguins 1	New York Islanders 3
Game 5	April 22	New York Islanders 4	Pittsburgh Penguins 2
Game 6	April 24	Pittsburgh Penguins 1	New York Islanders 4
Game 7	April 26	New York Islanders 1	Pittsburgh Penguins 0

CHAPTER 9:

FLYERS '75

The Islanders dig themselves into a humongous hole again, this time against the reigning Stanley Cup champion Broad Street Bullies in the Semi-Finals. Can they perform another miraculous comeback?

BILL TORREY: The next series we played was against Philadelphia. They had four or five days in between their series and were well rested. We had gone through a seven game series, and they caught us in the first two games [4-0 and 5-4] - we were very flat. It looked like it might be a runaway. They were a team that everybody was pointing towards for the Stanley Cup. It didn't look very good for us. We were down 3-0 [after dropping game three, 1-0].

EDDIE WESTFALL: Almost the same thing. After what we had accomplished, we didn't wake up I guess until the third game had been played. We were still in a coma - it was self-induced. [Laughs] I would have to think it's the same, I suppose if you study it, you can look back and see where it's not uncommon for teams - particularly underdog teams - that have become almost extinct and then come back to life.

JEAN POTVIN: It was the same thing. The Flyers had a very good team that year. They had a much better team than Pittsburgh had. They really outclassed us certainly in the first three games. It was a very physical series, because that's just the way the Flyers played. The Flyers were a very bruising team. But I'll tell you one thing - they never pushed us around. Because that's the year that Clark Gillies took on Dave Schultz, and he really did a number on him. It was a convincing win. I also remember Garry Howatt taking on Bob "Houndog" Kelly, who probably outweighed Garry by 30 or 40 pounds. And Garry got the best of him - really, the best of him. Bobby Nystrom was there, my brother - we had a tough team. And the Flyers knew not to screw around and intimidate us, because it didn't work.

They just beat us with good old hockey, because they had a heck of a team. You got Bobby Clarke, Bill Barber, Gary Dornhoefer, Rick MacLeish - who was I thought a highly underrated hockey player. So they had a very talented team, as well. Anyways, we were down three games to nothing, and here we go again. And the same thing - now we can joke about it a little bit more. Al says, "Let's just rewind the speech I gave you guys about a week and a half ago. Let's do this again. Come on, you've got to turn your head around. You've got to mentally get back to where we were when we won the last four. We have not played well. We've made some stupid plays, taken some bad penalties, and this is why we're in the hole that we're in again." So here we go - we start coming back.

BILLY HARRIS: We go, "Hey guys, we did it once more. Why can't we do it again?"

CLARK GILLIES: We had a lot of people shaking their heads, I'll tell you that. "What the hell is going on with these guys? Could this possibly happen, that we do this two series in a row, since nobody's done it since the '42 Leafs? And here we can do it twice in one season? That would be quite a miracle if that happened."

BOB NYSTROM: It was no different than the first. We had already experienced that, so we weren't intimidated by it. We felt that we could win the series, and take them to that seventh game.

JP PARISÉ: We won one [4-3], and then another one [5-1], and then we come back to Long Island for another one, and win that one [2-1].

GLENN "CHICO" RESCH: There were two moments. When Clark Gillies pummeled Dave Schultz in game five, then we won game six.

CLARK GILLIES: That whole thing with Schultzie had sort of been building all year long. Everybody was saying I'm "the big heavyweight" on the Islanders. We had a few skirmishes. And then when we played them in '75, I believe that was game five in Philly. We were up pretty substantially - it was late in the game. And Freddie Shero puts Bob Kelly, Dave Schultz, and Orest Kindrachuk out there against myself, Lorne Henning, and Billy MacMillan, I believe. It was basically Shero put Schultz out against me, so you knew right away that something was going to happen. We kind of looked at each other, and off we went. That was really the turning point as far as my career - could I go against the other tough guys in the league? Because Schultz at that time had the reputation of being *the* tough guy. And I beat him pretty good in that fight. I would have beat him a lot more, too, if Moose Dupont hadn't have grabbed me around the neck. He was down and out. I would have pounded him right into the ice if I had the chance. At that time, I kind of lost my cool. I knew what I was doing, but I was kind of free-for-all-ing at that time. I wasn't going to stop punching him until he was down to the ice, and that was when Dupont grabbed me around the neck. As it turns out, Schultzie and I ended up being pretty good friends after the whole thing was said and done, so that's kind of ironic.

BILLY HARRIS: If it's the same one I'm remembering, we were beating them, and they got all their goons out there. It was like the last shift of the game, and I'm on the ice. I get a tap on the ass, and here comes Clarkie out to play right wing, against Schultz. So Arbour was obviously sending him out to send a message. I think that's when it happened. They fought quite a bit, but that's the one thing I remember the most, because I'm standing there against Schultz, and you know they're going to start something, right? So you go, "Who are you going to end up with?" I usually ended up with Bob Kelly or somebody I knew. [Laughs]

AL ARBOUR: It meant a lot. Gillies, he would take on anybody. He was unbelievable. It was unreal. Philly was the toughest team in the league at the time, and Boston was after. There's no question about it - we had enough tough guys that we could handle ourselves.

BOB BOURNE: All of a sudden, they knew this was a team they weren't going to push around.

BILL TORREY: Long-term, we played the Flyers six times a year, and we had lots of confrontations - not only with Schultz, but they had two or three other guys that thought they were pretty tough. One thing about our team that was developing was we were getting bigger, and we were not only getting better - we were getting tougher. So we were not intimidated - that was not a factor in that series. After that, Schultz had a few tussles with Clarkie, but not very many.

BILLY HARRIS: Certain guys are there for that reason [to fight]. I was there to score to goals. If I broke my hand…I already broke my hand once in junior - I snapped my knuckle right off and I missed a couple of weeks. My dad told me, "You need an awfully long stick to score a goal from the penalty box."

JEAN POTVIN: It's 3-3. And then naturally, they brought in Kate Smith, their old favorite. [The Flyers] had an amazing record in the playoffs and regular season, that whenever they played her record of "God Bless America," the Flyers had been almost 100% invincible. I think at that time, they had won 35 times and lost one - something ridiculous like that. And for that special night, Mr. Snider, the owner of the Flyers, flew her in. She was retired I believe at that point in Florida, and she sang the national anthem. They rolled out a carpet immediately to the right of Chico Resch, and she came out there - and they might have even brought out an organ, where the guy played and she sang. I think Mr. Snider told her, "Look, the fans are going to go nuts, especially towards the end. Just stand there as long as you can and wave - don't move." And she seemed to stand there *forever.* Naturally, we tried to defuse that magic a little bit, by having Eddie, our captain, give her a bouquet of flowers. It was tulips or roses. Eventually, she came off, and they rolled the carpet.

GLENN "CHICO" RESCH: And I got to tell you, as great as I played in game seven of the Penguins series, I knew I had to play *big* in game seven against the Flyers. And they had Kate Smith, who is a legendary singer. Now, people don't even know who she is. But she stood right by my crease and sang the national anthem.

AL ARBOUR: Chico was really upset about the fact that she was in the net. It really disturbed him.

BILLY HARRIS: And the worst thing imaginable happened. It might have been on the first or second shift, Gary Dornhoefer gets the puck right at center ice, takes a wrist shot at Chico, and he blows it in from center ice.

GLENN "CHICO" RESCH: I can still see the first shift - Dornhoefer comes down the wing, and he slaps one. I saw it. Now, for a goalie, if it's on the ice, I've got it. If it's up another six inches, I got it. He put it just between that window - between the bottom of my glove and the top of my stick, but I kicked out and I've got to tell you, I felt it hit the stick. I knew I got a big chunk of it. And then I hear the crowd roaring. This is within the first minute. The puck is in the net. I look down, and I had gone to thinner sticks, and the stinking puck had hit right at the top of the blade and chipped out about a quarter inch piece of wood.

BILLY HARRIS: The crowd goes crazy. When you go into a visiting rink, you've got to try and take the crowd out of the game. Either get the first goal or play real close-checking hockey for the first ten minutes - just to get everybody into the game. They were already revved up with Kate Smith singing "God Bless America." And that was it, we never recovered from that first goal. We had a shot at them. We didn't get blown out, but we didn't win. And it was the ninth time we faced elimination. Like a cat's got nine lives - it was the ninth time we faced elimination, and we lost the ninth time.

EDDIE WESTFALL: It's weird how those things happen, when you think, "We almost did it twice," if it wasn't for a Gary Dornhoefer goal on Chico Resch at the beginning of the game. It was from just inside the blue line, as a matter of fact, I missed a check - I was trying to hammer him through the boards I think, and I probably went out of position to hit him. And I either got not enough of him or missed him completely. He fired it from inside the blue line, and it was in. That set us back a little bit, but as we would say in the dressing room after, "You didn't expect that the Philadelphia Flyers would go a whole game at home in the seventh without scoring a goal. Let's see if we can make sure that's the only one."

GLENN "CHICO" RESCH: I'm not making excuses - we battled back. But in those types of games, that first goal is *so* huge. I mean, it's one of my most agonizing moments, I would say. Because if we could have gotten the jump on them in that game, it would have been huge.

JEAN POTVIN: We came back and scored one, but the final score was 4-1, and that's when we were actually eliminated.

BILL TORREY: We came back pretty good in the third period and had some chances, but really, we ran out of strength. And as you know, they went on to win the Cup [against the Buffalo Sabres].

JEAN POTVIN: But it was a great run, and we gained a lot of experience and confidence for the following season, because of what we had just done for the first time in the playoffs. We were known as "the Cinderella Team."

EDDIE WESTFALL: That was the most exciting year. And I yield to my two Stanley Cups with the Boston Bruins, as exciting as the first one was, because it's the first time - from the time you were a little kid, to win a Stanley Cup. But if I had to pick one year out of the 18 I played, that '75 year in the playoffs was about as good as it could get. There wasn't a season I ever had that was more exciting, more fun, had more ups and downs than that one. Culminating in the end of the season and the playoffs. That was worth a career, to be a part of that.

GLENN "CHICO" RESCH: Al and Bill orchestrated the team perfectly through all those ups and downs those first playoffs.

GARY "BABA BOOEY" DELL'ABATE: The remarkable thought of the Islanders going to the Stanley Cup Finals that year was very Mets-like. It was sort of "worst to first." I remember being in ninth grade, after they had that big year, and suddenly, everybody was an Islanders fan. We had a kid, and his name was JP, and we always used to call him "JP Parisé."

JP PARISÉ: They had more better players than we did. They were tough - they were "workers," also. So they just had a little too much for us. I always wonder what would have happened if they would have turned Bryan Trottier pro at that time. Because Bryan had been called up and was with us for the playoffs, and they never played him. There was some thing about him being protected another year - I don't remember. Bryan was just a great player. As a kid, you could tell. I wonder if they had turned him pro, if we would have won that.

Semi-Finals (4-3):

Philadelphia Flyers over New York Islanders

Game 1	April 29	New York Islanders 0	Philadelphia Flyers 4
Game 2	May 1	New York Islanders 4	Philadelphia Flyers 5 (OT)
Game 3	May 4	Philadelphia Flyers 1	New York Islanders 0
Game 4	May 7	Philadelphia Flyers 3	New York Islanders 4 (OT)
Game 5	May 8	New York Islanders 5	Philadelphia Flyers 1
Game 6	May 11	Philadelphia Flyers 1	New York Islanders 2
Game 7	May 13	New York Islanders 1	Philadelphia Flyers 4

CHAPTER 10:

GREETINGS, MR. TROTTIER

With the arrival of center Bryan Trottier, the Islanders soon find out they just landed one of the best all-around players in the league.

BOB BOURNE: The year I got drafted was the first year the NHL ever allowed underage drafting, and that's when Bryan Trottier was drafted. He didn't play my first year, but he came in the next year, and he kind of turned that franchise around.

BILLY HARRIS: They brought him up before that, and he was playing junior. He came to practice with us. I'm going to the guys, "He could play right now and be our best player on the team." But they sent him back and made him play another year in junior. When he finally got to camp, he was unbelievable. I'd never seen anybody so strong on their feet. He could do it all.

CLARK GILLIES: I was confident Bryan was going to make a big difference, because I had played in junior against Bryan - he was in Swift Current and I was in Regina. We were actually drafted the same year. I was in the first round, and they took Bryan as an underage player in the second round - which was a real steal by Bill Torrey, as far as I'm concerned. I knew Bryan coming in was going to be a real positive addition to our team. I basically considered him a first round pick, because the following year, we probably would not have gotten him - he would have gone to somebody right off the bat. That's how good he was. So for Bill Torrey to take him in that second round and send him back to junior for another year was very smart. Right from the get-go, Bryan was on the power play, killing penalties. Just doing it all - like he did in junior.

EDDIE WESTFALL: They brought him in, and he practiced with us at Racquet and Rink, and I said to a couple of the guys - probably over a beer or something later - "This Trottier kid is a left-handed shooting Gordie Howe in the making." He was great. He was only probably 19 at that point, but you could see how he handled himself, and he was so strong on the puck. He just loved to play. You could tell immediately. And he was the politest, nicest young man.

GLENN "CHICO" RESCH: An interesting thing that happened was with Trots, Johnny Tonelli who came later, and Mark Messier and Rob Ramage and a lot of those 17-year-olds, got a lawyer, and sued the NHL, because they weren't allowing players to come into the NHL until 20. Y'know, "the 20-year-old draft." It was a labored thing. And the judge ruled it, "No, these players are eligible. They're voting, they can go to the army or war. They deserve to start making a living at 18. And so they had that anti-trust suit or whatever it was. So Trot's year, you had all the regular guys coming in, who would have been 19 and 20. It was a draft of 20-year-olds. And there were some 19-year-olds getting drafted, but mostly 20-year-olds. So now all of a sudden, you've got it upgraded where you got 18, 19, and 20-year-olds all in this one draft. So we get Trots in the second round. That was a huge, huge, huge timing for us.

BILL TORREY: In January, after the WHA started signing all these underage kids - taking them away from the NHL before they would have a chance to draft them - we had a Board of Governor's meeting, in which all the teams said they wanted to do something before all those kids were taken by the WHA. So it was decided that year and announced that NHL teams - this was in late January - would be allowed to draft one underage player in either the first or second round of the draft.

In that draft, we had the third pick of the draft, and we had pretty much decided by January/February that Clark Gillies was the player we wanted. We needed one more big piece up front, and he was the guy that we really wanted. Well, now all of a sudden, the rules change, and there were kids available now in the draft that wouldn't have been available otherwise. So we had to redo our thinking. Our western scout, Earl Ingarfield, and his assistant - who lived in Swift Current - insisted that I take a look at a kid from Swift Current, who was underage. We were looking for a bigger winger, we were also looking for another centerman. To make a long story short, I went out the first time to see Trots play. I got out at Swift Current, Saskatchewan, in the middle of a blizzard. The game in particular that I went to see Trots play, Stan Dunn the coach didn't put him on the ice until the third period. But they had a very, very strong team - a Memorial Cup potential team. They had a number of drafts that year - Tiger Williams was on that team, players of that maturity and size. Anyway, Bryan was the third line center.

He finally got on the ice in the third period, and he did score two goals - even with the limited ice time. He was not the only player that we looked at, but more and more, number one, we felt that Trots was attractive to us because he was little known and it was his first year of junior - he was playing on a strong team and not getting very much ice time. So when it came time to actually sit down and work out the draft, we listed two or three underage kids, one of which was Trots. When it came time for our third pick, we knew for sure Clark Gillies was going to go in the next one or two picks. And we also felt that those underage kids, there were a lot of the better ones that had not been scouted that thoroughly, because the league decision of even allowing them in the draft. So we went ahead and drafted Clark Gillies, and then when it got to the 22nd pick, there were five or six underage kids that had been drafted already. And there was young Bryan Trottier. We all liked his potential, we all liked everything we had learned about him and saw in him. So we took him next.

BRYAN TROTTIER [The Islanders' center from 1975-1990]: I'm from Val Marie, Saskatchewan. I played junior hockey in Swift Current and Lethbridge, and was drafted out of Swift Current in '74, I believe it was. I came to camp in the fall of '75, right after they had their first playoff run. It was a pretty exciting time. And ended up playing 15 years on the Island.

The underage draft was brand spanking new, because the World Hockey Association was signing 18-year-olds. They had what was "a secret draft" or "a silent draft," that didn't have the big hoopla like they have today. It was a phone draft. We had very limited exposure, communication. Everything was handled by telephone, so it was kind of interesting. We just made the best of it, and nobody complained. It was an exciting time, because the Cincinnati Stingers were knocking on the door, and when they knocked on the door, my name got thrown into the NHL hat. I had minimal experience or understanding of how it worked, but it was new for my family, too. Ignorance is bliss at some points, but it would have been nice to have had a little bit better understanding of the whole thing. But no complaints.

I was very young - I was only 17 at the time. My parents, they believed that I didn't belong playing against men yet. I don't think they wanted me to go and put myself in a position where I wasn't quite ready physically, let alone mentally. It turned out to be a wise decision for everybody. I was so young, and had a tremendous amount of respect for Al Arbour and Bill Torrey. They both were very convincing in the direction they wanted to take for my future. Acceptance was pretty easy, because I figured, "These guys have the experience. They know what they're talking about." My parents felt the same way, saying that another year of growth was going to be really good for me.

Earl Ingarfield was going to be my coach, so I felt excited about that, because he was one of the guys that drafted me. I figured I was in good hands - as far as an opportunity to learn and an opportunity to get the right kind of direction and coaching that I needed for that season. Wearing the "C" in junior and having a big leadership role, maturing physically and mentally, another year under my belt. Just normal growth - not so much from the standpoint of height/weight or anything like that. Just muscle growth, developmental skills, a ton of ice time.

It wasn't really their minor league team - I went back to the junior team I was drafted from. I just went back and played another year of junior, and the following winter, I went to training camp. So '74-'75 was just another year of junior hockey. It was really good, because like I said, I got a ton of ice time - close to 30 minutes a game. Under the tutelage of Earl Ingarfield, and a great city, Lethbridge. Really enjoyed that year in Lethbridge. Got to make a lot of new friends and good teammates. I think we over-achieved to some degree, and we maybe under-achieved in other areas. But overall, we really had a great group of guys. A lot of those guys ended up going to the NHL or are still involved in hockey in some way - Brian Sutter, Ron Delorme, Lorne Molleken.

JP PARISÉ: There was a period of time where Bryan Trottier was probably the best player in the National Hockey League. I can remember his first game in Long Island - he had three goals and five points [on October 11, 1975, against the Los Angeles Kings]. He was just a complete, good player. Strong and tough, and physical and smart. Oh my god, he was a good player. It didn't take him long, either. He must have gotten 80/90 points his first season [95 points]. He was going to be a Hall of Famer - you could tell that. He was just a nice kid that came from a little town, Val Marie.

JIM PICKARD: Trotter could play it basically any way you wanted to. But he was built like a fire hydrant, and he had such good hockey sense. He was just a tremendous player.

BRYAN TROTTIER: I had good teammates. Veterans like Eddie Westfall, JP Parisé, Gerry Hart. The young guys like Bob Nystrom, Clark Gillies, and Garry Howatt. God, it was just a standout group of guys that were very supportive. It just seemed like from the goaltenders out, Billy Smith and Chico Resch, everybody appreciated every little thing I did. It didn't matter what the situation was, I tried to contribute as much as possible. I think my style fit into Al's system a little bit - Al didn't yell at me very much. All in all, I felt welcomed. I felt like I was part of things. I think all of those things add to your confidence.

And lived with a really great family on Long Island. I didn't have to worry too much about meals or taking care of myself off the ice. I could just concentrate on hockey, have a great season, and let the chips fall where they will - as a 19-year-old kid just kind of getting used to Long Island, the National Hockey League, and new teammates. Trying to come out unscathed with my head on my shoulders, because I still felt like I was a kid against men. Some good things happened. Al put me in a situation to succeed. I think the recognition, it was just a really good opportunity here - a team that was on the rise. I felt really good about my role and how I could contribute, whether it was offensively, defensively, or taking a face-off. Just learning as fast as I possibly could, being a sponge - big ears, big eyes. The same as all the other kids that come into the league, and excited about a dream coming true, finally.

CHAPTER 11:

1975-76 AND 1976-77

The Islanders believe they have what it takes to get over the hump and land in the Stanley Cup Finals. But for two straight seasons, the Montreal Canadiens have something to say about it.

LORNE HENNING: After '75 is kind of when we made a name for ourselves and became a solid franchise.

EDDIE WESTFALL: In the big picture, we felt that we had arrived, after going to the Semi-Finals the year before. We didn't expect a whole lot the season before, but we accomplished a lot. So now, that changes the mood and the whole approach. Your expectations are now that we should be able to compete with anybody. And it wasn't cockiness as it was a confidence. You can be cocky after you've accomplished a whole lot. We were still in "the learning stage," and a few of the players - the younger players that were becoming very good quickly - still had a way to go.

JP PARISÉ: We had high expectations. Trottier came in, and the younger players were starting to get better - Clark Gillies, Bobby Bourne. All of a sudden, we were a better team, just for the fact that the guys that were there the year before got better and matured. We were competitive and we easily made the playoffs.

BOB LORIMER [The Islanders' defenseman from 1976-1981]: I grew up in Toronto and played all my minor hockey in the GTA - the Greater Toronto Area. Actually got drafted by the St. Catharines Blackhawks in major Junior A, and went to training camp and didn't make the team. So then I came back and played just Junior B hockey here in the Metro Toronto and Junior B league. Then was offered a college scholarship to play hockey at Michigan Tech. So I played two years at Michigan Tech and got drafted after my sophomore year, and completed my four years, and turned pro after my four years. So I was drafted in '73 - the same draft as Denis Potvin. I like to say that Denis was the first overall pick…and I was the first pick in the tenth round. [Laughs]

After I came out of college, I didn't get a contract with the Islanders. I went to training camp in Fort Worth, which was their highest minor league team at the time. I played in the International League in Muskegon for a year, had a fairly good year, and then signed a contract with the Islanders the following year. I was with the Islanders all through training camp, and then got sent down to Fort Worth, and I got hurt and missed a month in a half. Then I got playing again and got called up. My first game, I got hurt and lost my spleen, so I missed the rest of that year, and then the following year, I was up and down a little bit.

I remember we were playing Buffalo, and I went to hit Craig Ramsay, and I just remember he put his stick sideways at my stomach level. I hit him, went back to the bench, and went, "Boy, that really hurt," and played the rest of the game. And then a few of us were going out for a couple of beers and something to eat, and I had a really bad stomach ache, so I just went back to the hotel room. It got worse and worse. I phoned Ron Waske, our trainer, and said, "I've got a really bad stomach ache," and he said, "Why don't you go down to the front desk - it's probably nerves from your first game. You should see if they have Tums or something." I did, and it didn't work out. I phoned him again like two hours later, in the middle of the night, and he said, "I can't do anything for you. Why don't you go to the hospital and see what's going on." So I got in my rental car and drove to the hospital, and as I walked through the front door, I passed out right on the steps of the emergency room, because I had been bleeding internally since the hit happened. That was very lucky, because if I'd have stayed in my hotel room, that would have been it for my career…and my life, actually. So I had a very inauspicious start.

JEAN POTVIN: We were out-classed [by the Montreal Canadiens, who defeated the Islanders in the Semi-Finals in both 1975-76 and 1976-77]. We weren't ready. I don't think we had everything that it took to beat the Montreal Canadiens. And let's not forget, that Montreal team that won four Cups between '76 through '79 is recognized as maybe one of the top ten best teams ever, in the history of the NHL. Y'know, Guy Lafleur was the best player *in the world* at that time. We had Trottier, Bossy, Denis, Smitty, Chico, Gillies, Nystrom. We had a heck of a team. But not good enough to beat them.

AL ARBOUR: They had a better team than us. They had a great team, there's no doubt about it. We played well, but they played better.

BILL TORREY: Well, obviously the Canadiens were a more veteran team. They had a history of winning championships. Probably had a little more depth than we did - we were still in a building stage. And there is a learning curve. We were better during the regular season, we weren't better in the playoffs. Because of the success we had during the regular season, a lot of people began to start to write us off, as "They're never going to be winners" and so on. And there was increased pressure. The assumption is that a team like that is just always going to get better and better and better. Well, people get to know the team better, people get to understand what you're doing. There was not just one glaring reason. There were a lot of little pieces that needed to be worked on.

BRYAN TROTTIER: We were a team growing, [the Canadiens] were an established team. They had a great, great team. Without a doubt - goaltending, defense, offensive weapons, depth. And we couldn't compete. We weren't ready. We were a young team, a growing team, and learning how to win. And learning from other teams - great teams like the Canadiens. They were on a roll. They won four in a row and it was their time. Probably the heart of their whole team was right at the time when they were peaking as a team, as a group, as individuals. Larry Robinson was a perennial all-star, Guy Lafleur was a perennial all-star, Ken Dryden in the net. It just seemed like we weren't quite at their level yet.

EDDIE WESTFALL: Experience. We were still learning to be a good playoff team. And some of the younger players that had just arrived in '75, '76, and '77, they were not quite ready. I think Bossy came in '77, and he was tremendous, but he had to learn. There was a lot to learn yet about regular season hockey and playoff hockey - they're quite different. And players like Bryan Trottier, Clark Gillies, and Denis Potvin. [Potvin] was probably more than ready. And by then, it was established that Billy Smith was kind of "the go-to guy" in the goal. He was finding his way through it all, too. He would get distracted occasionally, but he had to learn as well as everybody. This is a whole different set of rules now, being in the playoffs.

BILLY HARRIS: Probably because they had five all-star defensemen, and Jacques Lemaire, Guy Lafleur, and Steve Shutt. They were just a solid team. We were getting close, we beat them a few times. I remember one game, I scored three goals and we lost 4-3. Another game, I scored the overtime winning goal in Montreal. We were close, but they just had too much depth. And we were still pretty young. We were just a little too young and maybe a little too intimidated.

CLARK GILLIES: It was always great playing the Canadiens, because you knew that you were going to be in a fast, high-tempo game. And they had a couple of guys on that team that could play tough, as well. But every time we played the Canadiens in the early years, I remember they were always very fast skating. In their normal fashion, they would get a 2-1 or 3-1 lead going into the third period, and it would basically be over. They would just shut you down. They were tough to play. It was good training for us, because ultimately, that's really the way we played - Al's thought process was "Take care of your own end, and the other end will take care of itself." So we would get a lead, and then basically go into another mode, and shut the other team down. That was a lot like Montreal, and that was a lot because Scotty Bowman, who coached them at the time, was one of Al's mentors. We basically followed that system pretty well, and we learned a lot from the Canadiens. We had some pretty good series against them. The two series we lost were pretty exciting. For us, anyway. If you get a chance to go up against a team like that - especially for me, early in my career - was a real treat. And we were able to take some real positives out of those series, and work them into later years.

GLENN "CHICO" RESCH: The interesting thing about the late '70s, we were the one team that that Canadiens feared. That one year, when they lost only ten games [it was actually eight games, during the 1976-77 regular season] and only lost two games in the playoffs - they were both to us.

JEAN POTVIN: Both years where they beat us and went on to win the Stanley Cup, my aunt or uncle would call, and say, "[The Canadiens] won the Stanley Cup again, and you know what they said that we thought was very nice? 'Who was your toughest competition on this march to the Stanley Cup?'" And both years, they apparently said, "The Islanders had a team that we worried about the most. Every game was close, and we feared these guys, because they just don't know how to quit. They are an up-and-coming team. I assure you - they're young, they're great, and they're going to win their share of Cups."

PATRICK DIVISION STANDINGS: 1975-76

TEAMS	W	L	T	POINTS
Philadelphia Flyers	51	13	16	118
New York Islanders	42	21	17	101
Atlanta Flames	35	33	12	82
New York Rangers	29	42	9	67

Preliminary Round (2-0):

New York Islanders over Vancouver Canucks

Game 1   April 6   Vancouver Canucks 3   New York Islanders 5
Game 2   April 8   New York Islanders 3   Vancouver Canucks 1

Quarter-Finals (4-2):

New York Islanders over Buffalo Sabres

Game 1	April 11	New York Islanders 3	Buffalo Sabres 5
Game 2	April 13	New York Islanders 2	Buffalo Sabres 3 (OT)
Game 3	April 15	Buffalo Sabres 3	New York Islanders 5
Game 4	April 17	Buffalo Sabres 2	New York Islanders 4
Game 5	April 20	New York Islanders 4	Buffalo Sabres 3
Game 6	April 22	Buffalo Sabres 2	New York Islanders 3

Semi-Finals (4-1):

Montreal Canadiens over New York Islanders

Game 1	April 27	New York Islanders 2	Montreal Canadiens 3
Game 2	April 29	New York Islanders 3	Montreal Canadiens 4
Game 3	May 1	Montreal Canadiens 3	New York Islanders 2
Game 4	May 4	Montreal Canadiens 2	New York Islanders 5
Game 5	May 6	New York Islanders 2	Montreal Canadiens 5

PATRICK DIVISION STANDINGS: 1976-77

TEAMS	W	L	T	POINTS
Philadelphia Flyers	48	16	16	112
New York Islanders	47	21	12	106
Atlanta Flames	34	34	12	80
New York Rangers	29	37	14	72

Preliminary Round (2-0):

New York Islanders over Chicago Blackhawks

Game 1	April 5	Chicago Blackhawks 2	New York Islanders 5
Game 2	April 7	Chicago Blackhawks 1	New York Islanders 2

Quarter-Finals (4-0):

New York Islanders over Buffalo Sabres

Game 1	April 11	Buffalo Sabres 2	New York Islanders 4
Game 2	April 13	Buffalo Sabres 2	New York Islanders 4
Game 3	April 15	New York Islanders 4	Buffalo Sabres 3
Game 4	April 17	New York Islanders 4	Buffalo Sabres 3

Semi-Finals (4-2):

Montreal Canadiens over New York Islanders

Game 1	April 23	New York Islanders 3	Montreal Canadiens 4
Game 2	April 26	New York Islanders 0	Montreal Canadiens 3
Game 3	April 28	Montreal Canadiens 3	New York Islanders 5
Game 4	April 30	Montreal Canadiens 4	New York Islanders 0
Game 5	May 3	New York Islanders 4	Montreal Canadiens 3 (OT)
Game 6	May 5	Montreal Canadiens 2	New York Islanders 1

CHAPTER 12:

FINANCIAL TROUBLES SOLVED

*After an ownership change, the Islanders' financial troubles
are solved, and the focus can return once more solely to
hockey.*

STAN FISCHLER: Unfortunately, Roy Boe had two teams - he had a
basketball team [the New York Nets, in addition to the Islanders], and
he didn't manage them both well. That's why somebody had to come
in to handle the money matters, because by the late '70s, it looked
like the Islanders might even fold.

BILL TORREY: There were always rumors. And since he had a
number of limited partners, some of them I think had ideas about
taking it over. There were some of his partners that were involved in
just the Islanders and were not interested in basketball, and felt that
Roy, when it came to money, the money went to basketball first and
to hockey second. We did have difficult times. We had to pay a four
million dollar indemnity on top of the six million dollars to get into
the league, and then we had to pay the Rangers four million dollars
for territorial indemnity. So, with interest and all, that proved to be
more than Roy could handle.

EDDIE WESTFALL: Roy Boe was the epitome of a salesman. He -
along with Torrey - sold me on the idea of coming to the Island and
helping them establish a franchise. And there was nothing that you
would ever not like about Roy Boe. He was just a wonderful guy. But
you could see that his background was selling, and he was very good
at it. And I don't mean high pressure, I mean just he was a good
salesman - he was well-versed, he knew how to talk, and he knew

how to present it. It was easy to tell Roy Boe was a person that really cared about the players and the fans. He was very enthusiastic. So, as you're trying to do something, you have in the back of your mind as a point, "Come on guys, look, if we're as good at doing our thing on the ice as Roy Boe is trying to do as an owner, we've got a long way to go. But let's see if we can't catch up." So it was an easy sell. I so enjoyed him. And he liked to be around with the players. He was a big fan.

BILLY HARRIS: A great guy. One of the all-time greats. He was excitable and loved hockey. He didn't know much about it - his real passion was basketball. But he was a great guy, and it's too bad that he got railroaded out. I knew where he lived in Westhampton - I'd go visit him. When I came back to New York and I was working on Long Island back in the '80s, I'd go out and see him. "Stop by any time and have a drink."

LORNE HENNING: The first few years, I know it was always a little bit of a concern - guys weren't going to get their paychecks. But we worked our way through it.

BILL TORREY: Eventually, the franchise was taken away, reorganized, and refinanced. And then John Pickett became the principal.

STAN FISCHLER: Pickett was a tough businessman, who knew what he wanted and got it. And he saved the team. He was a man more than anybody that was responsible for coming in and making the necessary fiscal adjustments. And now, he's basically a forgotten man. But they should have a statue of him in Uniondale.

CLAIRE ARBOUR: Well, Mr. Pickett saved the team from bankruptcy. We really respected him. His wife [Marilyn] was really the one who was a real Islander fan. She loved that team. I don't think Mr. Pickett knew too much about hockey, but the business end of it, he worked it out, and saved the team. We were ever so grateful for him.

EDDIE WESTFALL: John Pickett is a good friend. I knew his wife, Marilyn. Her last name was Seaman, and she and her father were one of the original limited partners of the Islanders. She was there from the very beginning - way before John Pickett got involved in the hockey team. She was an enthusiastic fan. She had two boys and a girl, and she was at the games all the time. She was involved, she was around, and she was a lot of fun. She was a real character. And then when John Pickett came in, we saw a lot more of her. But he was more of a business guy, he was "a numbers guy." He didn't come around in the dressing room so much. He enjoyed it all, but I think his vision was to do his best to build this thing up and get rid of the debt that team had. And I'll say this - I developed a friendship with the Picketts. I lived in Locust Valley at the time, and when I got married for the second time, I got married in the Picketts' backyard of their beautiful home, up there in Locust Valley. And Marilyn Pickett's father, Al Seaman, married us. [Laughs] He was the mayor of Upper Brookville.

BILL TORREY: John Pickett…you have to understand a little bit of the make up of Long Island. Much of our early support at the gate came from the north shore of Long Island. And the reason for that was first of all, Roy Boe knew a lot of people on the north shore. They had the money to buy season tickets, and they also came from schools and colleges that played hockey. And there were several outdoor rinks on Long Island, where even though they were Wall Street guys and businessmen, a lot of them played hockey. So they had a real interest in the game. And Roy Boe went to Yale - he knew a lot of them. So he could bring a lot of those guys to the games, and brought a lot of support that way.

Now, the biggest supporter that few people realize how important he was to getting hockey on Long Island was Nelson Doubleday. I knew Nelson from Oakland, when I was running the Seals. Nelson was an investor in the Oakland Seals. He went to Princeton - he wasn't a player in Princeton, but he knew all the hockey players. He loved the game. He was a Rangers season ticket holder and lived on Long Island. He probably was the most influential person in making up my mind to go there, rather than possibly go to Atlanta. So I knew him because of the Seals, and he convinced me that this was going to be good, and he was 100%

behind it. It just so happened that he was a good golf buddy of John Pickett.

NELSON DOUBLEDAY, JR [Partial shareholder of the Islanders]: I'd grown up being a Rangers fan, and I was always interested in hockey. I knew the owners starting out in Oakland, and that was where Torrey was. I just followed him around, and wound up with him in Long Island. Somebody asked me if I would be interested [in being a partial shareholder of the Islanders]. I was a hockey fan, I was interested in it, and that's how I got involved in it. I think it was kind of loosely done, and John Pickett was going to be very professional about how he handled it, so I said, "Yes, I'd be interested." He managed the finances and did it very, very well.

BILLY HARRIS: He was a partner on the team back then - he would come to a lot of our parties. He was a really great guy, Nelson Doubleday.

BILL TORREY: Pickett more or less turned the public aspect of the business [to Torrey]. He felt that was my responsibility as president and general manager.

STAN FISCHLER: Pickett shunned publicity, and he was quite content to let Torrey share in the spotlight, and to a lesser degree, Devellano. When necessary, he was around. What his job was, was to save the team. It was an awesome challenge, and he did that. So having saved the team and being in the process of putting it back on its feet, that's not the kind of thing that draws quotes or headlines. It was the kind of thing that you do in the background, and you let Torrey and Devellano put together their championship team.

BILL TORREY: John had good business contacts in New York, and was very instrumental in the improvement of our broadcast deal with Cablevision and Channel 9 in New York.

BILLY HARRIS: It was a nice family, it was a nice group. I think in this day and age, the teams are run like such a big business - they've got a staff of a hundred, they've got marketing, they're trying to raise money doing all kinds of other stuff. We only had five people in our front office. It was like a big family.

AL ARBOUR: John was a great owner. He was our savior, really - from bankruptcy. He was a great guy, until he divorced his wife, and then things started going downhill. After that, he moved to Florida, and I didn't see him.

BILLY HARRIS: I knew John and Marilyn pretty well. Marilyn was a great gal - she would always have Christmas parties for us. But then John turned out to be a real…he wasn't what he was. You could write a Hollywood script about that. He never went to Harvard, he never went to…he ended up selling the team but keeping the TV rights. I think he finally sold them off. He was a smart guy, a smart businessman. He ended up divorcing Marilyn I think and marrying his secretary, so what can you say about the guy?

JIM PICKARD: We were a young team. And slowly but surely, the pieces came together. As they say in the business, "You have to lose to learn how to win," and we certainly did that. I think in the regular season, our point total improved almost every year. And then the draft choices - the scouts did a fantastic job. The pieces just kept falling into place. Then when they got Mike Bossy. That really helped a hell of a lot.

CHAPTER 13:

GREETINGS, MR. BOSSY

With the arrival of right winger Mike Bossy, the Islanders soon find out they just landed one of the best goal scorers in the league.

CLAIRE ARBOUR: When they talked about recruiting Mike Bossy, Henry Saraceno was the scout, and he kept talking to them about Mike Bossy. And Al said to them, "I'd like to go watch him play." And he said, "No, I don't want you to watch him play. Just trust me, *he knows how to score.*"

AL ARBOUR: He was a great player, there's no question about that. Henry Saraceno would never let me see him play. I'd go there, and I'd say, "I've got to see Bossy play." And he says, "No way. You're coming out to dinner, and that's it." He'd take me out for dinner, and I never saw him play. Bill Torrey set it up. They took four right wingers before him [in the draft]. Imagine that? At that time, they didn't know. When his name came up, they said, "No, time out!" And Henry had a fit. Time out, my ass! [Laughs] I knew who we were going to get. We all knew.

BILL TORREY: Coming from Montreal, the name "Bossy" was well known in athletic circles. He had an uncle that was a rowing singles sculls champion, and was a great all-around athlete at West Hill High School. He had another uncle that played for Catholic High, and was a perennial champion in the high school league. So the Bossy name was certainly one that I was familiar with. But even more so, my Quebec scout, Henry Saraceno - I had him as a scout in Oakland before I came to the Island - kept telling me, "You've got to go see

Mike Bossy." Henry knew the family inside and out. He coached Mike Bossy as a Bantam, when he was twelve years old, knew him for two years, and loved Michael like a son. Mike Bossy - and to this day, nobody playing junior hockey has ever been able to do this - scored 70 or more goals in all four years he played junior hockey.

But there was a lot of thought that first of all, it was the Quebec League, which is not known as being as physically tough as the OHL [Ontario Hockey League] in the Western League. A lot of good scorers, but not big, strong guys. He wasn't known as a checker, he wasn't known to be a physical player in any way, so there were things about Mike that a lot of teams didn't...the Montreal Canadiens must have seen him play every game he ever played in junior, and they passed on him. But we were very fortunate. We were looking for a right winger, in particular, we were looking for more scoring. Those were our priorities. For the most part, when our scouts talked to Al and me about what our team needed the most, we needed a scoring winger - preferably, a right handed shot. Over the four years, I saw Mike play junior I don't know, 30 or 40 times. There was little doubt in my mind that he was a natural goal scorer. His shortcomings - lack of physical play, lack of overall defense. And obviously, Al had a reputation of demanding that from his players.

Jimmy Devellano wasn't convinced about Mike Bossy. He liked Red Foster - he led the OHL in scoring. He was a center and a red headed kid. And some of our other scouts were a little leery of him. But in the end, Henry just said, *"Hey."* And that year of the draft by the way, is the only year that the draft was not done in one area - everybody was hooked up on a telephone conference call. We did that draft by phone. It was the only time it's ever happened. I remember Henry walking into my office that morning, and he put a picture of Mike Bossy up on my bookcase, in back of my desk. We were drafting 15th. I turned to him, and I said, "Henry, there's no way that a guy that scored 75 or more goals for four straight years is going to not be taken before the 15th pick in the draft. We've got to look elsewhere." Anyway, we watched, and it just so happened that year in the draft there were a good number - six or seven - very good right wing prospects, which worked to our advantage. Big time.

Red Foster was a good all-around center. The only problem with him is late in his final year, he injured his knee, and that was a bit of a concern. But anyway, the debate in our office came down to two players - Red Foster or Mike Bossy. I turned to Al, and I said, "Al, do you want 'a home run hitter,' or do you want an all-around right handed shooting player/winger/centerman?" We decided we could gamble for the home run hitter, and we did. But we were very fortunate. The only reason Mike Bossy [was still available] was because teams didn't think he could handle the physical play of the NHL, and defensively, wasn't sound. There were *five* other right wingers taken in the draft prior to our taking Mike Bossy.

EDDIE WESTFALL: Apparently, Bossy was like the 22nd pick - I don't know whether that was the reason he wore "22" or not - but he wasn't an early pick, he was a later pick. Again, what a gem. You could just tell when he came to training camp. He was very quiet, and quite introverted - in the sense that he wasn't "Here I am. Out of my way." Quite the opposite. But you could tell right away this guy was gifted. I couldn't believe that that NHL scouts couldn't see in this guy that he had this unbelievable talent. He had great balance and strength. He wasn't a person that played physical hockey, but to do what he did on skates, he had to be so powerful. I always said, "He's a Nureyev on skates. He's like a sophisticated contortionist." He would be in an awkward position, and he could still get the puck away with a pass, or get a hell of a shot away in a position with his body, that god, most of us would just fall over. Tremendous feel with the puck. The kind of things that you say, "You can't teach those things. You have to learn them on your own and practice them." And he could do it.

BILLY HARRIS: Mike Bossy wouldn't be able to deal with the criticism [from Arbour], or the screaming and yelling and ranting and raving. He'd come in after one period and go around the room. He'd be yelling at me, "Hey Harry, you look like you're skating in a fucking sandbox!" Another time, he comes in, and goes, "Hey Potvin! I don't mind you carrying around a fucking piano on your back, but when you stop to play it…" [Laughs] Or, "You look like you're skating around with a bag of concrete on your back." So the next day at practice, we got a bag of concrete, we bring it out in the shopping buggy to the ice, and made Denis a presentation. If he said stuff like that to Mike Bossy, holy Christ. I don't know what Bossy would do.

CLARK GILLIES: In hindsight, obviously, it was very positive, but nobody was really sure. Although he set all kinds of scoring records in Quebec, he was passed over by a lot of teams, because they said he couldn't play defense. I guess Torrey at that time said, "We'll teach him how to play defense. We know he can score goals." He obviously proved that right off the bat. I was very fortunate to be put on a line with Bryan and Mike - I think it helped all of our careers, the three young guys that were really making a name for ourselves. From day one at practice, when Al put us on the same line, it was magical. Everything seemed to work, right off the bat. It turned out to be one of the great moves - again - that Torrey made. Taking a chance on a guy that nobody said could really play.

GLENN "CHICO" RESCH: Again, taken later in the draft. Had the reputation of scoring, but could be intimidated. The only thing that I remember about Boss is he was telling me in that training camp, he had a great off-the-wall fake to the outside/jump to the inside/pull the puck through the defender's legs or stick and legs. Guys were saying, "You can't do that at this level." And he said, "I don't know why I can't. I'm not going to do it *every* time." What people don't realize is unless you played the game, you think a guy like Bossy, Wayne Gretzky, and even Denis Savard, "We'll just pound them. Just drill them a few times." Right? Just try to do it a few times. These guys, from the time they were little kids, they knew how to keep their head up. They knew how to not put themselves in a position that you could really set them up to drill them. And unless you double team them...and even then, they knew it was coming. In all the days, the only time people could work Trots over - that I could see - was when he was in front of the net. And as you know, that eventually shortened his career. When he's standing there, you could crosscheck him. But coming off the wall or up the ice, I never saw anyone drill him like say, Scott Stevens did later to other players.

JP PARISÉ: He came in at a good time. They placed him right away with Bryan Trottier, who may have been the best player in the National Hockey League. And then you got Clark Gillies on the other side, allowing him to play, because Mike was not overtly physical. He was a sniper, but when you play with guys like that, the process of adjusting to the league comes a lot quicker. He was allowed to do things and shoot. But the more he played, the confidence came over, and all of a sudden, not only is he a shooter, but he's a good playmaker. And as it develops, he's just a good, sound hockey player. But the situation was great for Mike Bossy.

BRYAN TROTTIER: We had a pure goal scorer. A threat, every shift. A guy that wanted to score, a guy that wanted to be "the guy." He took a ton of pride in scoring goals, and a ton of pride in contributing as an offensive gun. That rubbed a few guys wrong at the time maybe, but as a roommate, a line-mate, and a friend, I saw the excitement of that - playing with a guy that was really hungry. Some people thought it was selfish, but I thought it was a pretty good selfish. It turned my game around, obviously, because I saw the game from a different set of eyes all of a sudden. So for me, it was pretty refreshing for our team, recognizing the value that he had. We tried everything to make sure we were setting him up or demanding a little bit more from him on the system side, because he was an offensive weapon, but we still needed him in the defensive zone. He was pretty dependable that way.

Underrated as far as a playmaker is concerned. They thought he was kind of one-dimensional. We just let the league and the press think that. We didn't care what everybody was saying about us, we just figured deception or what they don't know won't kill the world. We went about our business, thinking "We're going to find a way to make things work." It wasn't necessarily from management's point of view, because that area was pretty good - they let us figure out things by ourselves rather than just telling us. "You guys have got to figure it out a little bit by yourselves. You guys have got to grow up. You guys have got to be men and figure things out eventually." They allowed us to grow together, and I think that's healthy to some degree. But Mike was a key to that when he came to the team, because it was another dimension we had, another weapon. Timing is everything in that regard, because we were all still young enough. We were all in that same age group - there was like a three or four year difference in all of us. Especially in that core group.

CLARK GILLIES: Obviously, we didn't put up the same numbers, but we had a good line - we were very effective with myself, Trottier, and Billy Harris [known as "the LILCO Line"]. But in all fairness,

Mike Bossy, proved what a great goal scorer he was, and what magic touch he had around the net [with Bossy in place of Harris, the line was re-christened "the Trio Grande Line"]. Harry would admit he didn't have the same touch. But we were all young at that time, and it was fun to go out there with Billy and Bryan and do the same stuff. With Mike coming in, I guess Al figured he was a better fit for Bryan and I, and put him with us.

BILLY HARRIS: Well, he took my job on that line! [Laughs] When Boss showed up, he got that spot on that line, and then I was just bounced all over. Just bad timing on my behalf. But Bossy is a great player.

BRYAN TROTTIER: No slap to either guy [Harris and Bossy] - both great guys, really great friends of all of us. We love them both dearly. But probably the biggest difference was "We got a 50 goal scorer against a 35 goal scorer."

GLENN "CHICO" RESCH: To be a dynasty, to win Cups, you have to have elite players. And I would say the elite players in the game, if there's 20 teams, there might be two on each team. And they wouldn't all be forwards. It could be a forward and a defenseman, like Orr and Esposito. Trottier and Bossy made us an elite team.

CHAPTER 14:

1977-78

Everything seems perfectly in place for the Islanders to make a run at the Stanley Cup...until they meet the rough and tough Maple Leafs in the Quarter-Finals.

BILLY HARRIS: There were a couple of guys on the team that were assholes - I'm not going to say who they were - and they wanted Clarkie to be captain. Eddie just basically resigned his captaincy. I'd never been on a team in my life where they had a fuckin' vote. It was like pee wee. But Eddie was great. He'd been in Boston for ten or twelve years, won Cups there. He probably gave the team some credibility - more than anybody. They were probably jealous of him, because Eddie had his own airplane. Eddie liked to have fun. But he was a pretty good player in his own right. There was nobody better at taking face-offs - well, Trottier got to be the best - and he'd kill penalties and score the odd goal.

CLARK GILLIES: Eddie was captain from the beginning, when he was brought over from Boston. He was kind of "the elder statesman," so Torrey made Eddie the captain. He was captain up until '78, and then I remember a few of the guys on the team maybe didn't like his leadership qualities. Some of the older guys put a little bit of a coup together, and decided that we needed a new captain. Actually, they nominated Bryan Trottier and I. And then we had a vote, and I think I beat Trots by one vote, or else he would have been the captain. But I didn't like the circumstances under which I became captain. I have a lot of respect for Eddie Westfall. I didn't like the way the whole thing was pulled off - it just didn't feel right.

EDDIE WESTFALL: That wasn't my decision. I think what they wanted was one of the younger players to identify with the building nucleus of the team going forward. That was probably the thinking behind it. I'm only reading between the lines and I don't know for sure, but it might have been that was part of it, that they wanted to exorcise somebody into that position that identified. Or, knowing that my career was on its downside, that it would be better and easier for them to transition me out of the team if I wasn't the captain. But one thing that I remember saying to Torrey was, "You better be careful, because if the captaincy has the significance that I always held it as - because of my early years with the Bruins coming up, and the captains that I had when I was a player - if you make it 'a political football,' you won't do it right."

As it turned out, the first time around, it was really between Bryan Trottier and Clark Gillies. I said that I would not sit in the room, and they had the players voting on it, which was, again, quite different. So I'm sitting out at the Racquet and Rink, when the team voted. I forget who it was that came out and said they wanted me to come in, because they were deadlocked, and they wanted me to vote. I said, "Wait a minute. How stupid is that? You want *me* to pick the next captain of the team? I didn't feel very good about the way this thing was being handled, but I wasn't going to get in the way of it. Now, you want me to pick the next captain? *You're nuts.* I'm not doing it. You guys work it out." So that's really when it first came down, and it was Clark Gillies.

JP PARISÉ: At first, it was a complete surprise [when JP found out he was traded to the Cleveland Barons]. I got a call from a guy from Cleveland, and he said, "What do you think of the idea that you're going to be coming to Cleveland?" I said, *"What?"* I called Mr. Torrey, and asked him, "What is this rumor?" And he said, "JP, I am no closer to trading you than I was three years ago." That must have been close, because the following day I was gone! [Laughs] Of course, I was so friggin' disappointed, because I felt that the Islanders were coming along and they were going to have a great chance to be in the Stanley Cup.

But at the time, I was like 35 years old, and I didn't have much longer to be in the league. And being traded to the Cleveland Barons, who were at the bottom of the league, it just killed me. Was I angry? I suppose I was angry. But then I put my senses together, and I said, "With this team, I spent the best three years of my career. So how can I be angry with Torrey, who had just allowed me to play with good, young kids, and basically finish my career in great style?" Disappointed? Extremely disappointed. It broke my heart. But at the same time, you have to look at the big picture and say, "He gave me a chance that was just wonderful, and great, great memories. That's life, and go on." We've remained friends, and I'm forever thankful to him and Al Arbour for giving me the chance.

JEAN POTVIN: I was pretty upset and disappointed with that [Jean Potvin was also traded to the Cleveland Barons], because two years before that - 1975-76 - I had been the second highest scoring defenseman in the NHL. I had 72 points - the only guy that had more than me was my brother, Denis had 98 points. I was, rightfully so, asked to focus a little bit more on defense, so anyways, I thought I had made some good contributions with the team. But y'know, Bill Torrey and Al Arbour look at their team, and they felt that, "To become the best team in the NHL, we need another good center iceman." And Wayne Merrick is the guy they came up with. They decided to make the trade for Wayne Merrick, and at that point, they were being asked by Harry Howell, who was the general manager [of the Barons]. Harry wanted a little more experience on his team, so Bill gave me up and JP Parisé.

I remember when I was told that I was traded, I was very upset, very disappointed - because our first daughter had just been born. I was traded January 10th, 1978. Our daughter was born December 22nd, 1977. So she wasn't even 20 days old. And the other thing is there had been some very strong rumors - and many of those were true - that the Cleveland Barons were in serious financial difficulties. Having trouble paying their players and so on. And Bill assured me that that was no longer the case. The Gund brothers, George and Gordon Gund, had just bought the team, and they were a very, very wealthy family. I believe they owned the Cleveland Trust. So anyway, he goes, "No, no. That's not going to be the case. You don't have to worry about getting your payment or anything like that."

We ended up going there - JP and I - for the balance of the year, which was about four months. That was a horrible team, so it was very depressing - I had gone from a team that was on the up-and-up and was starting to make a lot of noise, and I'm being thrown aside to Cleveland. That summer, Cleveland financially was tight, but they weren't drawing fans, and they decided to merge with another team that was having problems drawing fans, and that was the Minnesota North Stars. So they decided, "OK, of the two cities, where do we move the team to?" And they felt that moving the team to Minnesota would have better results, because Minnesota is more of a hockey town than Cleveland. So they moved to Minnesota, but Minnesota didn't have much of a good team, either. Anyways, the year I got traded, what was going on with the Islanders in the background, the Islanders lost to Toronto in seven games [in the playoffs], which was a huge disappointment.

CLARK GILLIES: It was tough. We were - talent-wise - a better team [than the Toronto Maple Leafs]. We finished first [in the Patrick Division] that year. You go through learning stages in your career. That was a learning stage for us. We certainly had the ability to beat the Toronto Maple Leafs, but we - for some reason - didn't play the physical game we were supposed to play. If you look back, I think that's the biggest reason we lost. We didn't match up to them from a physical standpoint, and it was disheartening. It's really what beat us. But again, you take baby steps to get to the point you want to be, and that was another thing that we put in the memory bank, and said, "We can't let that happen again."

EDDIE WESTFALL: Believe it or not, Toronto out-muscled us. And I think they intimidated our team, which I was surprised with. I'd gotten hurt. When they beat us, I think I was sitting in the seats. But I thought that some of the players, like Darryl Sittler and Tiger Williams, went after Trottier and Bossy, and they physically intimidated us.

BILLY HARRIS: That goal they scored to beat us in overtime [in game seven], it wasn't a great goal. I think Chico came out, and Denis got caught up ice. Our big line is out on the ice, and they all got caught. It was just a shame, really. But a tough, physical series. Roger Neilson was a great coach, and he had those guys playing well above their head. I mean, I did have a real good opportunity in the overtime. I intercepted a pass from Turnbull to Glennie. I saw the pass coming, so I took a chance, and intercepted it. I caught Palmateer totally by surprise, but he was staying basically on the goal line, so he couldn't do anything - he couldn't come out and check me or anything. I couldn't deek him, because he's in deep in the net. So I went high glove side, and he basically hugged the left post, and said, "I'm going to give him that side, and hopefully he shoots there," and he beat me. But if I score that goal, we knock them out in overtime. And about two or three shifts later, they come down and score. I was pretty disappointed about that, because it would have been a great opportunity. Who knows - maybe history would have changed and they wouldn't have traded me. [Laughs]

GLENN "CHICO" RESCH: I've got to tell you, that's a bit like what happened to the Vancouver Canucks this year [2011]. We won our first three games at home, but they were all close battles. Their coach was Roger Neilson, and he had a physical, checking team. He had some really good players too - they would just keep coming at us. They went after Boss, I think Boss got hurt after game six. They kept pounding away. We scored the first goal [in game seven], and went up 1-0. And I can still remember, they got a goal in the middle of the second period on a power play, I think. We had a lot of chances. But Mike Palmateer - give him credit - he played really, really well.

And the two things I remember was one, before Lanny McDonald scored in overtime, Billy Harris had a breakaway, and I just remember thinking, "Billy, *don't shoot it half way up the net.*" Billy had a habit of taking the puck and snapping it, but it would always go right where goalies like it - at the height of the gloves. I remember he snapped it, and Palmateer stopped it. Then, on the winning goal, the puck went high up in the air, and Clarkie was telling me he was behind, and was going to jump up and glove it. He missed it, and Lanny McDonald was coming in and got it. I've got to say, I didn't see this clearly at all. I came out, and then Lanny scored. It was as crushing a defeat as you can have. That to me epitomized the term "sudden death overtime."

There was the song, "We Are the Champions," by Queen. We weren't playing it in our dressing room - they were playing it out on the speakers at our home games. And I remember the Leafs kind of mocking that, and playing it in their room. Which, it's fine, we might have done the same thing. But that was just totally heartbreaking.

AL ARBOUR: That was a crushing loss - I don't think we ever got over that. I think that goal was offside, too, but it doesn't matter anyway.

CLAIRE ARBOUR: What loss Al took the hardest? I think the one when Lanny McDonald scored in the overtime. If I look back, that was a toughie, because we were expected by then, there was such progression, and the team was making such advances, and there were expectations. It's funny, I don't remember loses as much as I remember victories. [Laughs] I guess you train yourself to forget those things. But I remember that one. That was a tough one.

LORNE HENNING: That was the physical part of it - they took over and took it to us. And I think there was always a question of whether we were physical enough.

JEAN POTVIN: If you looked at the Islanders' loss to Toronto, Toronto had a very physical team. And the Islanders, to a man, will admit - of course, I wasn't there, I had been traded - you could have guys like Gillies, Nystrom, my brother, say that they did not stick up for themselves probably the way they should have. And that resulting into that loss to the Toronto Maple Leafs. I remember watching one of the games in Toronto on TV, where Jerry Butler crosschecked from behind Mike Bossy. Mike Bossy went head first into the boards - they had to carry him out on a stretcher. That was towards the end of the second period of that game, and I thought the Islanders were going to come out and just, like, *war* in the third period. Well, the only guy that I remember doing anything was Garry Howatt, who I think got into three fights in the third period. Whether you want to call it revenge or try to get even with whoever. It probably still is today, but back in those days, if you had three majors in a game, you were automatically out of the game - game misconduct.

BRYAN TROTTIER: It wasn't our time. We were still learning how to win. Maybe some injuries along the way, there was still some growth in a lot of us. There was a hot goaltender on the other side. Those things happen. You learn that there are things you can't control, and you still have to overcome. Recognizing expectations or pressures and learning how to deal with those things. And just maturity.

GARY "BABA BOOEY" DELL'ABATE: They had played really well [during the regular season], and you had these great expectations. You're like, "OK, this is going to be the year." And then to lose in the first round, at home, seventh game in overtime...you figure, "OK, game seven is in your building. That one's got to be going to you." I remember that to be a devastating loss, because it was like, "OK...*so when is this going to happen?*"

PATRICK DIVISION STANDINGS: 1977-78

TEAMS	W	L	T	POINTS
New York Islanders	48	17	15	111
Philadelphia Flyers	45	20	15	105
Atlanta Flames	34	27	19	87
New York Rangers	30	37	13	73

Quarter-Finals (4-3):

Toronto Maple Leafs over New York Islanders

Game 1	April 17	Toronto Maple Leafs 1	New York Islanders 4
Game 2	April 19	Toronto Maple Leafs 2	New York Islanders 3 (OT)
Game 3	April 21	New York Islanders 0	Toronto Maple Leafs 2
Game 4	April 23	New York Islanders 1	Toronto Maple Leafs 3
Game 5	April 25	Toronto Maple Leafs 1	New York Islanders 2 (OT)
Game 6	April 27	New York Islanders 2	Toronto Maple Leafs 5
Game 7	April 29	Toronto Maple Leafs 2	New York Islanders 1 (OT)

CHAPTER 15:

1978-79

Everything seems perfectly in place for the Islanders to make a run at the Stanley Cup (sound familiar?)...until they meet their archrival, the Rangers, in the Semi-Finals.

GARY "BABA BOOEY" DELL'ABATE: You could see the team getting better, because you would see how much better they were playing during the regular season. They really were contenders. And then they would get to the playoffs, and it seemed like they were taking a lot of steps backwards. If your team goes to one game away from the Stanley Cup Finals, the expectation next year is to go further. You don't want to go backwards, you want to go forwards. And then, it seemed like they were getting the "choke" moniker. I remember I had a math teacher who was a huge Rangers fan, and we would always come in and go, "Wait 'til next year." And he'd say, "You guys sound like a bunch of Brooklyn Dodgers fans - 'Wait 'til next year'!" He would mock us and it would piss me off.

BOB LORIMER: The expectations were very high for everyone on the team, so it's a very good situation to come into, because every game means a lot when you have the expectation of being one of the better teams. We had a very, very strong regular season - we won the league title - with high expectations. In fact, I think we actually peaked too soon, because we were so strong and we had a fairly comfortable lead on top of the standings that we coasted a little bit at the end of the year, trying to prepare ourselves for the playoffs and rest up. That was probably what actually cost us.

BILLY HARRIS: We hated playing in the old Chicago Stadium [the Islanders faced the Blackhawks in the Quarter-Finals]. We're going, "Let's win this game, because you don't want to come back here and climb up these bloody steps." Because the locker rooms were in the basement, and the ladder…it wasn't even steps, it was like a ladder that you had to climb up to get on the ice.

BOB LORIMER: We had a lot of confidence that we were going to win. The expectation was that we had a better team than Chicago, and if we just played to our capability, we'd take that series fairly easily. And obviously, that's what happened [the Islanders swept the Blackhawks, 4-0]. That was going according to plan. We had a bye [in the first round] - in those days, if you were at the top of the heap, you got a bye. We had a lot of confidence going into play against the Rangers. Quite frankly, we didn't play up to our expectations. I think maybe the sweep over the Blackhawks was wrong in hindsight, because I think it maybe made us a little over-confident coming in against the Rangers.

BILLY HARRIS: The one thing about playing the Rangers - as much as we did - it was sort of ironic that they had Freddie Shero taking over, and they had Ron Greschner, Pat Hickey, and Dave Farrish. A lot of young guys, and Shero wanted them to live in the City. And they were partying big-time - I knew Dave Farrish pretty well. But these guys are from small towns, like Western Canada. They're yelling at the bench, "Hey, you bunch of hicks. Why don't you go back to Long Island! You belong on Long Island!" As if it made them better, that they played for the Rangers and we played for the Islanders. And these guys are *fucking hayseeds,* yelling at us to "Get back to Long Island." I looked at Greschner, and I go, "Well shit, if he's not one of the hick dirt farmers from out in Saskatchewan…"

CLARK GILLIES: It was typical Islander/Ranger hockey, except there was one big difference - John Davidson. A lot of people would say that John Davidson was the difference in the Rangers getting to the Cup that year. He was just an absolute star in goal, and I give him credit for being the reason why they beat us. They went on to the Stanley Cup Finals against Montreal [the Canadiens would beat the Rangers, 4-1], which is where we wanted to be at that time. But again, you look back and you analyze, and you say, "What areas did we need to improve on?" Again, it's a bit of a cliché, but you have to take your lumps and take some loses before you can figure out just exactly what you need to do to win.

BOB LORIMER: Part of it too was what helped us a lot in our "playoff successful years" was our power play worked very well. And if I remember in that series, our power play didn't work well, and JD played very well for the Rangers. He played *extremely* well in that series, and our power play wasn't clicking on all cylinders. That really hurt us. But I think in hindsight, we had one very strong scoring line, and if that line got shut down, we struggled to score with our other three lines. I think that was a big key - as long as the Rangers could shut down Trots' line, then they had a good chance against our other three lines. Obviously, management recognized that as well, and made the correction the following year.

EDDIE WESTFALL: Davidson, you couldn't put anything by him. With the Rangers, the difference was goaltending - Davidson lit it up, big-time. That was what everybody took away from that series, that maybe we didn't take them serious enough, as far as the team and the goaltending.

BILLY HARRIS: The way the guys played, everybody was *so* uptight. The expectations were so high. I think they realized that there were a few weaknesses, and they had to fill a few holes. The fact that it was the Rangers made it worse.

MIKE McEWEN [The Islanders' defenseman from 1981-1984]: We [McEwen was on the Rangers at the time] played six games, 360 minutes, and I think I heard a stat where 330 of the minutes were either tied or a one goal lead for either team. It was a really close series. It was a hard-fought series. I remember Ron Greschner's winning goal, we won [the deciding game six] 2-1. It was a shot from the point - it was in the second period, and that was the game-winner. I remember it was a typical shot from the point, and it went in. It was then that we had the feeling, *"We're going to beat these guys."* That and just their stunned look after the series. They were on the ice - especially Potvin - in disbelief.

AL ARBOUR: We weren't good enough. They didn't believe in themselves enough.

BRYAN TROTTIER: You don't go into any season thinking, "This is not our year." You figure, "We've got to give it our best shot." You don't know how many chances you're going to have. We believed we had as good a shot as anybody. We had a pretty good year. Again, it wasn't our time. We went into another hot goaltender. It just seemed like there were things we still had to learn. That was another one of those learning curves for us.

BOB BOURNE: We were very upset in '79 when we lost to them, even though they had a good team. The one thing we wanted to do was play Montreal in the Finals, and if we had, it would have been a heck of a series. We wanted to see how we'd do against a team like that. But it wasn't meant to be.

BOB NYSTROM: They were disappointing. I guess the early stardom was maybe not a good thing. Although it was a great experience, it probably gave us the idea that, "Hey, we can get here. It's not a problem." All of a sudden, we ran into teams that just said, *"No way."* Like Montreal - no question about it, they were on a roll, then we had Toronto, then we lost to the Rangers in '79. That was heartbreaking. But I think each one was a learning experience.

GLENN "CHICO" RESCH: That year that we lost to the Rangers, we had really played them well in the regular season. But the Rangers won the first game and we never really had much of a chance after that. It was kind of like, "What if?" That's the great thing about sports - you can say "What if," "We'll get you next time," "If this didn't happen," "You were lucky," "We were unlucky." You know what? That might be true, but the bottom line is look at the scoreboard. It is what it is.

GARY "BABA BOOEY" DELL'ABATE: There were two things going on - you had to take a lot of shit from the Rangers fans because the rivalry…the day the Islanders beat the Rangers four years earlier, the rivalry was born. But then on top of it, you were not only taking shit that the Rangers beat you, but you were also taking shit that your team was a bunch of choke artists, and they maybe got lucky one year, and nothing was going to happen. You felt like it was a team that underperformed in the playoffs.

BRYAN TROTTIER: It's a reflection, is how I look at it [Trottier winning the Hart Trophy in '79, as the NHL's "most valuable player"]. I don't look at it as something I achieved by myself. Most of those awards that happen - whether it's the scoring championship or someone recognizing your value to the team as the most valuable - I think again, it's another good reflection on our group. I was on a really good team, and we were finding ways to help and support each other. It could have been anybody.

STAN FISCHLER: No question, '78 and '79 were equally bad. It was like the Sedin twins - you can't tell one from the other, and they're both terrific. You couldn't separate '78 from '79. The '78 one should have been in the bag, and they blew it. It was one of the meanest series in the history of hockey. And it was blown at home and it was blown in overtime. And then, the Rangers one was the fact that it was *the Rangers*. I mean, the hated rival. Both ways, it was just terrible. Of course, the Rangers one happened at the Garden, which made it even worse.

EDDIE WESTFALL: When I think of the '78 and '79 teams, we were really poised to win a Cup either one of those years, when we got barrel-rolled by the Toronto Maple Leafs and the New York Rangers.

JIMMY DEVELLANO: Because it's not easy, that's why. And because they were still a relatively young team. And because they needed pieces. It was very methodically done, trust me. Bill Torrey did a terrific job in filling in the pieces. And we had a lot of long playoff runs. We had a couple upsets - not those many, really - but a couple. But our team got better each year. We were able to, as a management group, figure out where our weaknesses were.

BOB BOURNE: You have to learn how to lose before you can learn how to win. And we learned pretty hard. We were pretty disappointed in the late '70s there. But we stuck to our guns and kept getting better. We had a real "character" hockey team, so sooner or later, we were going to win.

STAN FISCHLER: They started out as terrific underdogs. They were underdogs for a reason - they weren't that good! So if you're not that good, you're not going to be making miracles every single year. It took time. Even when they got upset by the Leafs in '78, there was something missing - it was the goaltending was not good enough. Then in '79, the Rangers got lightning in a bottle. They were missing something, and the "something" was three-fold - one was the goaltending, one more mean defenseman, and one more center.

JIMMY DEVELLANO: Sure, we got upset a few times in the mid to late '70s. Disappointing of course. But the regular seasons were good, the team was young. There was no feeling of, "Oh, let's tear this fucking thing apart." Instead, it was, "Let's add something. Let's get something to add." And with that approach, we were eventually able to win it all.

PATRICK DIVISION STANDINGS: 1978-79

TEAMS	W	L	T	POINTS
New York Islanders	51	15	14	116
Philadelphia Flyers	40	25	15	95
New York Rangers	40	29	11	91
Atlanta Flames	41	31	8	90

Quarter-Finals (4-0):

New York Islanders over Chicago Blackhawks

Game 1	April 16	Chicago Blackhawks 2	New York Islanders 6
Game 2	April 18	Chicago Blackhawks 0	New York Islanders 1 (OT)
Game 3	April 20	New York Islanders 4	Chicago Blackhawks 0
Game 4	April 22	New York Islanders 3	Chicago Blackhawks 1

Semi-Finals (4-2):

New York Rangers over New York Islanders

Game 1 April 26 New York Rangers 4 New York Islanders   1
Game 2 April 28 New York Rangers 3 New York Islanders 4 (OT)
Game 3 May 1   New York Islanders 1 New York Rangers 3
Game 4 May 3   New York Islanders 3 New York Rangers 2 (OT)
Game 5 May 5   New York Rangers 4 New York Islanders 3
Game 6 May 8   New York Islanders 1 New York Rangers 2

CHAPTER 16:

1979-80

An apparent hangover from the previous year's playoff defeat seems to be affecting the Islanders' play for most of the 1979-80 regular season.

JEAN POTVIN: I remember Bill calling me about a week after the Islanders were eliminated by the Rangers, and I believe my contract was up with Minnesota. We had lunch at a restaurant in Huntington, and he asks me, "First of all, how's Lorraine? How are the kids?" I said, "Fine, they're doing fine." He says, "OK, here's the reason why I want to talk to you. If I was able to make a trade for you, and get your rights, would you be willing to come back to the New York Islanders?" I said, "Bill, are you kidding me? I'm not planning on going back to Minnesota. To tell you the truth, I think my career may be over. Of course I would. But let me ask you a question, I'll be very honest with you. You've got a hell of a team." He says, "Oh yeah, I've got a hell of a team. We got eliminated early two years in a row! There's something missing."

He said something that was pretty flattering. He said, "I called a number of the players in my office, and I said, 'One year, we get beat by Toronto, which is a huge upset. This year, we had an unbelievable regular season, and we lose to the Rangers. What the hell is missing? What's going on here?'" And I guess my name came up once or twice, and they said, "We really miss him in the locker room. He plays a key role there and he's very important to us. We love to have him around. He just has a very positive impact on all of us." So he mentioned that to me, and I said, "Geez, that's really complimentary. That's great." And he says, "Let me work on something, and if you're willing to come back, I'll try and see if I can swing a trade." So he did, and I wound up coming back to the Islanders.

EDDIE WESTFALL: Part way through that season [1979], I was still used for key face-offs and penalty killing, but my role as a regular player was diminished. I didn't really want to play under those circumstances - maybe with another team, my role on a regular basis would have been increased. But with this team, I was slowly being accessed out. I'll never forget, Nelson Doubleday - he was the guy that kept me from going back to Boston. I was on my own, I was single, and my kids were up in the Boston area. I had an airplane and was commuting the best I could those years I was playing. And Nelson said, "What do you want to do?" I said, "I think I'll go back up."

Harry Sinden came back in '72 after I had already left the Bruins, and he came back to be the general manager and president. He and I had stayed in touch. He's my oldest and dearest friend in hockey - I've known him even before he got married, when he was a kid. So he said, "You'll have a job with this organization." So I was anticipating maybe going back up to Boston. And Nelson said, "Wait a minute." Because back then, it was rather confusing - the Islanders had a broadcast team for the home games and a broadcast team for the away games, on WOR and SportsChannel. He said, "The fans are confused. They have two different [broadcasting] teams, and we want to just have one team doing the games. Why don't you do the color for the analyst part of the broadcast?" So I said, "Nelson, here's what I'll do. I'll try it for a year. If you like what I do and I like it, we'll talk about a contract beyond. If I don't like doing it or you don't like the way I do it, it'll just be one year, and I'll be out of here." So that's where it started.

I didn't have to put my stuff on and go to practice. [Laughs] You're at almost all the practices, and obviously, all the games. So it's a wonderful extension. A dear friend of mine up in Boston - when I had to leave Boston and come to Long Island, and I'm doing the pouty-wouty and holding my breath until I turn blue, and threatening to retire and quit - he said to me, "What are you going to do?" And I said, "Well, maybe I'll get into business." He said, "One thing you want to know right up front, if you get into a business, it's going to take you five years to figure out how the business is doing and get all the people in it. If you can stay in hockey, it's a lot better than trying to hack it out in another business. You don't know anybody in it and you don't know the business."

This worked twice - staying in hockey [as a player] with the Islanders and also staying in hockey when I retired as a player [as a broadcaster]. So I stayed in it, and I'm absolutely thrilled that I did. I had so much fun, because I knew the game. That was one of the interesting parts. When you do an interview, and you know what the answer is before you ask the question...but you had to find out what the other people in hockey felt about this. But trying to keep it simple, so the question was simple and the player knew the answer. That was always an interesting concept.

CLARK GILLIES: I held that [captain] position for two years, and those probably weren't my two best years. For whatever reason, I always felt some strange responsibility to be doing something that I wasn't comfortable with. I finally went in to see Al after the '79 season, and I said, "I'd like to give up the seat to somebody. The guy that it would probably fit best on would be Denis Potvin." He asked Denis if he wanted it, and Denis said, "Absolutely, yes."

LORNE HENNING: Clark is such a good team guy, and he just found it hard to get on guys. I think it was taking away from his game a little. It was pretty smooth [the transition from Gillies to Potvin as captain]. We had a lot of leaders on that team. A lot of guys chipped in, a lot of guys helped out. So it was a pretty good group effort. Denis was a leader in his own way, and Clarkie was still a leader.

BRYAN TROTTIER: That year was a tough season. It wasn't like we had the best year. We didn't feel like we were underachieving, we certainly weren't overachieving. But it was a time of introspection, where we were looking at ourselves individually and as a group, versus looking outside for answers. Those kind of things pull you together. And maybe there was some fear, and maybe there was some stress about the whole situation.

BILLY HARRIS: The biggest thing was just how the guys seemed to be uptight. We weren't playing that well. And I don't know if it was because of injuries or what. I don't really remember if some of the guys were hurt or one of the goalies was having a bad year.

BOB BOURNE: It was a struggle that year. One of the greatest things in my life ever happened - my son was born in November. But he was born with spina bifida. So it was a tough year for me mentally. I was so looking forward to our first son, and then he went through a lot of operations. For us, personally, it was a tough year. And then we had some guys hurt, but we kept going.

CLAIRE ARBOUR: I remember Bobby Bourne, his first child was born with spina bifida, and that was really something that…most of the players had healthy kids. That really brought everybody together, thinking, "Oh my gosh, *this is serious.*" The team got even closer. They learned to support one another.

BOB LORIMER: That's the year that Denis hurt his thumb. He missed like 30 or 40 games, and if you take the best defenseman in the league off your team, any team is going to struggle. Denis was obviously key, because not only did he make our power play click, but he was also a great penalty killer. So you take him out of the equation, and that left a big hole for us. But in hindsight, it may have helped us, because other guys on the team had to take on other roles and get more experience in roles that they probably wouldn't have gotten the ice time in those situations. So I think it actually helped us, and it helped Denis, because he came back and he was well-rested for the playoff drive. Sometimes, those things seem like the worst things that can happen, but actually, they can make your team stronger - because the expanded roles guys can get when they have to do things that they normally don't get the ice time for.

GLENN "CHICO" RESCH: You're hopeful every year, because you know you have a dynamic team. But of course, like teams say, it wouldn't have mattered if we were 15 points in first place after the first 40 games and we're blowing everybody away - you know it comes to the end of the season, when it comes to crunch time. So whatever happened, we started to struggle a little bit after Christmas. The fans got a little bit testy and I don't blame them. We were all feeling a little bit anxious. They were calling for Al's head a little bit, because fans don't know what's really going on - it wasn't Al.

BILLY HARRIS: One of the things that stood out, I remember it was in Edmonton, and Al sat out like four or five guys. And he sat me out - at least he talked to me before the game. But I had never missed a game, and he had broken my streak, on purpose. Just to prove to the team that personal records weren't important. Which I thought was pretty lame.

BOB NYSTROM: I truly believed that the management was going to disband the team - they were going to start making some moves.

LORNE HENNING: People were looking to Bill and Al to make a lot of changes. And credit to them, they didn't. Most organizations would strip a lot of pieces out of there and add pieces, but they knew what they had. And until you win, you had to get through that. And eventually, we got through it.

STAN FISCHLER: I never thought that deeply about it [that the team may be dismantled if they didn't win it all in '80], but I know that Torrey did. Obviously, if you keep missing when you're a favorite, then you have to question, "What is the problem?"

AL ARBOUR: I didn't think about that. I knew we were a good team - there was no question about that. We just had to get the right players.

JIMMY DEVELLANO: You had a pretty passionate general manager with a lot of authority in Bill Torrey. He had real good backing and a good worker in me. We both believed in Al Arbour. You can have a pretty damn good team and not win the Cup. And you shouldn't tear it apart - you really, really shouldn't. I don't know what the hell that proves. I gave that counsel to the San Jose Sharks two years ago. They came to me, because I had been through it twice - with the Islanders and with Detroit, when people thought we should have won and didn't. I said, "Don't listen to the press and don't listen to the fans. You've got a good team. You didn't finish first overall in the regular season by accident, OK? Just tweak your team. Add a piece or two. Don't tear it apart." While it was a little bit of frustrating times, we had an ownership in Pickett that liked Bill Torrey and liked the job he was doing.

BILL TORREY: We did not play well in the early part of the year. We had a lot of injuries and we were far from a finished product. But we were able to make a couple of changes, and made a deal during the year that certainly helped us. We started to get our solid core back.

BOB NYSTROM: I think that the two players that we got that year in the latter part of the season, Butch Goring and Ken Morrow, really put us over the top.

CHAPTER 17:

THE FINAL PIECES TO THE PUZZLE

A trade with the Los Angeles Kings sends a popular original Islander to the west coast. But the scrappy gentleman they get in return is often considered "the final piece to the puzzle."

BRYAN TROTTIER: Bill made some moves - whether good, bad, or indifferent - looking back, they turned out *phenomenal*. John Tonelli the year before, then you get Dave Langevin, Butch Goring, Ken Morrow, Duane Sutter, and Gord Lane that year. It was like a whole new set of chemistry that comes together, and guys just grabbing the rope - maybe in a different way. We have to as a group welcome [the new players], get them settled, and find a way to get that chemistry working. It all evolves, like a perfect storm.

STAN FISCHLER: I thought there would be some sort of trade, I didn't know anything about getting Goring. Let's face it - getting rid of Billy Harris was addition by subtraction. This guy just didn't live up to his expectations, and by the time he got traded, you knew he was not going to get any better. And ditto for Dave Lewis [Harris and Lewis were traded for Butch Goring, from the Los Angeles Kings, on March 10th]. But nobody imagined that Goring would be as terrific as he was. Goring is a guy that belongs in the Hall of Fame. Not only [was he the missing piece of the puzzle], but he produced. He made everybody around him better.

BILLY HARRIS: No [Billy didn't see the trade coming]. Bill Torrey called me - I think it was 1:00 in the morning. I thought he was joking. I remember the whole conversation. He sounded like he was a little bit shook up, because I'd known him a long time - he drafted me in '72. The only good thing I can say is that I got to play with Marcel Dionne, and I went to LA and I knew a lot of the guys I played with in junior or with the Islanders. It was a heck of team. To say that you played with Marcel Dionne - who I've known for quite a long time and is still a good friend - you don't appreciate how good a player he is until you play with him. And I'll tell you what, he was one of the all-time greats.

I got shipped to LA - they could have traded anybody, and it would have calmed the whole team down. Everybody was so uptight, and they were so worried that something was going to happen. Because we had been close for so many years, so they figured something was going to happen. And something did happen. But after that, everybody calmed down, and they walked away with it. So it was just a question of taking the pressure off. Guys like Bobby Nystrom and Bobby Bourne - in between periods, they're smoking cigarettes. I could handle pressure. But a lot of guys, it really affected them.

GLENN "CHICO" RESCH: Bill Torrey's very first pick ever was Billy Harris. He loved Billy Harris, and Billy played pretty well. I mean, did he become the dominant, elite player you hope when you draft one or two? No. But Billy was Billy, and he did it all. But I think that little glitch we had, when we went on that little bit of a losing skid there, showed Bill that he needed to do something about that center ice position. So he packaged Davey Lewis, who was a terrific, solid defenseman, and Billy. Much like he did with Minnesota years earlier, he put together an attractive enough package to get Butch Goring. Butch came in with fire and passion. And mostly, he had good hockey sense. He was a terrific player. We thought, *"Whoa."* And then Kenny Morrow joined us after the Olympics, and Kenny was unbelievably solid defensively. Oh my goodness, that guy never made a mistake!

JIM PICKARD: His name is Kenneth Arlington Morrow. So I always used to call him "Arlington." He was very quiet and unassuming.

KEN MORROW [The Islanders' defenseman from 1980-1989]: I'm from Flint, Michigan, which is about an hour north of Detroit. A big auto industry town, and like a lot of kids in Michigan, I started to play hockey when I was young - outdoors. We ended up building a small rink in our backyard. I have an older brother, and we both played hockey. My father got us involved. He was a baseball player, but he started coaching us in hockey. We just grew up like a lot of kids in Michigan and Canada, playing outside with our friends and playing youth hockey through the ranks. From there, the competition got better as I moved up through hockey. We started traveling to Detroit and Canada, playing on some travel teams. When I got up to the junior ranks, which is as a 16/17/18-year-old, I ended up trying out and making a team - the Detroit Junior Red Wings, which was one of the premiere Junior A-teams in the Detroit area. That got me started on the higher level of hockey. Played one year there, and got scouted by some college coaches, and got recruited to a couple of colleges.

I had two scholarship offers to go to schools, and chose to go to Bowling Green. I thought that was the pinnacle of my hockey career at that point - getting to play hockey. Went down to Bowling Green, four years there. The coach, Ron Mason, turned out to be the winningest college hockey coach in history, so I had some great coaching. I was drafted by the Islanders my freshman year, stayed in school. There wasn't really any choice for me - I had to stay in school. They didn't approach me about leaving early, I wasn't ready to leave early. Then I started getting noticed in college as far as USA Hockey. My first taste of international hockey was my junior year. I was an All-American that year, and they asked if I would come over and play in the World Championships, in Czechoslovakia in 1978. So that was the first time I'd ever done anything like that. I got asked again in '79, but decided that I wanted to stay in school that spring, and then got invited to the sports festivals, which they had in '78 and '79. In '79, they used that as the tryout for the Olympic team.

It's 30 years [since the 1980 US Men's Olympic Hockey team won the Gold Medal], and if anything, it's probably grown in stature. For me, it was a thrill of a lifetime. It was unexpected. We thought we were going to do OK. I think we were seeded sixth or seventh. Our goal going in was to make the final four - to make it to the medal round. We had to get off to a good start, and we did. We got to win those first couple of games, we tied Sweden, and we beat the Czechs.

Those were the two teams that we really had to do well against right off the bat. So that got the ball rolling for us. The game everyone remembers is the Russian game. I've never found the right words for it. We had so many things going for us at the time. I was on the ice for the last minute and a half of the game. That's something I'll always remember - trying to hold on to a one goal lead against that team.

I really didn't have any contact with the Islanders until after the Olympics. That's when I found out I was going to join them. As soon as the Olympics ended, I talked with Bill Torrey. I didn't know what was going to happen at that point. Your whole focus is on the Olympic team, so as soon as that ended, I didn't know if I was going to sign a pro contract. I didn't know what their plans were for me. I met with Bill Torrey, and he said, "We're bringing you right to Long Island." It was a thrill for me - within a week, I had won a Gold Medal and I had signed my first pro contract. The Gold Medal game was on Sunday [February 24th, against Finland], I went home for a couple of days, and then I was in Long Island either Wednesday or Thursday of that week - practicing with the team. And then I played my first game that following weekend. It all happened suddenly, and I was off on my pro career.

GORD LANE [The Islanders' defenseman from 1979-1985]: I'm from Brandon, Manitoba. I played junior hockey with the Wheat Kings - I think it was 1969 through...I was drafted in 1973 by the Pittsburgh Penguins. I was their ninth round pick. And then I was sent from Pittsburgh to their farm team in the IHL, in Fort Wayne. I was in Fort Wayne for probably three months and then traded to Dayton in the IHL, where Tommy McVie was coaching. I was there for two years, and then Tommy went up to the Washington Capitals, the following year, I was brought up too. I stayed there from 1976 through 1979. December 7th, 1979, I was traded to New York for Mike Kaszycki.

The 1979-1980 season, before I got there, I was surprised they even traded for me, because I was playing for *the Capitals* - not a real powerhouse at that time. And I wasn't even playing regularly. So I was a little bit surprised when I went there, because even though they were struggling, they were still a very dominant team. They had some great hockey players. I think I was only traded for because Denis had been injured - he tore up his thumb. I don't think they expected me to be there for a very long time. But when I got there, I just fell in and it was a breath of fresh air.

DUANE SUTTER [The Islanders' right winger from 1979-1987]: I came from a small town in Central Alberta - Viking - and grew up playing hockey there. Moved on to a little city, Red Deer, Alberta, played in Alberta Junior Hockey League there, as a 16 and 17-year-old. I headed into Lethbridge in the '78-'79 season, and played there in the Western Hockey League. I was drafted in August of '79 by the Islanders.

　　You go into your camp with your eyes wide open, trying to figure out who's who and what's what. I was very much aware of the fact that they had won the regular season championship the previous year, and obviously, they were a pretty darn good hockey team. Unfortunately, they had some growing pains through the playoff run, when the Rangers upset them. But they were a very determined group. Never a deficiency on the Islanders was character. They were a solid group of players with an intense hunger to get back and prove to the world that they were a very good hockey team.

　　I was sent back to the Western League to start the season, and then recalled November 28th of '79. Was able to stay up with the team the rest of the season. Fortunately, I was able to find a niche that I could add to the line-up, game in and game out.

DAVE LANGEVIN [The Islanders' defenseman from 1979-1985]: I'm from St. Paul, Minnesota. I got into hockey through my dad. In Minnesota, in the summers you play baseball, in the fall you play football, and in the winters, you play hockey. My dad built a rink in our yard. He was a good hockey player - he was one of the better players in St. Paul at that time. He played for Cretin High School. But at that time, hockey wasn't really a national sport in the US as it is now. There were eight of us kids, and it was probably better to have the kids do something in the winter than be in a house. We built a rink, and we played outside all winter. I didn't play indoor ice until I was probably in eighth grade. They just started to build indoor rinks down in the Metro area. So then I went to Hill High School - one of the premier high school hockey teams. We had a great coach that developed players, so we won a few state tournaments when I was in high school. We just played because we loved it - we didn't know anything about professional hockey or anything like that. The North Stars came in '67, and then I think the big thing that changed the need for hockey players was when the WHA came in, and we had the Minnesota Fighting Saints.

I played up at the University of Minnesota Duluth, I got a scholarship from Duluth, and then I played four years there. I was drafted when I was 20 years old. The draft at that time was when you were 20…actually, the year that I was drafted was the first year that they changed it from 20 to 18. So my draft year, we had three years of players being drafted. I was projected to go in the first [round], and then with three more groups of kids going, everybody was bumped back. It was just the start of the US player being drafted, and they needed a lot of players, because they had two leagues going. I was drafted by the New York Islanders and the Edmonton Oilers. When I was with Edmonton, they were flirting at the time with the NHL and the WHA merging. At that time, we were all thinking, "Well, what's going to happen? Do I stay with Edmonton or do I go to New York?"

It worked out that each team could protect two skaters and two goalies, and all the other players, the NHL team that drafted you had a right to claim you back. With Edmonton, Wayne Gretzky was an automatic choice they were going to protect, and it was between me and Bengt Gustafsson. And they chose Bengt Gustafsson. Eventually, they lost him anyways, because Edmonton cheated. They wanted to protect me, but New York said, "No. You had your chance." So that's how I became a New York Islander, was through the merger draft. I came out in the summer and we talked with Mr. Torrey and Mr. Arbour, and I signed with the New York Islanders in probably July. My wife and I bought a house in Fort Salonga. We made New York our home.

My first training camp, the first day that I got there, there was a big team meeting, and I was wondering, "What the heck is going on here?" That's when Clark Gillies gave up his captain [title]. It was very emotional for him. And I'm wondering, *"What the heck did I get myself into here?* Maybe I should have just stayed in Edmonton!" I was watching New York as I was playing with Edmonton, thinking, "Eventually, I want to get there." So I was following them. I really didn't know the impact of that ['79 playoff] loss until I got there. At that time, the Islanders and Rangers hated each other. I don't know if it's like that anymore, but there were teams that you actually *hated* the players, and you wouldn't even want to see them in the summer and say hi. We had a few teams like that at the time - Philadelphia.

JEAN POTVIN: Dave Langevin was a huge, positive impact. He was a welcome addition to the Islanders. And Kenny Morrow was huge - he immediately played like a champion. I mean, there was no learning curve with him. Kenny was no "Bobby Orr type," but defensively, he was flawless. And Dave Langevin added a lot of muscle to us. We called him "Bam Bam," because he'd always be banging guys against the boards or in front of the net. So OK, these guys, like us, we were not Mike Bossy, Bryan Trottier, Denis Potvin, or Billy Smith. But we brought something else to the team. I don't care what anybody says - when you're playing a team sport, it's not just five superstars who win it. You have to have a surrounding cast, and everyone has a role to play - whether it's to play defensively, to be a checker, or to be a penalty killer like Lorne Henning, along with Butchie. Butchie was one of the best penalty killers in the NHL, but hardly anybody knew that, because who saw the LA Kings play back in those days? They'd never be on TV. So yeah, these are pieces to the puzzle.

DAVE LANGEVIN: We tried to get more balanced, because they had one line. They had Trots, Boss, and Clark as their line. Even watching today, most teams with one line can't win the Stanley Cup. And if you play two lines, you're never going to win a Stanley Cup. Because you just don't have the strength - teams can key in on two lines. And if it's four defense, you're not going to have four offensive. Just the wear and tear, you're not as fresh. As the series go long, the fatigue factor sets in, you have injuries. You lose one player with four defense, things don't get any better - you could see with Vancouver last year [2010-11]. They lost a couple of defensemen, it's over.

LORNE HENNING: I think the first part of March, we were right on the bubble of being out of the playoffs - I think we were 16th or 17th. We went out to California, and we bonded. The guys went through a lot of stuff. And since we went through the big trade that everybody talks about - getting Butchie, which was "the missing piece" - then we got on a roll and got big goals by a lot of different guys. It's amazing how we had so many heroes. Everybody chipped in - it was a total team effort.

KEN MORROW: I think my first game was March 1st. The season had been a bit of a disappointment for the team. Denis Potvin came back and played his first game from injury, [and was] was my first game. About a week or two after I came was the trade for Butch Goring, and that really jump-started the team.

BOB BOURNE: I believe it was ten straight games we went at the end of the season without losing [twelve games]. We got on a roll and we got our confidence, and we felt that we could win that year. Everything was in place. Smitty was playing really well.

DAVE LANGEVIN: I think you give a lot of credit to Bill and Al, as, "OK, let's go a different route with this. Let's get this season going. We'll get new people, we'll start filling our needs." And what happened there is it all came together at the end. I don't think we lost a game the last three weeks of the season. We were unstoppable. We were confident.

GLENN "CHICO" RESCH: You just said, "OK, really good team. A team that could win the Cup anyway." But now, you've just added a couple of incredible more players. We *knew* this was going to be our time. I know I went the last thirteen games of the season undefeated, and Smitty had a nice stretch going in.

BOB NYSTROM: We played a little bit different that year. We didn't have a great year - there's no question about that. When you look at how we finished the year, it was on a real positive note. We were just starting to come into our own.

GARY "BABA BOOEY" DELL'ABATE: I remember not caring that much [about the regular season], because you were waiting for the playoffs. At the time, it seemed like almost every team got in the playoffs, so it was like once you got to the playoffs, everything was different. I always remember, "Who is the weird guy with the weird helmet?" Which was Goring. I remember Goring playing really well - you could see them starting to play better at the end of the season. I think I remember going to a game very close to the end of the season that year, when they played the Rangers. I think Gillies beat the shit out of Espo, which was very exciting for us. They were scrappy, and you were like, "OK, let's get to the playoffs and see what happens."

DAVE LANGEVIN: I think Bill and Al, they finally realized that the regular season doesn't mean anything - other than you have to get in the playoffs, that's number one. I think the year before, they felt that they had to be the number one...you're trying to gain respect and notoriety in the league, that you're the top team in the league. Sometimes when you do that, you're not getting a balanced team. You're going at such a high clip that you're worrying so much about winning that when the playoffs come, you're not prepared for the playoffs. And I remember that was one thing that I picked up, hearing conversations of Al and Bill during that time, was "We didn't care about the regular season. *We're building for the playoffs."*

AL ARBOUR: We were gearing ourselves for the playoffs. Once we got in the playoffs, it didn't matter. We just had to play our game, and we had to play better than the other team. We had to stand up for ourselves and go and fight. We did what we had to do.

BILL TORREY: A lot of people wrote us off going into the playoffs in '80.

PATRICK DIVISION STANDINGS: 1979-80

TEAMS	W	L	T	POINTS
Philadelphia Flyers	48	12	20	116
New York Islanders	39	28	13	91
New York Rangers	38	32	10	86
Atlanta Flames	35	32	13	83
Washington Capitals	27	40	13	67

CHAPTER 18:

PLAYOFFS '80

After a disappointing regular season, the Islanders manage to put it all together in time for the 1980 playoffs, against the Kings, Bruins, and Sabres.

KEN MORROW: The first round that year, against the LA Kings, it was a best of five at that time. The Islanders still had this monkey on their back, as far as having lost the last couple of years in the playoffs when they were the favorites.

BOB LORIMER: That's a dangerous series, because of the Dionne line, with Charlie Simmer and Dave Taylor. Dionne won the scoring title that year, and they may have had the most points of any line in the league. And the travel was difficult as well, when you're flying back and forth [coast to coast]. So we didn't take them lightly, because we knew they could score. We wanted to get the series over as quickly as possible, because that could really put you behind the eight ball early in the playoffs. With the travel you had, it could make it very difficult for the remainder of the playoffs.

AL ARBOUR: It was an important game, the first game - to give the guys confidence, and they knew they could do it.

DUANE SUTTER: That was a good series. I remember just the match-up, because with Butch Goring coming to us from LA, that threw a little different spin on the whole series. Butch obviously wanted to prove them wrong, and could offer some of the coaches a lot of insight into what to expect or which buttons to push.

JEAN POTVIN: That series, it was also strange in a way, because we were playing against two very good friends - Dave Lewis and Billy Harris. They certainly wanted to show the Islanders organization that they'd made a mistake. So they would have loved nothing more than to beat us.

BILLY HARRIS: That was just really a weird feeling coming out for the pre-game skate [for game one at the Coliseum]. And then all the fans…I saw some of my signs up there from the fan club. It was quite an emotional thing.

BOB BOURNE: Well, we were scared to death, because we beat them the first game at home pretty handily [8-1], then they killed us in game two [6-3], in our own building. When we went to LA, we went out there with a lot of resolve, and we decided it was time to buckle up and get at it.

KEN MORROW: So we were 1-1 going out to LA in a five game series. All of a sudden, things are getting a little dicey. We were down 3-0 in that third game out in LA, and had a dramatic comeback, and tied it 3-3. I actually ended up scoring in overtime in that game. My first pro goal was an overtime goal against the Kings.

JEAN POTVIN: The thing that sticks out there is Kenny Morrow scoring an overtime goal. And Kenny I believe finished his career scoring something like four overtime goals. Some of the greatest goal scorers in the history of the NHL haven't scored four overtime goals!

DAVE LANGEVIN: Billy Smith became "the goalie" then. Before that, I think Glenn Resch was the goalie of record pretty much in the playoffs before. Smitty was kind of "the back-up guy." And then when he got his chance, the rest is history. And I think having his confidence…well, he was a fiery guy, too. He just didn't want to lose. And I give credit to Bill and Al again - they said, "OK. We're going a different route. We'll give Smitty a chance. He was the number two, and now we're going to give him the number one." And he ran with it.

STAN FISCHLER: First of all, Chico was actually preceded by Billy Smith. At the beginning, Billy was very crude. I myself did not think that he would amount to any significance as a big league goalie. But I underestimated his fortitude, his ability to battle. Chico was much more of a fun-loving guy. Did not have the overt intensity that Smitty had. But then again, *nobody* had that kind of intensity, because he's one of a kind. Chico won a lot of big games for them. He was the hero when they came from the three game deficit and beat Pittsburgh in '75. But I believe Chico's downfall began when the Islanders lost to underdog Toronto in '78, and Chico was beaten in overtime. That was a stigma.

Then the next year, it was Smitty that got beaten by the Rangers. But there was something much more dynamic as a personality in Smith. I believe that both Al Arbour and Bill Torrey thought less of Chico because he was a chatterbox. He was a great guy with the media, whereas Smitty was more brooding. He would talk and was often outspoken, but I think the management believed that Smitty was more dedicated. Now, that doesn't mean that he was. But this was the impression that I believe that they got. Of course, when it got to the playoffs in 1980, Smitty was front and center. I don't know this for a fact, but my guess is that Al Arbour was more of a Smitty fan - in terms of winning big games - than he was with Chico.

LORNE HENNING: Certainly, Smitty got in, took the ball, and ran with it. I think Al decided that Bill was going to get the first shot. Smitty was chomping at the bit and he was ready to go.

AL ARBOUR: I made a decision to use the better goaltender. But you couldn't play Smitty in the course of the season too much. That's why I kept movement around, because with Smitty, he was always in there - he wanted more money all the time! He got a big head, so you had to play the other goaltenders a lot during the course of the season. And we knew that Billy Smith would play every game in the playoffs.

KEN MORROW: And then we won the next game the next night, 6-0 [which clinched the series for the Islanders]. It was a huge win for the team. It could have been another disappointing playoff loss.

DUANE SUTTER: We had some injuries and there were some unsung heroes in that series - if I remember correctly, Alex McKendry came up and played, and contributed. A lot of people forget that we had a championship team down in the Central Hockey League, in Indianapolis, so there were a lot of good players down there, as well.

BOB NYSTROM: We got a little bit of a scare with LA there. That preliminary round, where we won it three to one, I've got to tell you, we were a little nervous on that one.

LORNE HENNING: There was a lot of pressure on us to win, and the guys felt it early on. In the playoffs, once you get going, you relax a little bit. The first round, you really feel the heat. I think the guys [felt] like you're supposed to win, and they kept it close. Until we got through that round and we started to relax a little more, for sure, it was a pretty intense round.

BILLY HARRIS: No, I didn't really follow [the Islanders in the playoffs] that closely, unless they were on TV. Because usually after the season, I have a summer home up here. I'd usually go down south and go fishing with a buddy of mine - he's got a big boat in the Bahamas. We'd fish for about a month, and then I'd get back up here and the playoffs were still on, so I'd usually watch the Finals.

BOB NYSTROM: But I would have to say of each one of those series, the one that put us over the top was the Boston series. Because Boston thought they were going to run us right out of the building.

STAN FISCHLER: The Toronto series [in '78] was dirty. It started with Lorne Henning - it wasn't deliberate, but he poked Borje Salming, and Salming went out of the series. It was just *vicious*. That was when Bossy nearly got killed - I forget which Leaf knocked him over. It was mean. The thing about the Bruins series was there were a lot fights. You had goalie fights, you had Gillies and Terry O'Reilly. But it didn't have the viciousness of the Leafs series. The Leafs series it was game after game - every single game. *Seven games*. It was crazy.

GLENN "CHICO" RESCH: The big brawl series with Boston. Where we were coming out of the series two years earlier against Toronto, the reputation was, "Oh, you can intimidate these Islanders." And again, you might have thought that, because really, Toronto beat us up physically. But again, Boss got hurt, we didn't have that dynamic second line, so what they didn't realize was we were a different team, and I think they found that out.

Clark Gillies, who everybody loved, was a laid back guy. He'll do confrontation, but he doesn't go looking for it. He knew in that series that it was he and O'Reilly. I remember after the big brawl and a couple of fights in the first two games in Boston, we came back for game three, and I heard somebody dry-heaving in the stall next to me in the bathroom, and I said, "Who's that?" He said, "Clarkie." I said, "What's going on? Do you have the flu?" "No, I just got a little bit of a nervous stomach. I know Big Terry's coming after me again tonight!" That summed up what the players had to do to win that series - they really had to go out of their comfort zone. And that's why I respect that team. Everybody went out of their comfort zone to win that series.

CLARK GILLIES: Bobby Nystrom and I were roommates, and he told me, "We're not going to let that happen again. We're going to match up - you're probably going to be against Terry O'Reilly, I'm going to be against John Wensink, and Howatt will probably be against Stan Jonathan. We're all going to have somebody that we're going to have to take care of." We'd always had physical games against Boston. And sure enough, that's exactly what happened.

BOB BOURNE: They had the toughest team I'd ever seen. Philly was a tough team, but nothing compared to the Boston Bruins. They had more individual tough players, but we were a really tough team, too. That's where guys like Gordie Lane stepped up and really made us a team.

DUANE SUTTER: The Boston series was a big series, because it was also another big hurdle for the Islanders - not only as an organization, but probably most importantly in the dressing room. A lot of folks around the league thought there was no chance we would stand up to them in the physical game, and we had two or three brawls in that series - line brawls - that again, gave us another level of confidence.

BRYAN TROTTIER: Bobby took on Wensink, Clark ended up fighting [O'Reilly]. Every game after that, they thought, "OK, we're not taking a backseat to the Islanders on this physical aspect." It just seemed like it was a group - especially our toughest guys, our guys that carried that load, were just absolutely phenomenal. It seemed like the more they threw at us, the bigger we responded as a team, because we felt, "Hey, *it's not that bad.*" I think that was a big thing for the team. The other thing was the play of Billy Smith. Against Los Angeles, he made some key saves at the key time, and you need that from your goaltender. He wasn't just a battler with the fists - he was a battler all the way through. And then in Boston, he just slammed the door.

AL ARBOUR: That was a hard-fought series, there's no question about it. I remember Andy Kallur, he's the type of guy that never said a word. I came in the dressing room, and he said, "Leave it to 'Killer' - the Killer's going to get them all! I'm going to beat the hell out of them!" He couldn't beat anybody. [Laughs] The guys went out there, and just kicked the hell out of the Bruins. O'Reilly, most of the summer, his face was swollen. They stood up, and they played very well.

BOB BOURNE: We won the first game in overtime [2-1], and then we had that big brawl in the second game [which the Islanders won again in overtime, 5-4], and we just showed everybody in the league that we were not going to be pushed around anymore. I think that really turned our team around.

CLARK GILLIES: Actually, the first game in that series was very passive. There might have been one minor penalty. And then all hell broke loose in the first period of the second game. We stood up to them, we beat them. There was a brawl at the end of the first period of the second game, which I think brought our team together in such a big way. Bobby Lorimer had a big gash under his eye, and I don't think he even cared if he got stitches or not - he just wanted to go back out there. But everybody came into the dressing room, and said,

"That's what we need to do to win, boys." And we just went on. Everybody knew at that point that this team could also play physical, so you better be careful with how you approach this team. We had a tough roster - myself, Nystrom, Howatt, Lane, Lorimer, and a couple of other guys that could go pretty good. It was one of the learning bumps that we had to get over. And we did.

DAVE LANGEVIN: We got the series down 3-0 [after a 5-3 Islanders victory], and we come home and we can finish the series in four, because every game was a brawl - everybody was involved in something and it was very physical. Just mentally, it was like, *"Oh my god."* Every game was like that. Then we come home and we lose to Boston [4-3 in overtime]. I wanted to get sick, just thinking, "We could have got this thing over with. But now, we've got to go back there for game five." I think we were down 2-0, and then I think Al Secord picked a fight with Clark Gillies, and Clark just kicked his butt, and it ignited us again. We beat them 4-2. So that was the one where we became a team where no matter what people threw at us, no matter how much they wanted to fight us or intimidate us, everybody stood up to them. Even the little guys, they stood up for themselves, and everybody stuck up for each other. I think that was a turning point for the rest of the playoffs and for the Islander organization. And the team. It got rid of that stigma that we could get intimidated.

BOB NYSTROM: I think that we handled ourselves extremely well against a very, very tough hockey club, and we ended up beating them four games to one.

BRYAN TROTTIER: Then we get up against Buffalo, and I still remember in Buffalo, when Bobby had to shut down Rick Martin, and Billy Smith says, "We're going to intimidate them in a different way. Not physically. We're going to intimidate them by not being intimidated by their offense." Gilbert Perreault was a huge factor, and it just seemed like there was no way to slow him down one-on-one. But as a trio, it was neat to see how the team managed to do that. There were big short-handed goals in Buffalo. Al was very strict, he was like, "I don't want anybody taking any penalties." And Gordie Lane up and takes a five minute right off the hop, and we get two short-handed goals out of it! It was little things like that, that just happened. Maybe coincidental, serendipity, whatever you want to call it. But it worked out in our favor.

CLARK GILLIES: I don't want to say it was easy, but after going through the hell that we went through with the Bruins…we had to play hard. The games weren't as physical. The games didn't take the wear and tear on you like the Bruins games did.

BOB NYSTROM: That series was a little bit different. Both of the buildings are very, very similar. I would have to say that Boston was the tougher of the two teams. But Buffalo had some incredibly talented players - they had Richard Martin, Rene Robert, and Gilbert Perreault. And certainly from a goaltending standpoint, they had an excellent goaltender, also [in 1980, Buffalo goaltenders Bob Sauvé and Don Edwards shared the Vezina Trophy]. We knew it was going to be a tough series. But we were pretty confident.

AL ARBOUR: I put Nystrom over on Martin, and he scared the hell out of Martin! That was it.

DAVE LANGEVIN: One of the biggest things in that playoff run for us in '80 was how well we did on the road. I think we were the seventh seed, so every series - except for the LA one - we had to start on the road. And every series, we won the first two games. Buffalo was "The French Connection" line. I think they had more firepower than Boston. They still had their big guys - Jerry Korab and Larry Playfair. The had some big, strong, mean defensemen, and they had some forwards that were physical, too. But they didn't have the tough guys like Boston had.

After what we did with Boston, nobody was going to intimidate us. I think *we* became the intimidators. They knew that, "OK, if they want to fight we can fight." And we probably had better fighters than anybody in the league, but it was just never a collective team toughness. It used to be, "We'll let Clark, Garry, and Bobby Ny go do the fighting." But the only way a team is going to be affective is if you have 20 guys willing to fight. Whether you want to or not. It's not whether you win the fight, it's just that teams know you're willing to stand up and go toe-to-toe. Every player. And you can't defend against that.

BOB LORIMER: It was a tough series, because they were a very dangerous team on the power play. You had to be careful with your physical game, because of the fact that they could score so well on the power play.

JEAN POTVIN: We obviously focused on the French Connection line. And the guy we focused on the most was Gilbert Perreault. Rick Martin was basically a gunner - as a shooter I think on the left wing. But the guy that made it all happen, with his playmaking ability, his speed, his razzle dazzle, was Gilbert Perreault. And Gilbert Perreault was excellent in many things. Once he was let loose, he was almost impossible to stop, because of his speed, size, strength. You know when you see a defenseman go back for the puck in his own zone, and he goes behind his net and he stops there, and everybody kind of positions themselves, and center icemen will pick up speed, go behind the net, pick up the puck and start up ice with a full head of steam? Well, when Gilbert Perreault would do that, he would be hitting his blue line on his way to our end of the rink at full speed. And I still believe he was the toughest player to stop - one-on-one - when he had that full speed going.

Naturally, when they played at home at Buffalo, they had the home ice advantage, so they could put out Gilbert Perreault's line against our fourth line. And then we'd quickly have to change on the fly. But Al would say, "If that happens and you're out there against him and you don't have a chance to get out, I have complete confidence that each and every one of you guys can do the job. But that said, if you see Gilbert Perreault winding up - so he's getting ready to get a head of steam, go behind the net, pick up the loose puck from the defenseman, and start up ice - I want you to head to that side of the net where he's going to come out. And I want you to force him wide and squeeze him into the boards. Slow him down, so that he's got to either pass the puck or dump it out. I'd rather have Rick Martin carry the puck, because they're not playmakers the way Gilbert Perreault is. So that is what we would do.

We would not allow him to take that puck behind the net, build up a head of steam - because he'd be on a full head of steam by the time he got to the face-off dot, to the right of his goalie! I remember one game in New York, where we missed - we didn't do that. He went back there, picked up the puck, he went through our whole team, and scored. So the thing I remember the most is how we keyed on that whole line, but we keyed significantly more than I think we keyed on any other player we ever played against that year in the playoffs that year, and that was Gilbert Perreault. Because he could destroy you. He was like a one-man wrecking crew, if you let him go. Al also emphasized, "Take the body. If you're going to check a player, don't worry about him passing the puck. Just don't let him get by you - get a piece of him."

BOB BOURNE: We went in and won the first game [4-1] - we scored a couple of short-handed goals. Once we won that first game in their building, we really felt we could win it. We handled them pretty good in our building, and then they came back from 3-1 down, it was 3-2, and we had to have a good game in the sixth game to win [5-2].

LORNE HENNING: My oldest son was born after I think the fifth game, so I stayed behind. He was born, I went into the game, and I got a short-handed goal that night! So that's what stuck out for me. Personally, it was satisfying.

BOB LORIMER: I remember that was probably the only winning goal I've ever scored in my life - in the sixth game, to put us in the Stanley Cup Finals. I didn't score very many goals, and that was one of the times I got into "the offensive mode." Probably because there was a delayed penalty at the time - that was probably the only reason I could do that.

CLARK GILLIES: We took all the disappointments and all the things we should have done, and we finally did them. I think that was probably the message we said to each other after we beat Buffalo, was, "OK boys, we've done what it takes to get this far. Now, let's do what it takes to go all the way."

GORD LANE: We were never respected. I think I remember reading in the newspaper wherever we went...other than that first round, where I think we were expected to beat Los Angeles. After that, you would go to Boston or Buffalo, and the newspapers or writers would never give us any kind of credibility. That's what stood out for me quite a bit - the way that we were always the underdog going into all those series.

CLARK GILLIES: At the end of the rainbow, who do you get? You get the Philadelphia Flyers! [Laughs] You're damned if you do and you're damned if you don't.

Preliminary Round (3-1):

New York Islanders over Los Angeles Kings

Game 1	April 8	Los Angeles Kings 1	New York Islanders 8
Game 2	April 9	Los Angeles Kings 6	New York Islanders 3
Game 3	April 11	New York Islanders 4	Los Angeles Kings 3 (OT)
Game 4	April 12	New York Islanders 6	Los Angeles Kings 0

Quarter-Finals (4-1):

New York Islanders over Boston Bruins

Game 1	April 16	New York Islanders 2	Boston Bruins 1(OT)
Game 2	April 17	New York Islanders 5	Boston Bruins 4(OT)
Game 3	April 19	Boston Bruins 3	New York Islanders 5
Game 4	April 21	Boston Bruins 4	New York Islanders 3 (OT)
Game 5	April 22	New York Islanders 4	Boston Bruins 2

Semi-Finals (4-2):

New York Islanders over Buffalo Sabres

Game 1	April 29	New York Islanders 4	Buffalo Sabres 1
Game 2	May 1	New York Islanders 2	Buffalo Sabres 1(2OT)
Game 3	May 3	Buffalo Sabres 4	New York Islanders 7
Game 4	May 6	Buffalo Sabres 7	New York Islanders 4
Game 5	May 8	New York Islanders 0	Buffalo Sabres 2
Game 6	May 10	Buffalo Sabres 2	New York Islanders 5

CHAPTER 19:

STANLEY CUP '80

The Islanders finally reach the Stanley Cup Finals! One small problem - the season's winningest NHL team, the Flyers, stand in the way.

KEN MORROW: What a team [the Flyers] had. That was the team that went 35 games undefeated that year - without a loss. They set the record. They had it all - scoring, toughness. Everything. And they had guys that had won the Cup back in the mid '70s.

CLARK GILLIES: It's tough to compare [the Flyers teams of the '70s to the 1980 team]. The '80 guys were tough. They had some really tough guys - Paul Holmgren, Bob Kelly. They were still a tough, physical team. The Broad Street Bullies of the early '70s, they had the reputation of Schultzie, Mad Dog Kelly, Eddie Van Impe, Moose Dupont, and the whole crew. A lot of those guys were still around when we played them. I think as a whole, we were a little younger and a little more talented. I don't know…I wouldn't say we were hungrier, but after our two disappointments in '78 and '79, maybe we felt it was our time, and proved that.

BRYAN TROTTIER: Against Philadelphia, it was just like, "Well, if we're going to try and beat 'the Broad Street Bullies of the past,' we'll play any game that's necessary." As a group, it was neat to feel that confidence in the room - through the whole playoffs. It was just one thing after another that happened all the time. Like a key play.

GORD LANE: I remember with Bobby Nystrom and myself, during the typical regular hockey season, for a 7:30 hockey game, you'd show up at 6:00 or 5:30. When we got to the Stanley Cup Playoffs, we were showing up at 1:30, just because you wanted to get there and you wanted to get the thing going. You couldn't sleep, you couldn't eat. That Finals, I weighed 176 pounds, just because you never ate - you were always nervous. You always had that fear of losing.

CLARK GILLIES: It was our first experience in that situation, that type of pressure. Mostly what I remember is a lot of sleepless afternoon game naps - you were supposed to be getting rest, and all you do is roll around in a pool of sweat, waiting to get up. And most of the time at night, you don't sleep. It's hard to explain to the average human being how all you do is toss and turn, and the whole game is going over and over in your head. It's very stressful, but you wake up and you go do your job. We knew we matched up very well against the Flyers. They had beaten us in the Patrick Division in the regular season, but we knew that our team was very capable of playing and beating the Flyers. It was just a matter of getting into it and getting the experience.

BOB BOURNE: Going into Philly, we knew it was going to be a war. It was a heck of a series, but we also felt like we were the better hockey team. Things just turned out for us. We had to play each other ten times that year, so we were very familiar with them. You had Bobby Clarke, Reggie Leach, and Billy Barber - that big line. And then they had a great checking line. They had MacLeish on the second line, who could score. And a pretty good defense, led by the Watson brothers - Joey and Jimmy. But they weren't really mobile, and we were a quick team.

DUANE SUTTER: We didn't really think too much about that as players [if the press favored the Flyers over the Islanders]. We knew obviously to get to the Finals, it was going to be a war, and probably a series more similar to the Boston series. We knew we had come through that series with high marks, and a gain in the level of confidence. We knew it was going to be a tough series, and there was a lot of motivation - especially coming out of the same division said a lot for the Patrick Division, how many good teams were in that division. It was a physical series, and their goaltending gave them a boost all the way though - Pete Peeters had played very well. I think one of our objectives was to stay out of the penalty box, and continue to have a good power play contributing game in and game out. The other thing was we felt that we had more experience in the net, and that somehow, we would get to the Philadelphia goaltending.

LORNE HENNING: You go through that and it's a long process. Guys are tired and worn out. You've got to stay away from injuries and guys are banged up. We had a lot of guys that were hurt - shoulders and knees. It is a marathon. And to get there, you put a lot aside.

BOB LORIMER: At that point in time, because the playoffs are such a grind, it's almost like the emotional element is not as great as in the earlier rounds. I think in the earlier rounds, you can have a lot of upsets, because emotion can overcome talent. So I always thought that as you go further down in the playoffs, the more talented teams usually win out, because you're not playing on as much emotion. That emotional tank has been drained, so you're relying more on your skill level. We thought we had more skill level than the Flyers. And what was really key for us was our power play, it really worked well for us that series - I think we were working on like a 30% clip or something. And that negated some of the physical play of Philly, because they knew they couldn't take liberties, because of our ability to score on the power play.

JEAN POTVIN: I remember the Islanders' power play being unbelievably dominant. I think the Islanders scored 15 power play goals in six games. That's like two and a half goals a game on the power play! So the Islanders' power play was absolutely *deadly*. And that was one of the things that Al Arbour - being the great coach that he was - kept harping on us, especially. And it started with the Bruins - "Do *not* get suckered into getting a stupid retaliation penalty. Because when the referee is looking at the play, and he sees movement out of the corner of his eye, he may see that guy slash you. If you retaliate, he will see movement. He'll turn, and he will not have seen his slash, but he will have seen you slash him back. And then we end up in the box. It will not be acceptable - do not be selfish. You're going to take your lumps and you're going to shut up, because you're doing it for the sake of the team. You're doing it for your teammates. To go out there and take a penalty that is going to cost us a game or a power play goal against is something that I will not stand for."

So we learned to - at times - turn the other cheek. And the Flyers, especially Bobby Clarke…Bobby Clarke was a great player. But man, what a pain in the ass he was. He would do anything to get you to take a stupid penalty. Because Bobby Clarke was not a fighter, but he was a chippy player. And he would slash you on the ankles, he would stick you in the back of the leg where there's no padding, to try and get you to take a stupid penalty. Then he would just laugh at you as you were going to the penalty box. So we were able to hold our cool. And Al had said that going into that series against the Flyers - "If we can hold our cool, they will take their share of penalties. And the best way to get them to stop playing cheap hockey is by scoring a goal and taking advantage of their penalties." And boy, did we take advantage of the penalties.

BRYAN TROTTIER: Just some key plays by individuals at the right time. Real hard-nosed hockey by guys that made it their mission, like Tonelli, Nystrom, Gillies, Sutter, Goring, Bourne, and Kallur. Guys just doing what they had to do. The power play was an effective tool. Philly was maybe a little more undisciplined than they should have been. We made them pay on the power play. There was a lot of neat things happening that way, too. Mike came back, and played with a sore thumb throughout the whole playoffs, and he still contributed offensively. We'd go to bed at night and just giggle, "Things are falling into place for us here. Let's ride the wave."

CLARK GILLIES: That was just more of the same - we had to play physical, we had to play smart, we had to have everybody going full-speed, or else we weren't going to beat that team. Philly had a pretty good hockey team at that time. If we didn't come out and play to the best of our ability, and a little above that, we weren't going to beat that team.

DAVE LANGEVIN: What it came down to is I think five on five, both teams were pretty equal. But where we really kicked their butt was on the power play. I think that's the key to any Stanley Cup team - five on five. Because if you're up against let's say, a Bossy, you're going to play good defense against them. You can try and stop them, but on the power play, there's nothing you can do. I think we got a lot of big goals on the power play. And then when you start playing that way, other teams have to back off. They can't be as physical, or they're thinking, "We can't get penalties." And the more you think about it, probably the more you do it. I think that was a key - our specialty players on the power play came through. And then Billy Smith was great for the playoffs, too. You've got to have a goaltender in the playoffs.

BOB NYSTROM: It was a tough series, also. Listen, we had fought and had brawls - we really battled with Philadelphia. We found them to be our second rival, next to the Rangers. The only thing that I would have to say is that we had their respect to a certain extent, because we had many skirmishes. But I think the one thing that really helped us in that series was our power play. What ended up happening was they were afraid to take penalties, because we would score on the power play. So therefore, it was a tough series, but it really wasn't a dirty series. They were known to be intimidators, and we had a pretty tough team also. But it was a lot cleaner than I expected.

CLARK GILLIES: We won the first game in Philly [4-3] - a big win for us. Denis Potvin scored on a power play in overtime. To get that first win under our belts was *huge*.

BOB BOURNE: Denis scoring in overtime in the first game, once we got that first game, we felt like we could win the series.

BOB NYSTROM: It's always good to win in Philadelphia. [Laughs] I don't care if it's now or then, it's a tough place to play, because the fans are into it. Again, they play a style of game that epitomizes Philadelphia - tough, hard-hitting, fighting, scraping. To win in that building - especially in the first game of the Stanley Cup - was a good one.

AL ARBOUR: We just played our regular game. The guys were confident and we knew we were good. They just went out and did their job.

JEAN POTVIN: It was another bruising series. I don't think you ever played the Philadelphia Flyers and didn't come out of there with black and blue marks. Naturally, they had a great, great team. But we were ready to win. We were just bubbling with confidence - not over-confidence, but we had accomplished a lot.

KEN MORROW: The battles, the fatigue. "The survival of the fittest," that's what it comes down to. That final series, you're trying to make it through and trying to win. It had been a long year for me at that point, so I was kind of riding the wave on adrenaline. Really just physically beaten up and exhausted at that point - mentally, too. But again, the thrill of a lifetime for me, never thinking I'd be in a Stanley Cup Finals.

DAVE LANGEVIN: We split in Philly [the Flyers took game two, 8-3], then we came home and won two [6-2 and 5-2].

GARY "BABA BOOEY" DELL'ABATE: I went to the first Islanders home game. I remember my brother and I walking up there, scalping tickets, walking in, and the Coliseum being sold out and really rocking.

DAVE LANGEVIN: Then we lost there [6-3], and then we came home [for game six]. I think we were very confident then, because they were in our conference, and we played them like 18 times that season - with preseason. There was nothing they could do that could fool us. You know everybody so well, you play them so many times. The Islanders always did well against the Flyers. Their biggest asset was their intimidation, and they couldn't intimidate us.

GARY "BABA BOOEY" DELL'ABATE: The thing that I remember about that series more than anything was when they went into game six, it was a Saturday afternoon. I wanted to go to the game more than anything, but I had a job - I worked at a Mobil gas station on Old Country Road, right by the Wantagh State Parkway. So I couldn't go to the game. I had a shitty little black and white TV, that I kept at the gas station to watch. I remember it was a national broadcast - it would have had to have been, or else I wouldn't have been able to get it on that TV. I remember watching the game, and cars would pull in for gas, and I remember thinking, *"Who the fuck isn't watching this game?"* I was annoyed! I was making people wait to get their gas pumped until a whistle blew. People were beeping at me, and I was like, "Fuck that, the Islanders are on. I'm watching the game."

BOB NYSTROM: I remember skating out and getting such an ovation on the ice. We came out for warm ups...my throat was quivering. It almost brought tears to my eyes - that's how excited I was and how good it felt to be in front of a sold out building, jam-packed. And they're standing there, cheering for the longest time.

GLENN "CHICO" RESCH: It's never easy to win the Cup. You kind of grab hold of the series, and you think, "Hmmm. We're going to win this thing." We're up 3-1, but going to Philly. They played a really good game, and it's 3-2. Both teams know now, in game six at Nassau, it's kind of "for the series." I'm not saying we wouldn't have won in Philly if we'd lost at home, but I would not have wanted to go there, because of the bounces and everything. And then of course, you remember that we got an "off-side goal" - an obvious off-side goal.

DUANE SUTTER: I scored a disputed goal that a lot of people said was off-side. Maybe it was, maybe it wasn't. [Laughs] And then it's 4-2 after two, and we were quite comfortable with that lead.

LORNE HENNING: Smitty played a lot of games. I think in [game six], he was starting to get tired. We had the momentum. Then they were coming back.

GLENN "CHICO" RESCH: Credit to the Flyers, we were up 4-2 going into the third period, and they tie it. It was a nervous time in that dressing room. But Smitty came out confident.

BOB NYSTROM: When we walked in between the second and third period, we were high-fiving. How quickly that turned around when we went back out for the third. We thought we had it in the bag, and then all of a sudden, they come back and tie it up.

CLARK GILLIES: I remember going into the third period, being up 4-2. [Laughs] Sitting in the locker room between the second and third period, going, "Oh god, all we have to do is get another one and shut them down, and we've got the Stanley Cup!" They got a couple of good goals in the third period. It was a hell of a third period for both teams.

STAN FISCHLER: They were all over [Smith]. Smitty saved them.

LORNE HENNING: I think a few doubts were creeping in again after we let them come back in the third. To win it in our building...I don't think anybody was looking forward to going back to their building.

BOB NYSTROM: Needless to say, we did not want to go back to Philadelphia, because we felt that was a *tremendous* disadvantage.

CLARK GILLIES: You go into overtime. You're home and you say, "We had this thing...what's to say we can't go out and get it back?"

CHAPTER 20:

"THE GOAL"

What were you doing at roughly 5:00pm on May 24th, 1980? Bob Nystrom and his fellow teammates certainly remember...

BOB NYSTROM: I remember sitting in the locker room [between the third period and overtime], and I went in the back room, and was just fooling around in the stick room with a scalpel, and I carved a notch in my stick. We always had a way of saying in the locker room, "Who's going to be the hero?" And everyone would say, "I'm going to be the hero!" I remember just sitting there, thinking about the game, fiddling around with the little scalpel, carved a notch, and I said, *"I'm going to get the winner here."* I was lucky enough to be put in that position, just a super pass by Johnny T. It's something that you dream about as a kid. It really is.

It's interesting, because I played with John Tonelli a lot. We used to do these two on two drills - we were just sick of them. Johnny and I always tried to crisscross. Nine times out of ten, it wouldn't work. On this particular case, all you try to do is get one defenseman to step up a little bit, and then the other guy can sneak behind him. And that's exactly what Johnny did - he got [Bob] Dailey to kind of bite on it. Then I was able to sneak by him and go to the front of the net. The one thing that I remember more than anything is watching the puck come to me from Tonelli, and thinking about what I was going to do with it. About five thoughts went through my head - stop it, go back the other way. And then I just decided, "It's coming fast enough, I'm just going to deflect it."

STAN FISCHLER: What I remember about it is that the guy who was the architect of the goal, everybody forgets, was Lorne Henning. What everybody also forgets is Henning normally should not have been playing in that spot - it belonged to Wayne Merrick. That was the Banana Line, where Wayne Merrick was the center, and he was a good center. So it was Henning setting up Tonelli, who set up Nystrom.

LORNE HENNING: The neutral zone, the pass, and then them going in on a two on one. I was kind of trailing, and to see it all happen in front of me was pretty special. Especially when who knows in overtime - anything can happen. We had a lot of success in overtime, and Bobby I think had four overtime goals. And then the pile in the corner after it happened, and then all the fans. I mean, I was in the dressing room three hours later, *still* in my hockey equipment. It seemed like half the building was in the dressing room. Now, everything is security - you can't get near anybody. But back in those days, fans were almost as excited as we were. They were a big part of it. I think [the "Banana Line" name] was just from practice, they always had the yellow jerseys, so they were "the Banana Line." It wasn't anything more than that. They had green jerseys, white, and then they happened to have the yellow line. They hated being called "the Yellow Line," so then it was the Banana Line.

DUANE SUTTER: You could see it developing when Lorne Henning got the puck down at the other end, and chipped it up the boards to Johnny T. I think they had missed a two on one like that earlier in the game - almost an identical play. The depth that we had, it could have been any of the three lines that scored. But some unsung heroes, like that whole line - Lorne Henning, John Tonelli, and Bobby Nystrom. It was a perfect ending. Once it was all said and done, just the relief of the stress and the tension and the emotions that you let go at the time, you don't realize how wrapped you are in it until it really happens. The release of the emotions. And everybody handles it in different ways. It was certainly the biggest thrill of my life.

DAVE LANGEVIN: The overtime goal, I was out there for that goal. Me and Stefan Persson were out there. If you ever see on TV when something big happens in a sporting event, it gets quiet all of a sudden. From the blue line to behind the net, I have no idea what happened. It was complete silence. And then all of a sudden, we were in the corner. Stefan was on my back, and I could hear the fans. That's exactly how it happened. You win, you get there, and it was probably one of the greatest feelings you could ever have.

STAN FISCHLER: It was the biggest goal in the history of the franchise at that point. Previously, the biggest goal was Parisé's.

GARY "BABA BOOEY" DELL'ABATE: I do remember watching TV when Nystrom scored the goal, but on a black and white TV, with aluminum foil for an antenna, so it probably looked a lot like the moon landing. But I remember being ecstatic, just ecstatic. Being so happy.

AL ARBOUR: It was really outstanding to win that first Cup. Just great. *Super.*

BILL TORREY: Anybody who was there and saw the game or gone through what we had gone through in our organization will never forget it. First of all, it was a clean play - it was a well-executed play. Lorne Henning made a very smart interception at center ice, made a good play to Johnny Tonelli, and Tonelli put it right on Ny's stick. Ny didn't actually shoot the puck, he deflected it. It was such a perfect pass. And for Bobby Ny, he was an original Islander. He was drafted in our first draft. I made him work with a figure skating coach to improve his skating that first year, and I thought he was going to punch me out when I first suggested it! But he improved. He worked *so* hard. He was tough as nails, but he could score goals. Bobby Nystrom was an underrated player. And teams feared him, because they knew damn well he'd go through a brick wall if he had to. In a sense, it was déjà vu. He was the right guy to get the winning goal.

JIMMY DEVELLANO: It was for me [one of the most exciting endings of an NHL game], but I wouldn't say that would be universal. You might not think that if you're a Detroit fan, or a Montreal fan, or a Ranger fan. If you're a Ranger fan, you think the greatest game you ever saw was game seven in 1994. Only to the Islander fan was that the greatest game. It was the greatest game for me personally, because what it meant was that I would get a Stanley Cup ring. And people in hockey, we live for Stanley Cup rings. Also, it meant that I would get my name on the Stanley Cup. And you know, none of us are so brazen to think that we'd do it more than once. We'd be happy just to do it once. May 24th, 1980, around 5:00 in the afternoon. That's when it happened.

CLARK GILLIES: To be honest with you, I'd just come off the ice when Bobby went on the ice. I basically had my head down, trying to catch my breath when he scored. So I didn't really see it - I had to watch it on the replay afterwards to really see how the goal was scored. Obviously, when we scored, we just went crazy and went on the ice to congratulate [each other]. That was a huge moment. That is probably my greatest memory of that whole series.

KEN MORROW: I came back to the bench after a shift, sitting on the bench, and I was bent over, trying to catch my breath, to get ready for the next shift. And I heard this tremendous roar from the crowd. I didn't see it! Bryan was on the bench also, so I literally - from a bent over position - leapt over the boards in one jump, was on the ice, and Bryan was coming off the bench too. The other guys had piled into the corner, and Bryan and I grabbed each other. I don't know if he lifted me or I lifted him, but there's a great picture of us holding each other up in the air. Just relief was really the first thing for me. Relief that it was over - that was the first emotion. Not that we had won, but not to play anymore! Kind of a feeling of disbelief, having been through a Gold Medal, and then to go through that three months later.

GORD LANE: I was just so happy somebody did it. You were so exhausted, I remember the first period, Kenny Morrow and I were out there killing a five on three penalty, and I could not even shoot the puck from one side of the ice to the other side. I was just so tired all the time. And I think that clinching goal, it wasn't so much that we won, I was just happy it was over.

JEAN POTVIN: It was amazing. My dad had had that dream to play in the NHL years before. My dad actually went to the Detroit Red Wings training camp, and he broke his back in training camp, and that ended his career - I think in 1939. He had had big time dreams of playing in the NHL, and never made it. So now, he's got not one but *two* sons playing in the NHL, and on top of that, playing on the same team, and then on top of that, winning the Cup. My dad could not have been more proud. And the same thing with my mother. She had not grown up playing hockey, but she had grown up [where] everybody in Canada is a big hockey fan - whether you play the game or not. So yeah, it was a tremendous amount of satisfaction for our entire family. And our older brother, Bob, had flown in for the Finals, so it was like a dream come true.

GLENN "CHICO" RESCH: For all the players, the moments after that...you're on the ice, you go into the dressing room. It's all emotion. That's why I say players that are really intense and had to battle to win a championship for the first time, why they don't sound very intelligent when they're doing interviews after - "I love these guys. Oh these are the best guys." It's because it's just *emotion*. The brain has shut down. It's not even about thinking, it's about the emotion of relief, excitement. "We did it!" It's a dream come true. Whatever those raw, joyful emotions are, they just shoot out like a volcano.

EDDIE WESTFALL: The one I didn't cover [as a broadcaster] was their first one! That was a bit of a disaster for us as broadcasters. They took the game away from us and put it on CBS, I think it was. The sponsors were really upset - people that paid for sponsorship all season long and got usurped at the end. John Pickett was so upset that he said, "As long as I have any say, that's never going to happen again."

BRUCE BENNETT: The early Stanley Cup years, you'd have anywhere from 30 to 40 photographers in the building for those games. Trying to take myself out of being a fan, being a Long Islander, I still think back to that first Stanley Cup victory. As much as you try to separate yourself from what's going on there so you can keep yourself at an even keel and concentrate on shooting, it was a very difficult thing to do then.

I often think back to that Stanley Cup - I've photographed 30 Stanley Cup presentations through the years, and that first one was special to me. Not only because I was a Long Islander and it was the first one of that dynasty that the Islanders built, but in trying to separate myself from what was going on there so that I could concentrate on shooting, it was very odd where you can trick your body into turning senses off. So you're just focusing on you and the Stanley Cup. The noise in that building was so unbelievably loud during the Cup presentation, that you sort of had to do something like turn your ears off and not concentrate on that - just focus on you and whoever is carrying the Stanley Cup. And what I remember most is once in a while you'd slip and hear how loud it was in that building. It wasn't until after I left the ice and going to the locker room - as soon as I jumped the boards and got into that little tunnel, my senses opened up, and I realized my ears hurt!

Virtually, every Stanley Cup game I go to - the final game - you'll be shooting next to a fan or a local photographer, and they always say the same thing. "Wow...have you ever heard a building this loud before?" And you go, "Well, y'know..." Everybody in their home building is always like, "Wow, this is the loudest it's ever been for a Stanley Cup Final." But in my mind anyway, 1980 was when it was the loudest.

BOB BOURNE: Once you win that first one, no one can take that ring away from you. It's a proud moment. Probably one of the greatest moments of my life.

DAVE LANGEVIN: The thing about winning a Stanley Cup, it makes all the heartaches and the injuries and all the training you've done in your whole life...the Stanley Cup makes it all worth it.

JEAN POTVIN: To win that Stanley Cup, for me, up until that time, there had been no bigger thrill in sports. None. As I said earlier, as a young kid, you grow up in Canada, there's not really any football on TV, there's no baseball, there's no basketball. Hockey *is* Canada - especially back then. You had like three channels, and one of them was 'Hockey Night in Canada.' One in English and one in French. I remember having so many dreams as a kid, just watching Jean Béliveau raise the Stanley Cup. And Jean Béliveau was my idol. It's a dream that you never allowed yourself to have. And then to all of a sudden, to get that Cup in the locker room and close to the door to the media for I think it was like ten minutes. The league said, "You can have ten minutes to yourselves, drink a little bit of champagne, have a good time. But then the media's got to come in." It's amazing, there was not a dry eye in that room. And you'd look around the room, and everybody had cuts, bruises, stitches, and black and blue marks. It was just like the warriors or gladiators that came through.

BILL TORREY: Any time a team wins its first Stanley Cup...winning the Cup is always a special event. No matter where, when. In all the years I've been in this league, winning the Stanley Cup, one team at the end of the year, after going through months and months of trials and tribulations, it's always special. Your first one is obviously a little bit extra special. And particularly, since we were the only team that played in a market with another team, and a very strong organization. An organization that obviously hadn't won a Stanley Cup in a long time, and New York was starved for a winner. So it made our winning a Cup in seven years something very special.

GORD LANE: What stood out was when we left the rink, the game was an early afternoon game, and after it was done, we stayed inside the arena for probably a couple of hours. I remember leaving the rink and Meadowbrook Parkway was at a standstill. The cars had stopped, and people were out of their cars, honking their horns. People were just stopped in the roads everywhere.

GARY "BABA BOOEY" DELL'ABATE: Then it was a Saturday night, and we all sort of gravitated to Hempstead Turnpike. Everybody just drove up and down the Turnpike, and kept beeping their horn with [sings the "Lets Go Islanders" tune]. I remember everybody being really happy. It was really exciting and really great. It was a Saturday night, it gave us something to do. We were excited. Nothing like that had ever happened before - "The Stanley Cup...oh my god!"

CLAIRE ARBOUR: Poor Bill Torrey - we all converged on his place in Cold Spring Harbor! We lived in Cold Spring Harbor too, a couple of streets over from him. Nothing had been planned, but we all wound up at his house. It was a very intimate party, because it was just the team and the wives, and that was it. It's just something that we will never forget.

RON WASKE: At the end of the party at the Coliseum, we had locked the Stanley Cup in the training room, and they all left to go to a party at Bill Torrey's house…and they left the Cup! So Jim Pickard, I, and our wives, we threw it in the back seat of my old, beat-up Dodge Station Wagon, and we were driving down the Long Island Expressway towards Torrey's house - with the Stanley Cup in the backseat.

GLENN "CHICO" RESCH: We went to Bill Torrey's for a big party. That was still enjoyable. But already, that mountain top experience of emotion is already starting to dissipate. And I always say this is why I think players stay up so late after they win a championship, because when you go to sleep and wake up the next morning, it's not the same. Then each day, it dissipates a little bit more. And then some time during that off season, people start saying, "Ah, but can they do it again?" So the past has already occurred, and you'd like to live it in the present. Your focus gets pushed to change. And now 30 years later, it's still a really nice feeling, but unfortunately, it's not a life-changing experience…I mean, it can be. Along with other factors, it can be a life-changing experience. But just winning the Cup doesn't make you all of a sudden feel like you're a different person, you know what I mean?

Again, it's a perspective thing. For me, it made me more reflective. I became more god-centered after that. I realized that god was as big a part of that as we were. And I'm 32, so I'm thinking, "My career is starting to get on." And I'd only played a few games, and Smitty played really well. I wasn't just a young kid coming up. For me, it was different than some guys. It was more of a reflective time for me. So spiritually, things got really better because of it, and I'm thankful for that. I didn't get puffed up, not that I should have. 1980 was a special time for me, because we won the Cup and my life changed spiritually, and I became a Christian. Because before that, I didn't have any spiritual interest. That's another whole story, but all these situations occurring for everybody that were different. It was different for everybody, but it's such an intense time of your life. It was like when Timmy Thomas won the Vezina and the Stanley Cup this year [2011]. He got up and thanked his teammates and family, and he said, "Oh, and by the way, I want to thank the lord, because this year was so incredible, and he gave me the talent, the opportunity, and the experience."

CLAIRE ARBOUR: And that first parade - they didn't know where to go and what to do with us. [Laughs] Because it wasn't easy on Long Island - it's just a bunch of little towns.

GARY "BABA BOOEY" DELL'ABATE: The parade that year started all the way in the back of Mitchell Field, and all the guys were in these antique cars. So my buddy - who had gone to school for photography - and I, we had our Nikon cameras, we were going to take some kick ass pictures. We decided to go early on the parade route, because we thought we'd get better pictures. And what happened was we were so early on the parade route that the cars had just come out and there weren't those many people there. So you pretty much could walk up to the car and shake the guys' hands. Which is what we did. So I have pictures of every single guy on the team, in their antique car, with me, shaking hands. We were way in the back, before they even got to Hempstead Turnpike. I think I pulled these pictures for possible use in my own book [2010's 'They Call Me Baba Booey'], and we didn't end up using them. But the one I remember for sure - I have a picture of me and Chico Resch, in this antique car. It's a riot!

BOB LORIMER: That was so nice to share with all your family and also all the great fans in Long Island. Long Island is obviously different than a lot of cities - there's not a "downtown court" to speak of. But I just remember all the fans being there. Long Island always seemed to not be a corporate crowd, but more of a true fan crowd, where you have individuals that buy season tickets and they have their own personal involvement, instead of a corporate involvement. That was special to reward those people that had been so loyal to the franchise and so supportive of the franchise - with their own money versus corporate money. And also, to have all the families there as well was nice, because you're sequestered from your family for so long in the playoffs. It's nice for them to be able to experience a very special moment.

CLARK GILLIES: Nothing! [In response to the question, "What do you remember about the ensuing victory parade?] We had a pretty good time leading up to that parade. I just remember piling into the trucks…no, the first one was in little antique cars. I don't think anybody knew what to expect, never had a parade of that magnitude. When we got into those cars and got closer to the Coliseum, everybody started crowding in. I think the cops finally realized, "Oh boy. This is bigger than we thought it was going to be." We finally got to the Coliseum, and went downstairs through the ramp, came upstairs onto a platform, where all the people were standing out there. We had to leave and go back in the building, because people were pushing forward so hard, the people in the front up against the fence were getting squished. And they said, "Somebody's going to get hurt here if we don't stop this." So we went back in the building, and the crowd…I guess somebody apologized to them. There weren't any big speeches or anything like that - for safety reasons, we had to shut it down. That's when the next year, instead of putting us in little model T-Ford cars, we went in the big trucks in went down Hempstead Turnpike, which was a little more controllable.

GLENN "CHICO" RESCH: The parade was great. It was good for Long Island. I'd never played anywhere else. If you named the guys of how many their first team was the Islanders in terms of the NHL, there was a ton of us. You're not going to see that as much anymore with free agency. But for us, it was really like a bond that had occurred with our fans, because we were mostly a lot of farm kids, a lot of Saskatchewan kids. But as you know, New York people, when you get to know them, they're a lot like the guys back home in the little towns on the prairies or the Midwest. It was a blast sharing that with them. It was the best of times for hockey players on Long Island.

KEN MORROW: I didn't even consider that [how special it was to win both the Gold Medal and the Stanley Cup in the same year]. I was always somebody that didn't look behind, I always tried to look ahead. I never got caught up in the Gold Medal/Stanley Cup thing. Even all the years we were winning, I was always looking ahead - trying to keep my job first of all, and just trying to win games, and extend my career.

LORNE HENNING: When you finally get there and win it, it's something you always remember. 30 or 40 years later, it's like it just happened yesterday. You really get a bond when you go through something like that.

BOB NYSTROM: I guess you get a little thoughtful about things, and for a while, I always said, "I wonder what would have happened if I didn't score that goal?" I don't like to think about that end of it, but I do think of it, and every once in a while, I see a picture or a video clip of it. It's a magical moment. It got us started on the first one, and I'm just so thankful that I was put in that position. I've been remembered - even though I've been out of the game for a lot of years.

DAVE LANGEVIN: I'd say Philadelphia was probably the toughest Final we had.

KEN MORROW: That year, we had to go through Boston who was the fourth seed, then Buffalo who was the second seed, and Philly who was the first seed. So we ended up beating three of the four top seeds that year.

AL ARBOUR: Winning the Cup the first year was the instrument that got us going. The guys figured, "Nobody's going to beat us. There's no way." And they played that way all the way through.

DAVE LANGEVIN: I remember after we won against Philadelphia, we went to Bill Torrey's house, and we were sitting around the pool. And Torrey says, "Well, *now we've just got to win four or five of these in a row.*" We all kind of looked at him, and said, "Can we enjoy this one first?" [Laughs] We're all sitting there with ice bags and all numb. Just physically beat. But yeah, it all came true.

Stanley Cup Finals (4-2):

New York Islanders over Philadelphia Flyers

Game 1 May 13   New York Islanders 4   Philadelphia Flyers 3 (OT)
Game 2 May 15   New York Islanders 3   Philadelphia Flyers 8
Game 3 May 17   Philadelphia Flyers 2   New York Islanders 6
Game 4 May 19   Philadelphia Flyers 2   New York Islanders 5
Game 5 May 22   New York Islanders 3   Philadelphia Flyers 6
Game 6 May 24   Philadelphia Flyers 4   New York Islanders 5 (OT)

Conn Smythe Trophy: Bryan Trottier (12 G, 17 A, 29 P)

CHAPTER 21:

1980-81

Can the Islanders repeat as Stanley Cup champs? It's looking promising, as the team breezes through the regular season as the NHL's winningest team, in addition to Mike Bossy setting an impressive goal scoring record.

DAVE LANGEVIN: Going into that season, I wanted to do it again. That's a feeling that you never want to lose. There was never any doubt.

KEN MORROW: We never felt that way [confident about a repeat Stanley Cup win] - Al Arbour didn't allow that, and the team wasn't…the guys weren't built that way. It was, "Let's continue this. We've got a lot to prove." Never rested on what we did. And I think you can tell. The biggest thing was that the pressure was off the guys that had been there. And the confidence that winning a championship gives you, it gives you a confidence inside that if you're in a tight game, you're going to win it. If you need a big goal, somebody's going to score it. You see it in other sports, too. That's what makes it hard to knock off the champion, because they have that confidence. I think that's what our team had. So guys that were in the primes of their careers, all of a sudden had this "championship confidence." We went through the next three years, and I tell people I remember winning games on a nightly basis…we were *destroying* teams. We were beating teams 6-1, 7-2. Everything was clicking. We were playing like a dynasty team.

BOB NYSTROM: The regular season is such a long, tough season. It's really hard to get back in the flow of things. It seemed like we had just quit playing, for heaven's sakes, and we're back at it again. But realistically, we felt like we owned the Stanley Cup. We just wanted to make sure that we went out to defend it and were able to hold on to it.

BOB BOURNE: We had such a solid team. Such a tough team. We could play any game any team wanted us to play. We felt like we could repeat. We knew there were some good teams coming up, and certainly, we knew Minnesota had a good team that year. But we just felt we could win it all again. We were probably more confident than all the time I was there.

LORNE HENNING: Al approached me [to become a coach]. I had a chance to go to a couple of other teams. At the time, I was just penalty killing, so I figured if I go to another team and it doesn't work out, and I go down to the minors...although I retired pretty young, it was an opportunity to get into coaching. He brought it up. We banged heads a few times, so it was kind of surprising to me. But I guess Al saw something there, and we had some great chemistry together for a lot of years, and a lot of laughs. A lot of fun. It was obviously a thrill for me to work under Al. I don't think people saw the other side of Al when you're playing for him. You don't see that he's a funny, funny, funny man, and had a great sense of humor. But he was pretty intense and strict and a disciplinarian when you played for him. It was kind of nice to see the other side of Al and have a few laughs. It was a great ride for me, just learning from him.

In the playoffs [of '81], I coached. In the regular season, I didn't play a lot of games. So for me, it was a great transition. Normally, when you're a player and then you get thrown in as a coach with your peers, it's always tough. But Al was very supportive, and threw me right into it, and let me run a lot of practices. And the guys were good, too. I tried to throw some different drills in there, just to keep them interested. They were receptive to it, and I think the change was good for them, too. Al was the one that was really supportive and helped me out. He was very instrumental in my career, that's for sure.

JIGGS McDONALD [The Islanders' television broadcaster]: It was Eddie that suggested to Nassau Sports Productions and John O. Pickett that I be the guy [to join Westfall in the broadcast booth]. I knew of Eddie - I followed his career and had seen him certainly in Los Angeles and in Atlanta. But I knew his brother, George. George was every bit as good of a player as Eddie, just the timing - the expansion, the growth of the league - he didn't get that opportunity because of age. The other brother that I knew was Stan. Stan had played some senior hockey, and then went into officiating in Ontario. I knew two of the brothers and then got to know Eddie real well.

The 1980-81 season was my first. The team having won the Cup, there was a lot of speculation or feeling that they would go undefeated - they wouldn't lose a game all season! Well, there were a couple of stretches there, where you said, "They're going to have to make some changes," or they weren't clicking on all cylinders. But it was a learning experience from my standpoint, that this team or that group of individuals knew exactly what they had to do, how to pace themselves, how to be ready. The most important part of the year was what came in April and May.

EDDIE WESTFALL: I hired Jiggs. [Laughs] I was made the vice president of Nassau Sports Productions, and Jiggs had been a friend of mine, my brothers, and my mom and dad for years, up in Ontario, where we were all living around and playing hockey. Jiggs was running around with his tape recorder and broadcasting hockey games in these little towns. When they started the team out in Los Angeles [the Kings], he started his NHL career there. Then in '72, when the Islanders started and the Atlanta Flames, Jiggs moved out to Atlanta. So he was working there, and I used to see him and talk with him. So when they decided the broadcast thing that I mentioned with the Islanders, I guess Jiggs knew about it, so he applied. I said to the people, "Here's the guy. If we're going to do this changing, this is the guy you want to get."

JIGGS McDONALD: This is the perfect spot for a broadcaster - [McDonald hails from] the village of Ayr [pronounced "Air"], Ontario, which is probably 75 miles west of Toronto. It sits right in between Kitchener to the north and Brantford - Gretzky's hometown - to the south. My joke line is it was easy to get into radio because they were so big back then, you could just take the back off and crawl right into them! I had a fascination with radio from the time I was probably five/six/seven - those impressionable years. I listened a lot. I can't say hockey or play-by-play was in the back of my mind at that time. I wanted to be on the radio, I wanted to be a disc jockey. Loved it, but I guess the one stint that brought everything into total focus for me was a six-week stint. I left a radio station and went to work for a larger station, larger community news station, and it was a seven second format. That's all you could talk! I recognized you couldn't do a whole lot, other than the time of day, the temperature, is it going to rain or not, or news. It just wasn't for me.

That had followed two years of play-by-play - doing some baseball, local community hockey. I knew that's what I really wanted to get back to, and had the opportunity to go back to the station that I had left, with my tail between my legs and on bended knee. I got into the radio business in '56 I think it was, and left in '67, to go to LA, to be the voice of the LA Kings. Five years - what I refer to as "my college education," working for Jack Kent Cooke. Eight years in Atlanta. And when Atlanta was in the process of being sold, there was all kinds of rumors at the time that Coca Cola, Delta, Ted Turner would join together and keep the team there. That didn't happen, and the Islander opportunity came along. It was one of maybe two or three opportunities I had, but it was the only one that was going to offer full play-by-play. I said, "Well, they just won the Stanley Cup. Bill Torrey told me to come along and that I would enjoy this, because they were going to win it for many years." The play-by-play thing I enjoyed myself - the opportunity to be creative, to paint the picture, is something I really enjoyed.

EDDIE WESTFALL: When he went to LA is when he got his name "Jiggs." That was Jack Kent Cooke - he was a fellow Canadian from the Winnipeg area, I believe. He owned the Los Angeles Kings, and when he bought the team and was developing the team and the broadcasts, Jiggs had applied and they hired him. He was the one that said, "Your name is Kenneth. Kenneth McDonald isn't really catchy enough. We've got to get you a [new name]." If I've got it right, it was the cartoon characters in the paper, 'Jiggs and Maggie' [the cartoon strip was also known as 'Bringing Up Father']. Jiggs said to him, I get a kick out of the comic strip, 'Jiggs and Maggie,' and Jack Kent Cooke said, "That's it! That'll fit - *Jiggs McDonald.*"

STAN FISCHLER: Each year, Torrey would make a change or two, which was a positive one. Never stay with what you have. A guy like Billy Carroll came onto the team. He was like Gordie Lane - he was one of the best penalty killers I've ever seen. Low-key, over-shadowed by the other guys.

BOB LORIMER: We had won a few very important games early in the season against our main rivals, and the feeling was we won those games, and we were very confident and played very well. Getting the "must win" games. It was almost like from Christmas on, we just knew we were going to win. It wasn't cockiness, it was just a confidence, that if we played well and stayed healthy, we were going to win. *Nobody* was going to beat us. If we didn't have any injuries and if we played to our capabilities, we knew our best was good enough, and that was important.

STAN FISCHLER: We used to drive out to the games, a bunch of us in the production team and television team. And we always would wonder not whether they would win or lose, but by what score would they win because it was such a good team.

BRYAN TROTTIER: Opportunity presented itself, and Mike jumped all over it [for Bossy to accomplish scoring 50 goals in 50 games]. He made the declaration publicly, that he was going after it. When he made that declaration, I remember the team rallied hard around it. All of us felt, "If Mike achieves it, it's going to be as much a team thing," and Mike was awesome about it.

CLARK GILLIES: Geez, 50 goals in a season is one thing, *but 50 goals in 50 games*...it was pretty amazing. I was part of a lot of those goals. I got to watch most of that, because I was still playing with Butch Goring at that time. He would never cease to amaze. And Mike, when it came to scoring goals, I don't think there was anything he enjoyed more in life than scoring goals. Growing up in Montreal as he did, to have an opportunity to tie or possibly break Rocket Richard's record, that was something that I'm sure was very special in his mind. And something he wanted in a big way.

BILL TORREY: There had only been one guy to do it before him, so you know how difficult something like that is to accomplish. The interesting thing about Mike Bossy was he always said - from day one - that he was going to score 50 goals in 50 games. And coming from Montreal, where the Rocket was from, it was an added incentive for Mike. It was something that he wanted to obtain, and said he was going to. Mike was a very, very confident athlete. He wasn't a braggart and he wasn't a big loud mouth guy. But he was very confident from the very first day. And he did it. He had amazing eyes and he had amazing hands. In an instant...you'd see Mike in a game, and you'd go, "Come on Boss, *wake up*. You're not doing anything." And then all of a sudden, boom! He'd score two goals in the flick of an eye.

BOB BOURNE: I remember the 50th. We were playing Quebec [on January 24th], and he had to get two in the last game to do it. It doesn't surprise me that he did it. What I remember the most about that game is his 50th goal and how it was set up. It was his typical shot, a couple of inches off the ice, right in the five hole. We were really proud of him.

AL ARBOUR: He had to score with three minutes or something like that. The way he did it was just unbelievable. He was just on the ice all the time. Just an unbelievable play - Trottier gave him the puck.

BOB NYSTROM: We didn't think he was going to get it. We were so concerned that we wanted him to do it in the worst way. Then he got the 50th, and I remember him dancing. Absolutely incredible. But hey, there's no one that deserved it more. He was some goal scorer, and to accomplish 50 goals in 50 games...I mean, now, I think there are people that have had *70 goals*. But in those days, 50 goals in 50 games was quite an accomplishment.

BOB BOURNE: The thing with Mike too - he played in the tough games, he scored in the tough games. He was always there for us.

DAVE LANGEVIN: He was not afraid to get in there. He would come out after games with bloody lips and cuts on his face, and you'd never hear him complain. He was - in his own way - one of the tough guys on the team. He'd never whined, he just went in there. When you score like that guy, you have to pound on him. If you let him loose, then he's going to hurt you. He's got to be in "the top ten ever goal scorers in the NHL."

STAN FISCHLER: There was always a question of whether Bossy could handle the tough play. And by that time, you could see how special he was. The only problem that Bossy had was not with Bossy, it was the fact that Wayne Gretzky had now really taken over and anything good that Bossy did was in a sense overshadowed by Gretzky. However, you now had one of the great lines of all-time, you had one of the great natural scorers of all-time in his prime, and a clutch scorer.

DUANE SUTTER: We had our ups and downs, as most teams do after you go through a big Stanley Cup run. The team will have a hiccup here and there. Mr. Torrey and Mr. Arbour kept us honest. They were obviously the architects of the team, but they showed great leadership throughout the whole Stanley Cup era. They kept us on our toes, by moving players in and out from the minors, and up. Tweaking the line-up with a trade or two later at the deadline. I think that was the Colorado trade, with Chico Resch and Steve Tambellini, and Mike McEwen coming in. That was just enough of a little bit of a tweak to get us over the hump again.

GLENN "CHICO" RESCH: We played Vancouver [on March 7th], in the last game before they stopped the trading deadline, and Gordie Lane broke his finger. They needed a defenseman, and as it turned out, they got Mike McEwen. I didn't see it coming. We're practicing that Monday of the day of the trade, and I remember Al came into the washroom, and he looked a little agonized. Of course, he was in on what was going on. I had no idea it was me and Steve Tambellini, but I said, "Hey, it's got to be a tough day," and he said, "Yeah, it's a tough day for everybody." Nothing had been announced.

So we got on the bus, and we're going to Winnipeg. But the bus doesn't leave. And then all of a sudden, my friend Lorne Henning comes on, who is know an assistant coach, and says, "Al wants to see you." And I said, "Hmmm. [Chico and Steve] are gone, aren't we?"

And he says, *"Yeah."* So then we went in, and Al, true to his classy nature, was crying and feeling bad. We'd all grown up together.

The most poignant moment in my departure from Long Island was when we had come out of Cantiague Park, the practice rink, our bags were sitting on the sidewalk, the bus had left, and a couple of fans had volunteered to watch our belongings while we were in talking to Al. And that was it. Steve and I went home, and two days later, we pulled on a Colorado Rockies jersey and beat the Rangers 4-3 - Steve got the game-winning goal, and I had a terrific game. It was kind of appropriate that our first game after being traded was in New York against the Rangers. And it was tough, it was a really hard move. That was a place that no one wanted to leave.

MIKE McEWEN: I was in Colorado, and there were rumors I was going to Montreal. I was in Washington, and it was right at the trade deadline. I had come back from the morning skate, and my agent had called. I talked to him and I talked to the Rockies' general manager, Billy MacMillan, and then I talked to Bill Torrey. It's 12:10, and I was traded to the Islanders. I'd come out of my room, and Joel Quenneville - the coach of the Blackhawks now, I played with him on a few different teams in the NHL - he's walking down the hall. And if you know Herbie [Quenneville's nickname], he's real loose and real quick-witted. A real funny guy. I'm looking at him, and I go, "Hey Herbie, I just got traded to the Islanders!" He's kind of doing his gate, he's walking down, and without missing a beat, he throws his hand at me, and goes, "Congratulations. You just won the lottery." That was the first words I heard after I got traded. And I was like, "Y'know...*you're right!"*

I was born in Northern Ontario, in Hornepayne, to a hockey family - we had a rink in our backyard. I moved to Toronto when I was seven, went up through the Toronto system, played junior Marlboros. Won a Canadian Memorial Cup, and got drafted by the Rangers, traded to Colorado, Colorado to the Islanders. My first game with them was in Winnipeg, and we played pretty well - we won. I played against them with the Rangers all the time, we went through the '79 series. I knew them all pretty well, as far as on the ice. A good group of guys, fun to be with. Different. But they had a lot of good things going.

JEAN POTVIN: It was just total dominance. I mean, we had the guns. Clarkie had scored like 35 goals or something, Trottier was probably close to 45/50 himself, Bossy I think ended up with…is that the year he finished with like 61 goals or something like that? Might even be more than that, because he scored 50 in 50 [Bossy scored 68 goals during the regular season]. We just had so many weapons. Tonelli had a big year, and I think that was the year Denis scored 30 goals during the regular season. So the big line was big. And then we had very welcomed additions, like Brent Sutter, and continued to have Butch, who was still in his prime. Dave Langevin was only getting better, Kenny Morrow the same thing. Stefan Persson doing a great job with my brother on the power play. Tomas Jonsson, Anders Kallur, Nystrom was doing his thing, Wayne Merrick. The Islanders were just so dominating that playoff year.

PATRICK DIVISION STANDINGS: 1980-81

TEAMS	W	L	T	POINTS
New York Islanders	48	18	14	110
Philadelphia Flyers	41	24	15	97
Calgary Flames	39	27	14	92
New York Rangers	30	36	14	74
Washington Capitals	26	36	18	70

CHAPTER 22:

PLAYOFFS '81

The Maple Leafs, Oilers, and Rangers are no match for the mighty Islanders in the '81 playoffs.

DUANE SUTTER: The Maple Leafs had been a pain in the ass for the organization in previous playoff series. The Oilers were an up-and-coming team with a lot of young talent and high expectations. But much like the Islanders had been two or three years before, they hadn't learned how to win and lose yet. The Rangers was a huge rivalry - again, going back to "the upset series" two years before. They were all tight series - a lot tighter than the final series scores were. But again, we stuck together. We found a way to win.

MIKE McEWEN: We were a pretty well oiled machine at the time. [Laughs] The Edmonton series was probably the toughest - I think they sort of surprised us with their talent level. We just played. The Rangers, those were good, solid games. They had Herb Brooks at the time, and he had a whole different system, and they had to adjust to that. I just remember thinking, "This team didn't have a weakness." Potvin and Morrow were a pair and obviously very good. I was really impressed with Langevin and Persson. Stefan Persson may be the most underrated player on that team. I think the guy maybe made two mistakes all year long. He was just so consistent and so good. Langevin, for two years there, he was the best defenseman I ever saw play the game. I mean, Potvin was there too, but Langevin…people don't know how good this guy is. He was *that good.*

KEN MORROW: Toronto, again, it was a best of five series, and we outscored them badly. We really blew them out. Never easy, but the

Oilers series, 4-2, that was kind of the start of their young group of guys - they had Messier, Gretzky, and all those guys. They just hadn't won anything at that point, but they were on the rise. I had another overtime goal [in game five], so that was my second overtime goal. The Rangers, 4-0. The big rivalry, but we were on a roll at that time.

BOB NYSTROM: It definitely was [revenge on the Leafs for beating the Islanders in the '78 playoffs]. That's one of the things that we wanted to do. It was incredibly important for us. And also, to beat the Oilers was quite an accomplishment, because they had a hell of a team. But I think Toronto was the most enjoyable. We beat the Rangers that year, too. We lost two games to the Oilers. I think we were rolling pretty good by that time.

BOB LORIMER: The Oilers had knocked the Canadiens off in the first round, which was a big upset at the time. So we knew the talent level, and that they were "the up-and-coming team," and that we had better win, because it wouldn't be too long before they were going to be starting to dominate, as well. I think just at that point in time they weren't quite as cohesive as a team, because they had so many younger players. But you knew it was just a matter of time, and that they would be dominant with the skill level they had. And I think that got us through that series, the fact that we just had a little bit more experience.

BOB BOURNE: That was the series where you could tell they were coming on, and they were very talented. A little bit inexperienced at the time. We knew how to play great defense, and they weren't quite there yet. That was a fun series.

CLARK GILLIES: Gretzky was very young at that time. He was only 20 years old. They had so many young guys - Messier, Coffey, Kurri, Fuhr. They were all just young kids, and they had a lot of learning to do. They were just like us - they had to go through some times where I'm sure they thought they were going to just step in and beat us, but I think experience at that time was worth its weight in gold. They played us tough, but I think we just ultimately knew that if we persevered and kept doing what we were doing, that we were going to beat that young team. But they put that in the memory banks, trust me. You knew they were going to be back, and bigger and better as time went on. It was nice to get them when they were younger.

DAVE LANGEVIN: A lot of players I didn't play with [when Langevin played on the Oilers from 1976-1979]. They drafted very well - they built a great organization there. Well, if you have Wayne Gretzky, it's not tough to build around him! But I think the biggest addition they got was Mark Messier. Because then, you've got two players, you've got two lines. It's tough to stop two lines. They kind of built the way we did. You've got the four very good lines, they got good goaltending. Yeah, it was fun playing against them. I just figured any way I looked at it, I was going to win some Stanley Cups - if I would have stayed in Edmonton I would have won some, and if I was in New York, I won some too. [Laughs] But Edmonton was…I had a lot of great memories up there, my wife and I. It was difficult to go back - I never really wanted to leave there. But you know what? I went to New York and I loved it there.

BOB BOURNE: The Rangers had a heck of a hockey team at the time.

DUANE SUTTER: A lot of times through the Rangers, we used a lot of their media coverage and hype as internal motivation. We were more of a quiet group with the media. We never really got over-confident. We could use a lot of what we were hearing out of the city as motivation. We were a pretty intense group going into that series.

CLARK GILLIES: It was always special beating the Rangers, don't get me wrong. That never gets old. I don't care if we were both in last place, beating the Rangers was beautiful. And I'm sure they feel the same way. But as far as the Rangers were concerned, I don't think any more special feeling than really we needed to win that series. At that time, Toronto was really no match for us. We had just grown so much as a team that when you're averaging like five goals a game and your goaltender is only giving up two-and-a-half, it pretty much tells you that if you go and play the way you're capable of playing, you're going to win most games. And that's really what our thought process was - if we play up to our ability and play the way we're capable of playing, then there's not many teams out there that are going to have a chance of beating us.

Preliminary Round (3-0):

New York Islanders over Toronto Maple Leafs

Game 1 April 8   Toronto Maple Leafs 2   New York Islanders 9
Game 2 April 9   Toronto Maple Leafs 1   New York Islanders 5
Game 3 April 11   New York Islanders 6   Toronto Maple Leafs 1

Quarter-Finals (4-2):

New York Islanders over Edmonton Oilers

Game 1 April 16   Edmonton Oilers 2   New York Islanders 8
Game 2 April 17   Edmonton Oilers 3   New York Islanders 6
Game 3 April 19   New York Islanders 2   Edmonton Oilers 5
Game 4 April 20   New York Islanders 5   Edmonton Oilers 4 (OT)
Game 5 April 22   Edmonton Oilers 4   New York Islanders 3
Game 6 April 24   New York Islanders 5   Edmonton Oilers 2

Semi-Finals (4-0):

New York Islanders over New York Rangers

Game 1 April 28   New York Rangers 2   New York Islanders 5
Game 2 April 30   New York Rangers 3   New York Islanders 7
Game 3 May 2   New York Islanders 5   New York Rangers 1
Game 4 May 5   New York Islanders 5   New York Rangers 2

CHAPTER 23:

STANLEY CUP '81

Can the North Stars dethrone the Islanders as reigning Stanley Cup champs?

BILL TORREY: There's always a little bit of a letdown after you've succeeded. You see it in all sports - baseball, football. Teams have a hard time winning consecutively. It hasn't happened that often, other than Montreal over the years. Other than one player, we were pretty much the same team we were the year before. We finished very strong, and ended up playing the Minnesota North Stars in the Finals. We knew that they had the potential to play very well.

JEAN POTVIN: It's very tough to repeat, because everybody is gunning for you. Everybody knows when you're playing against the best, you want to knock them off the top of the mountain. We were just as hungry that second year as we had been the first year. The benefit now was that I think every player on that team had been better than they were the year before. Plus, very importantly, we had the experience of knowing how to win, and we knew how to win under every circumstance. We could play the game any way you wanted.

So we went into Minnesota. There was never a threat, but the guy we were most concerned about was Dino Ciccarelli. He was a real, real sniper. A real mugger. You could not intimidate him. He was maybe 5'9", but he was *tough.* It was just a really great year, and again, the remarkable thing about that team I believe was that the desire level I thought if anything, increased because it was a quiet confidence we had. We didn't have that quiet confidence the first year. That first year, a lot of times, you played with fear.

LORNE HENNING: They had the great run against Boston, with Ciccarelli and Steve Payne, and they had a lot of hype. One thing about our team was so competitive, and I think coming in, people were hyping the North Stars, because they beat the Bruins and they had a lot of young guns. I think it was a real challenge for us, and our team always responded when we were challenged.

BOB NYSTROM: Dino Ciccarelli was a lot of that team, and certainly, the goaltending. But we had a pretty good series there. There's no place better to play a Stanley Cup Finals than Minnesota - the people there are just so into hockey. It was a great series. But again, I think we were cooking on all cylinders.

BRYAN TROTTIER: Again, I think contributions from a lot of the players. It was a neat time for Minnesota. For us, it was pretty fresh, to see them achieve and go as far into the playoffs as they did was kind of like we were saying, "This is a reflection. They surprised some teams. We've got to be prepared for *no* surprises." Even Mike McEwen got caught up in the whole thing - it was fun to share that experience with a few new teammates on the team that joined us. It was kind of neat to see the determination on our faces, as a team that was going to defend the Cup. And if someone was going to beat us, they'd have to wrestle it away. The confidence level for our team was pretty high.

DUANE SUTTER: I remember their big line - Bobby Smith, Al MacAdam, and Steve Payne. Al tried playing Butch Goring - and I think it was myself and Clark Gillies - against them as much as we could. A lot of that was we figured we could get under their skin and sway the momentum our way, if we kept them off the scoreboard five on five, we had a pretty good chance to win. It wasn't the match up game in, game out, or shift after shift, but certainly, it did play a factor in the series. Again, our big line contributed huge, our power play was outstanding, and our goaltending was outstanding.

MIKE McEWEN: We went up three games to nothing [by scores of 6-3, 6-3, and 7-5], we played the fourth game in Minnesota, and we lost 4-2. We had our team doctor and his wife behind our bench, and Billy Smith, going off the ice after that game…you can't touch

Smitty or talk to Smitty during the game or before a game. So he's going off the ice, and you've got to walk about ten feet, and then you start going up stairs. And once you walk the ten feet, you're right there by the people behind the bench. The doctor's wife was leaning over, giving everybody a pat on the shoulder, and she unfortunately gave Smitty a pat on the shoulder. I was about two guys behind him, and he just - with his stick - came right over top and whacked her on the forearm! *Hard.* As I'm going back, she's in pain, and the doctor's looking at her arm. Don't talk to Smitty after a game - it's not good.

DAVE LANGEVIN: The North Stars…I'm from Minnesota, and it was kind of nice to win. I coach now - a high school team with Curt Giles, who played with the North Stars. He brings that up once in a while, and I just say, "Curt, the difference between you and us is we knew we were going to win, and you *hoped* to win."

MIKE McEWEN: I think I got the last goal of the fifth game, and made Bryan Trottier the all-time point leader for the playoffs. What I remember about that goal is I took the shot from the point, and I think it was Tonelli or Gillies basically just hit the goalie. Knocked him off his angle. He couldn't recover and the puck went in the net. Back then, that stuff wasn't called. He was a little bit out of crease, so he just hit the goalie, and that's a goal.

GORD LANE: We expected to win that. I don't think we went into it with the same apprehension that we went in with that first one against Philadelphia, because Philadelphia had won the regular season - they had that longest streak without losing. But when we played against Minnesota, I think we expected to win. I don't think it was nearly as stressful as the initial one.

JEAN POTVIN: That was the year that Butchie won the Conn Smythe Trophy.

BILL TORREY: We finally finished them off in five. We played with confidence and we had a little tougher road. The games were close, they were good scoring games. But you could see we were a bigger/stronger team than they were.

GARY "BABA BOOEY" DELL'ABATE: All the years that the Islanders won their Stanley Cups, I was at Adelphi, in communications. I always equate typing a term paper [with the Islanders' Stanley Cup runs], because May was when I had to work on my term paper. So I would be up all night, but I would have the game on. I would type up the pages in the kitchen, but keep the living room TV on, and I was constantly running away from my paper, because I'd hear *"He scores!"* And I'd always go back and watch replays. And then, I was at Adelphi in the editing room for editing movies and stuff, in the attic of one of the buildings. I had a transistor radio, but I couldn't get a signal in any of the rooms I was in. I would have to walk down the hall to where the windows were. So what I would do is edit for a while - for 15 minutes - and then leave the editing room to listen to the game for five minutes. I'd go back and forth and back and forth. I was looking through my old stuff and I saw a term paper, typed up on this typewriter that I had, and it always reminds me of the Islanders.

JEAN POTVIN: Bill Torrey called me in his office after the season was over, and we reveled over how much fun this was, and how much fun it had been, and how he really greatly appreciated me coming back in a diminished role. But Al had told me when I came back from Minnesota, "Look, I don't know what the hell you do in that locker room, but it's a very positive effect. Whether you play or not, I want you to go out for the warm-ups - regular season and playoffs. Because I know what you can do. If I have anybody that's not playing well, if any of the kids get hurt or they're not developing the way I want them to, I know you can step in and do the job, totally. But even when you're not playing, I'd like you to go out for the warm-up." Which means I'd be getting dressed with the players, getting prepared for the games before just like they would - putting on my uniform. We go out for the warm-up, after the warm-up, he says, "If you're not dressing, take your equipment off, but I don't want you to go in the showers until they go on the ice. Do whatever the hell you do before the game, get them pumped up, get them ready to go." That's what I would do.

We reminisced on a lot of that stuff. And he said, "Look Jeanie, I can't tell you how much I appreciate the role you played. You put your ego aside, and you weren't sitting there pouting, because you didn't play as much as you knew you could. To tell you the truth, you still have some very good hockey left in you." Because at that time, I was only 32, and was still in very good physical condition. Look at guys today, they retire in their forties. He says, "Look, the team has obviously developed very well, and all of our young kids are doing very well - Kenny Morrow, Tomas Jonsson. I can only have so many guys on the roster. We'd like you to stay with the organization, but it won't be as a player. Now, on the other hand, if you would like to continue to play, I don't want to stop you. There are seven teams that are interested in you, and I will make the trade happen. No matter where you want to go, I'll make the trade happen."

He said, "Talk to Lorraine. Think about it for a couple of days. This is early summer, we've got time. If you want to come back in a week, come back in a week, and we'll chat." I said, "Well, before I go, what would be my role?" Then he said, "Al would like you to be maybe an assistant coach." I said, "Nah, I'm really not interested in that." "Scouting?" "Nah, I'm not interested in that, either." He says, "Well, you know how you like to talk? Maybe you can do on the radio the color commentating." So I said, "OK, fine." I went home and talked to my wife, and that was a quick conversation. It's like, "What am I going to do, honey? I'm going to sell the house, go to Pittsburgh for three years, or Washington, or Winnipeg, or wherever?" And back in those days, the money was not what it is today. Today, you say, "Look Lorraine, I can make another million and a half dollars a year if I go here, if I go there. Well, I'm going! You stay here with the kids if you want, but I'm not missing out on that kind of money!" In those days, the average salary in the NHL I believe was $65-75,000.

We had made some nice friends, some good contacts on Long Island. As a matter of fact, in the summer of '78, I signed a contract, and by then I was about 28 years old - I had decided to take my Series 7 Exam, to become a licensed, registered stockbroker. I had passed that, so I had that in my back pocket. And I figured, "That's what I want to get involved with after I retire from hockey." So anyway, I decided, "We like it here. Why are we going to sell the house and move to some other place? Then where are we in three years?" So I went back to Bill, and I said, "OK, let's talk shop. Doing radio is good, I'm also going to start working at this retail stock brokerage place. I'll do both jobs while I develop a book of business. But I'd love to get involved - I think this team still has another couple of Cups in it. It would be fun doing the radio broadcasting of that team." So we agreed on a contract, and the rest is history. I was watching from up there, doing the color commentating with Barry Landers as my sidekick, doing play-by-play.

JIM PICKARD: I remember in the summer, maybe after our second Cup, Ronnie Waske was over on my back deck, around the afternoon. We were probably having a couple of cold ones, and he goes, "Ah, it's a shame you can't win the Cup every year" or "It's a shame we don't play more." It was just how we all came together. It was such a fun group. A lot of battles - not in-house. It was just such a great group of guys. As we went along, we got tighter and tighter.

Stanley Cup Finals (4-1):

New York Islanders over Minnesota North Stars

Game 1	May 12	Minnesota North Stars 3	New York Islanders 6
Game 2	May 14	Minnesota North Stars 3	New York Islanders 6
Game 3	May 17	New York Islanders 7	Minnesota North Stars 5
Game 4	May 19	New York Islanders 2	Minnesota North Stars 4
Game 5	May 21	Minnesota North Stars 1	New York Islanders 5

Conn Smythe Trophy: Butch Goring (10 G, 10 A, 20 P)

CHAPTER 24:

1981-82

The Islanders breeze once more through the regular season as the NHL's winningest team, and in the process, set a regular season record.

BOB LORIMER: I'd talked to my agent during the summer, because I was thinking about buying a house. So I asked him to see if they had any inkling if they were going to trade me. And at the time, they didn't. So I bought a new house. And then six weeks later, got traded in training camp, because the Islanders got an offer they really couldn't refuse - it ended up being a first round draft pick. And that draft pick they eventually used to pick Pat LaFontaine [in 1983]. So it was obviously a tremendous deal for the Islanders. If I remember correctly, there was a deal that Colorado made, that swapped from a late first round pick to a third overall pick, which ended up being Pat LaFontaine. So it ended up being Dave Cameron and myself got traded for the third overall pick. The announcers, whenever I watch a game on TV, say "The worst deal in hockey history!" I don't think the trade was exactly how they remember it.

KEN MORROW: At that time, we set the record for consecutive wins. I think it was 15 [from January 21-February 20]. That made it so much fun, because not only were we going through those Stanley Cup years, but we had the Mike Bossy thing going on, and then the 15 game winning streak. Just a lot of good things happened for the team.

BILL TORREY: The Flyers [in 1979-80] didn't lose in thirty-something games - but didn't reach 15 consecutive wins. It was good in a way, because when you're already a two-time champ, you have a tendency to be a little complacent at times. But once we started on this streak, it was something that the guys zeroed in on. Once we got eight, nine, ten, it kind of caught their attention. It was something they wanted to accomplish.

CLARK GILLIES: The streak was kind of neat. That was like, "Holy shit, this could go on forever!" And then all of a sudden, it got to the point where we'd won seven or eight...and we had won five or six games in a row before, that wasn't a big deal. Then it became ten, and everybody said, "15 is the record." And then everybody was like, "Alright. Let's see what we can do with this thing."

BRYAN TROTTIER: I don't remember a lot about it, because it wasn't something that was on our minds - it kind of happened. All of a sudden, it became headlines. "THE ISLANDERS WITHIN 3" or "THE ISLANDERS WITHIN 4," I can't remember when it started. None of us made it a mission, it was just one of those things that presented itself.

BOB BOURNE: I remember part of that, because we were getting up to number nine and number ten, and there were no overtime wins in that time. I believe the record was fourteen at the time. It was just another feather in our hat. We were a great hockey team and our thought before going into every game is, "We should win *every* game." There were times during that season that we had letdowns. I remember Montreal only lost eight games one season [1976-77], and one of our goals was to not lose any more than that and set a record. But I know we ended up losing more than eight [the Islanders would lose 16 games that year]. It was just a real good, overall season for us. It's funny, because we did believe if we didn't win a game, it was because we didn't work as hard as we should have. It was just a lot of fun. It was so nice coming to the rink. You talk to every hockey player, and when you go to the rink knowing you should win every game, it's a pretty good feeling.

DUANE SUTTER: It looked like we weren't going to do it - Colorado had us down at home [in what would be the potential 15th win, on February 20]. Chico was the goalie. We scored two late goals to win it.

BRYAN TROTTIER: The Rockies were the team that made it the most dramatic, because it was Chico Resch in the net on the other end, and Tonelli comes down and blasts a goal. There wasn't much time left in the game [47 seconds]. So it was a very dramatic 15th win, against a team that was probably not the most scariest at the time, but they played a hell of a game. We were just on a bit of a roll, and some good things were happening. Again, I don't remember it ever being a mission, like "Come on guys, let's go after this!" I don't remember that. But when it presented itself, it was like, "OK, let's focus on this a little bit more." But it wasn't the prize, it wasn't "the holy grail."

BOB NYSTROM: John Tonelli scoring on Chico Resch. I hate to say that, but again, we were fighting. I don't remember all the specifics, but we were going into the third period there, and I remember Johnny T going down the left side. He came up with so many big goals for us. He ended up taking a slap shot, and it was Bobby Lorimer who might have been trying to block the shot. Johnny ended up scoring, and we beat the record. It was absolutely incredible. What it really says about the team is we just had a way of...and I kind of equate ourselves to the Yankees, or even now to the Jets - you find a way to win. There's some teams out there that find a way to lose.

GLENN "CHICO" RESCH: *Agonizing.* I was so bummed. Well, how about this, I don't know how many years it's been, but I can still see the play forming right now. I can see the Islanders defenseman coming out to my right outside the net, and I'm thinking, "Boys, don't forecheck. Play it safe." We go for the forecheck, they get it, and I can still see the puck go to the left boards to Johnny Tonelli, and Bobby Lorimer - who ironically, was an ex-Islander - went down early. It was just between the top of the circle and the blue line. But again, he's anxious to block it. And then Johnny Tonelli unleashes it, and it's going to hit Bobby Lorimer up high. So he kind of goes to his right, and if that stinking puck didn't just come by a shin-pad, and I was down looking for it, and Johnny put it just above my stick between my legs. Oh my goodness. The ironic thing was it was the same end and a very similar feeling to Lanny MacDonald scoring in '78. I can still see the boys jumping in the corner and going bonkers. But you know what? I'm glad it was them and not somebody else. It was awesome homecoming though, I do remember that - the fans were very, very nice to me. So yeah, it was a good full circle there.

CLARK GILLIES: That night we left and went to Pittsburgh. I think we might have *over-celebrated* the 15th win a little bit, and Pittsburgh beat us the next night [4-3]. It was fun while it lasted. I thought that record would last for a really long time, but Pittsburgh ended up getting 17 [in 1992-93].

JIGGS McDONALD: I don't think - and this isn't really only because of the 15 consecutive games - there was ever a better-balanced team throughout the National Hockey League than there was that year. And everybody bought into it. To the best of my knowledge, nobody complained about their ice time, or who they were playing with, or not happy with not being on the power play, or not being used on the penalty kill. It was the epitome of what "team" really means.

DUANE SUTTER: That's probably a record that a lot of people don't remember - those 15 consecutive wins were done in regulation. 60 minutes of hockey. Now that record doesn't stand, because Pittsburgh broke it initially, *with overtime games.* That was a huge run. It took a little bit of time to gather ourselves again, to get back into "playoff mode," and build some momentum going into the playoffs.

PATRICK DIVISION STANDINGS: 1981-82

TEAMS	W	L	T	POINTS
New York Islanders	54	16	10	118
New York Rangers	39	27	14	92
Philadelphia Flyers	38	31	11	87
Pittsburgh Penguins	31	36	13	75
Washington Capitals	26	41	13	65

CHAPTER 25:

PLAYOFFS '82

After the Penguins provide a major scare in the Division Semi-Finals, the Islanders get back to business against the Rangers and Nordiques.

DUANE SUTTER: The Penguins were a pretty skilled team. They had a good balance of skill and grit. They matched up pretty well against us. Their goaltending was surprisingly good in that series [Michel Dion was the Penguins' goalie]. We thought we could get to them, but again, it was timely goals, timely saves. They did put a lot of pressure on us.

KEN MORROW: The Penguins played us real tough. They had some good players on that team, some snipers - Rick Kehoe and Randy Carlyle.

DAVE LANGEVIN: At that time they were "best of five." When it's best of five, anything can happen. I think that's why they went to best of seven, because too many good teams were losing in the first rounds. It doesn't take much to get one fluke goal and one fluke win, and then everything turns.

BOB NYSTROM: I missed the first four games, because I had pulled my groin. I remember sitting up in the stands and watching the first two games. I'm looking at the scores right now on my computer - we won 8-1 and 7-2. And then we go into Pittsburgh, and it was like someone just shut us down.

JIGGS McDONALD: Game three, let's go back to game three. They had won with relative ease the first two games. It was just a runaway, the first two games on Long Island. You go into Pittsburgh, it's the Saturday night before Easter Sunday, and we're going home right after the game - we're chartering. We're walking across the street…when I say "we," I mean Eddie and myself, but the players too are taking their overnight bags to the arena, because they get on the bus and go to the airport right after. The Penguins players are driving into the parking lot of the arena, seeing this confident bunch, and saying to themselves, "Oh yeah? *Really?"* Lost game three in overtime [2-1]. So they lose game three, and now have to march across the street back to the hotel, re-check in, stay, and wake up Easter Sunday morning to the church bells ringing, not being home, and getting ready for game four - which they got blown out that night [5-2]. Came home for game five, and are trailing.

CLARK GILLIES: That thing was totally unexpected - the fifth game, that is. We destroyed them in the first two games on Long Island. So everybody just assumed - that word "assume," right? - that we would go in, destroy them in the third game, and have some time to rest. Little did we know that we'd drop two down there and come back, and be faced with being down 3-1 in that fifth game, with five minutes to go.

GORD LANE: I remember sitting on the bench in that fifth game on the Island, when we were down 3-1. And I remember coming off a shift and looked at the bench and Anders was looking at me. Anders just said, "Well, what do we do now?" Meaning, we were never in that situation before.

BOB NYSTROM: I think it was 3-1, and I got a penalty. I walked into the penalty box and sat down there, and Jack Rafferty said to me, "I can't believe it's over." And I said, "Well, it's not over *yet."*

KEN MORROW: They really had us on the ropes. Was that the game that Al Arbour switched goalies?

BRYAN TROTTIER: I think that's kind of an Al Arbour rule - he used the goaltender warm-up as an opportunity to rest the power play.

It just turned out we were a minute into the power play, and he pulled the goalie. I think he gave the power play a good two minute rest, while the guys were warming up the other goalie. And the power play goes out and scores a goal. It worked out. Had it not scored a goal, it would have been futile. But the fact that it worked, it became a ploy for a lot of other teams to do. And then the league changed the rule, because other teams were just using it as an opportunity to rest the power play.

CLARK GILLIES: Of all the things I tell people about, "What does it take to win the Stanley Cup?", I say, "There's three things. You've got to be good enough, obviously. You've got to be healthy. And maybe most important of all, you've got to be really lucky." We're sitting on the bench with five minutes to go, going, "Holy cow. It wasn't supposed to end his way." And we're shaking our heads as to what happened. We were all on the bench going, "Come on, boys. It shouldn't end right now!" And sure enough, Mike McEwen made it 3-2, and then John Tonelli scored with not very much time left to tie it up.

KEN MORROW: And then we score on a dump-in and a crazy bounce over Randy Carlyle's stick. I think it might have been John Tonelli or somebody came in and scored.

GORD LANE: Kenny and I always used to kid each other - "Which one had the best dump-in from center ice?" Obviously, we were not the offensive guys like Denis and Stef. I remember coming on the ice, and I think the puck went to Kenny. He threw it over to me, and I got to center ice, dumped it in - like we always do - to Randy Carlyle. Randy was going back to get it, it bounced off the boards strangely, over his stick, Johnny was just going into the net, right onto his stick, and he stuck it in. As far as an assist, it was by accident - I just threw it in.

BRYAN TROTTIER: A lot of drama. It seemed like there were situations and fortune that smiled on us. A key power play at the right time. A fortunate hop over Randy Carlyle's stick, on a dump in. Those things don't always happen. It was one of those things were Al would say, *"We need to take advantage of the breaks."* And those were the breaks, and we took advantage of them. It's no reflection on Pittsburgh, as much as it is the hockey gods smiled on us that day. We took advantage of it.

GORD LANE: The winning goal will always stand out in my mind, because Denis was beat. Bullard, Kehoe, and another other guy that was on the left side, they went down on Kenny Morrow, three on one. Bullard faked the shot and went around Kenny, and it was three on zero!

CLARK GILLIES: Mike Bullard had Smitty totally out of the net. He took a shot and hit the goalpost, and I believe right on the heels of that, John Tonelli went down and scored right after that. We were basically finished. Mike Bullard...talk about being lucky - he just totally screwed up and hit the goalpost, and we ended up winning that game. Now, how we won it, I don't know. Well, I do know - we were very lucky. By all rights, they should have beat us in that fifth game. If that would have happened, we'd still be shaking our heads, because who knows if we would have been able to come back and rebound after that. It was almost over against Pittsburgh in that first round.

BOB NYSTROM: I remember that game so vividly, because it was my first game back, and going in on a breakaway...on pretty much a breakaway, in overtime. I remember I had the goalie beat and I wanted to put it in on my backhand, and Pat Boutette pulled me down from behind. I lost the puck, Johnny T got the puck - I was laying on my back - and he put the puck in, right over top of me, in the top corner of the net. Oh my god, it was such a great memory.

AL ARBOUR: It was on par [with Nystrom's Cup-clinching goal in 1980]. That was a great game, there's no question about it.

MIKE McEWEN: The overtime goal I got an assist on. It was really strange, because the same play happened in Junior against Randy Carlyle. When we won the Memorial Cup, we beat his team in the Semi-Finals. But he comes in from the point, he's wide open for some reason, he's able to walk in to the top of the circle and I'm in front of the net. I see him, I go out, he takes a slap shot, I go down and block the shot, get up, and I hit Tonelli on a breakaway pass. He goes down and takes a shot, Nystrom got the rebound, and Tonelli put it in for the winner. It was the same play in junior when I was 18 - Randy Carlyle walking in and it was overtime. In junior, I passed to John Anderson - who played in the NHL - he went down and scored, and we won the series. It was weird.

KEN MORROW: Just a typical John Tonelli goal. I think it kind of typified what our team was. I mean, Bryan Trottier and Mike Bossy were the face of the team, and they carried us, but it was John Tonelli, Bob Nystrom, Wayne Merrick, Duane Sutter, Gordie Lane, and those types of players who were the unsung heroes that we had. Any one of those guys would step up and make a big play and score a big goal. And that was John Tonelli in that game.

DUANE SUTTER: We were always a confident group. There was never any doubts of that. Again, it was playing for the break. The grinders, or *the soldiers* dug in, and we were able to sneak out. A lot of that series was a blur, and a lot of that was because I was hurt. I was playing, but I was hurt.

BOB BOURNE: When I look back now, every team that has a dynasty, there is a game or a series that you might have got a little bit lucky.

LORNE HENNING: You could see the change of emotion through the whole series - we were on a high, then they were on a high. So it was once we got that goal to get within one, we just took off. But there was so much pressure there for us to win.

DAVE LANGEVIN: That would have been a tough one to lose. It's different losing in the Stanley Cup Finals than it is losing in like the first round. Usually, the first round is the toughest round typically, because the teams aren't as good - they don't have any system, they're just kind of all over the place, and it's hard to set up systems to play against them. And they don't have anything to lose - they don't have any pressure on them.

GARY "BABA BOOEY" DELL'ABATE: I remember that series vividly. I remember being at my neighbor's house - we were all big

Islanders fans. In fact, my next door neighbor that I grew up with, his uncle was a really big politician - Joe Margiotta. Joe Margiotta used to get these awesome tickets - center ice, fourth row back. So I used to go with them a lot to the games, too. I remember being there, and his younger brother throwing stuff around the house, like, "I can't believe they're blowing this!" It really looked like it was over. And then they scored and went on.

STAN FISCHLER: That was - of the entire run - easily the scariest one. It looked so bad. First of all, the Penguins' goalie played the series of his life, Michel Dion. He was just out of his mind. And usually, what we would do is at the end of each period, when I did the between period interviews, we would give a gift away. We had a writer from Pittsburgh, and the game looked like it was so dead for the Islanders, we gave him all the gifts we had, because we figured this was the end. Of course, the way they came back was as arresting a comeback as I've ever seen. It was really part of the fabric of this team - the comeback-ability. It was the foot soldiers - it was Nystrom and Tonelli. They had that blend. They had the virtuosos like Bossy, and then you had the foot soldiers.

JIMMY DEVELLANO: Oh my god, we nearly blew it. My thoughts were it was very nerve-racking, because it would have clipped our Cups off at two. Not that that was so bad. But we had such a good team in '81-'82. I don't know what we had - 119 points, 121 points? [118 points] We were the best team in the league. We nearly got upset in round one. I remember sitting there very nervously. But guess what? We didn't get upset. We won it. And it would have changed the course of history, because the Islanders hold some very outstanding records.

STAN FISCHLER: The greatest comeback of all time was the '42 Leafs, but that's a whole different situation. This was as great a comeback that I'd ever seen, because we thought they were dead.

GORD LANE: All the Stanley Cups, all the stuff we won - I think that was likely the biggest series that really stands out in my mind.

MIKE McEWEN: I remember the Rangers, I thought I played pretty well that series. I got hurt against the Rangers. I went in the corner with Barry Beck, and my arm was out, and ended up going against the glass. He saw it, and drilled right into my elbow, and hyper extended my elbow. I had to play the rest of the playoffs with a sling on my arm. I remember the Rangers were a tough series, but we'd sit in that room before a game, and go, "We've got to go out and *dominate.*" And we knew we could dominate. That's just a weird feeling - you're sitting there in the NHL playoffs, and you know you can dominate a game and take it over.

DUANE SUTTER: If I remember correctly, that line was a crucial line for us - Tonelli, Nystrom, and Merrick, and whoever else slipped into the center ice position. Again, any time we played the Rangers, we had a little bit different type of motivation, just because they were "of the proximity," and of the Rangers/Islanders rivalry [the Islanders would beat the Rangers, four games to two, to advance to the Conference Finals].

BOB BOURNE: The Quebec Nordiques were tough. We thought we were in tough with them, because the Šťastnýs were playing so well. And playing in Quebec City was no fun either - it was a tough building to play in. They were fast and strong, but every time we came back to our building, it didn't matter. All those four years that we were in our building, we weren't winning 2-1 or 1-0, we were winning 5-1. We really took control of games in our building. And then we'd go on the road and we'd play a really tight defensive game, and we could score. It wasn't just Trots or Boss or Clarkie - we had so many guys who could score. We had scoring from the fourth line a lot of years.

DUANE SUTTER: The Quebec series, we thought it would be a lot tighter series, because they had come through some tough series of their own, and they were an extremely skilled group. Again, probably the difference in that series was the goaltending.

CLARK GILLIES: I do remember playing Quebec...vaguely. That's just one of those things where we breezed right through [the Islanders swept the Nordiques in four games]. Other than the Rangers series, there obviously wasn't much in our way.

Division Semi-Finals (3-2):

New York Islanders over Pittsburgh Penguins

Game 1 April 7   Pittsburgh Penguins 1 New York Islanders 8
Game 2 April 8   Pittsburgh Penguins 2 New York Islanders 7
Game 3 April 10   New York Islanders 1   Pittsburgh Penguins 2 (OT)
Game 4 April 11   New York Islanders 2   Pittsburgh Penguins 5
Game 5 April 13   Pittsburgh Penguins 3 New York Islanders 4 (OT)

Division Finals (4-2):

New York Islanders over New York Rangers

Game 1 April 15   New York Rangers 5   New York Islanders 4
Game 2 April 16   New York Rangers 2   New York Islanders 7
Game 3 April 18   New York Islanders 4 New York Rangers 3 (OT)
Game 4 April 19   New York Islanders 5 New York Rangers 3
Game 5 April 21   New York Rangers 4   New York Islanders 2
Game 6 April 23   New York Islanders 5 New York Rangers 3

Conference Finals (4-0):

New York Islanders over Quebec Nordiques

Game 1 April 27   Quebec Nordiques 1   New York Islanders 4
Game 2 April 29   Quebec Nordiques 2   New York Islanders 5
Game 3 May 1   New York Islanders 5 Quebec Nordiques 4 (OT)
Game 4 May 4   New York Islanders 4 Quebec Nordiques 2

CHAPTER 26:

STANLEY CUP '82

Can the Canucks dethrone the Islanders as reigning Stanley Cup champs?

BOB BOURNE: I remember sitting in Billy Smith's house, watching Vancouver and Chicago play [in the Conference Finals]. We were waiting to see who we were going to play. Vancouver beat Chicago. We looked at their team, and just felt that we were a much better hockey team and very confident going into that final series.

KEN MORROW: There was a lot of hysteria at the time for Vancouver. It was the first time they had been in the Finals, and they had beaten some good teams out west [the Calgary Flames and the Los Angeles Kings]. They had "the terrible towels" going - the white towels in the coliseum. They were tough, they had a good team. They had Tiger Williams, some good players.

AL ARBOUR: I remember the waving the towels when Roger Neilson was coaching them. The towels started in Vancouver.

DUANE SUTTER: That had come out of one of their previous series, where they thought they had been screwed out of a goal. I think it one of the series previous to the Finals. And Roger Neilson had held that towel up, and was waving it. So that just became a tradition out there.

BOB BOURNE: I remember the towels. It was pretty intimidating - skating around in warm ups. But by that time, we were pretty seasoned with playing in somebody else's building in a Stanley Cup Final. We knew what to expect. We were pretty business-like in those days. We just went out and played our game and stuck to our game plan. Al Arbour's big thing was, "If the building falls in, you still go out there and play and stick to our game plan."

BILL TORREY: More than anything else, [goaltender] Richard Brodeur - who we had traded away - became what was known that season as "King Richard." He was really the backbone of their team. They were a big team, but they weren't a high-scoring team, and he had one of those seasons for the books. But quite frankly, what beat them…there were a lot of things - we were a better team, we had better depth. But what *really* beat them - Billy Smith was better. I think all the attention that Brodeur got, it was a little spur for Billy. Because in the end, the difference clearly was that Billy Smith didn't let us get beat.

STAN FISCHLER: That first game, I remember I brought my oldest son, Ben, to that game, and that was scary because Vancouver was on a tremendous roll. Terrific roll. Sort of like the Bruins [in 2011]. And they almost won that first game [the Islanders beat the Canucks in overtime, 6-5]. Had they won that first game, they could very well have won that series. The fact that the Islanders could come back every series is a symbol, and that series was Bossy getting that late goal, which was so important - the Harold Snepsts mistake.

CLARK GILLIES: He made the mistake of putting it right on Mike Bossy's stick. About two seconds later, it was in the net and we won that game.

BRYAN TROTTIER: Mike fired a bullet over Brodeur's shoulder, and we just never looked back after that. I thought they were very undisciplined as a team. I think Roger Neilson amped them up a little too much, to the point they were taking a lot of unnecessary penalties. We just let them. We were like, "OK. *No retaliation,* guys." They took a lot of penalties, and again, our power play stayed real hot.

DAVE LANGEVIN: There was a lot of verbal jabbing back and forth by more Vancouver than us - thinking they were ready to win. I just think that's what they had to do to talk themselves into it. But they gave us a scare the first game. Then after that, it was pretty much history. They didn't give us much after that. Bossy took over.

DUANE SUTTER: Boss had an incredible series.

STAN FISCHLER: And then Bossy scoring that goal when he was flying in the air [in game three]. That was a trademark.

JIGGS McDONALD: The Bossy goal, of course, when he was diving headfirst into the ice, that was just an incredible play. At that time, I don't think any of us had seen a goal scored in mid-air like that in full-flight. Yeah, there had been the Bobby Orr goal [the 1970 Cup-clinching goal in overtime], but Mike was closer to the ice, that's where he scored it - Bobby was tripped after he had shot the puck.

BOB NYSTROM: That to me was one of the most incredible goals I've ever seen. Not from the standpoint from going through and beating everybody, but he's just stretched out. And it was good from my standpoint, because my parents live close to there, so they were able to see all the games. [Laughs] But it was a tough series, also. I have to say that Vancouver played us pretty tough that year.

DUANE SUTTER: A big part of that Stanley Cup run was Brent [Duane's brother] was finally there. He didn't play a lot, he got sat through a couple of playoff series. Winning the first Stanley Cup in '80 was a huge thrill, and something I'll never forget. But to win one with your brother, that's even more special. Winning in Canada...the first two Stanley Cups, my parents had come and watched a couple of games, but had never been with us when we won, and they were with us out in Vancouver. And along with Brent, it had [a special meaning].

AL ARBOUR: It was really something to beat the Vancouver Canucks. We beat them four straight.

CLARK GILLIES: They weren't blow-outs on our part, but we played our game to a T, and went through the four games. And it ended the way it should.

GORD LANE: Probably the same kind of situation as Minnesota - we just expected to win. You look at our line-up and look at theirs. We have five potential Hall of Famers. We had Arbour and we had a crew that could basically play whatever you wanted. It wasn't what we wanted - whatever *you* wanted. If you want to fight? Alright, we'll fight. If you want to play? Alright, we'll play. But we will eventually win.

KEN MORROW: That might have been the best our team has ever been.

JIGGS McDONALD: That was the one that they won on the road. That one, to me, the significance of winning on the road, yup, they won at home, they knew what that was all about. But the flight back from Vancouver, I recall being down in the dressing room and people from the NHL saying, "Now, *the Cup goes in the case, it goes in the belly of the plane.*" Well, it didn't. It was in the plane. It sat strapped in...well, it moved around, but it was there. And the number of guys who spent personal time, just came, sat with the Cup, arm around the Cup. A couple of them in tears. I think there was more quality time or more personal time spent with the Cup in that case than there had been with winning it at home, because the celebration is going on, you've got places to go, things to do. But here, you have that four and a half/five-hour flight across country in the middle of the night. And the Stanley Cup - the ultimate holy grail of hockey - right there with you. It was unreal.

BRYAN TROTTIER: That was unique, just in that sense - to win the Cup on the road for the first time. It was different. It felt like a long ride home that night, because I was sick as a dog. I had a flu bug or something. The next day I felt great, but that whole ride home, was just like, *"Ugh."* There was so much celebration on the plane, and all I kept saying was, "Oh man, I think I'm going to throw up." And I had a headache. I was sick to my stomach. I'd wake up every once in a while and look at the guys partying, and was like, "I want to join them...but I can't."

BRUCE BENNETT: As a team photographer during those years, rarely would I travel with the team. Basically, my job was to cover the home games, and maybe once a season, I would take a road trip. When the Islanders played out in Vancouver for the Stanley Cup, they had flown me out there to cover [game four]. And that kind of experience was such a special thing, because it didn't happen very often. One of my best memories was an overnight trip, coming back from Vancouver after the Islanders won that Stanley Cup. Although the few stragglers like myself were toward the front of the plane, you could peak and hear what was going on towards the back of the plane. I'd run through once or twice to shoot some pictures, but didn't really want to disturb the partying that was going on.

We landed at dawn at LaGuardia, at the Marine Terminal, and there were a few thousand fans there to greet us. I pushed myself toward the front of the plane to be one of the first people out, so I could photograph the players coming out. The crowd was going wild and I realized that Clark Gillies had opened the back door of the airplane, was showing the Stanley Cup, and was waving a white shirt - like they had done in Vancouver, for the local team there. And the crowd was just going *wild*. I photographed the players as they were coming down onto the tarmac, and Tomas Jonsson had climbed up a staircase that they would push up to the airplane, and was waving to the fans as the sun rose behind him. It made for such a great photo. And those fans, who had probably stayed up all night - like the Islanders had stayed up all night - had such a treat to see the players and to see the Stanley Cup at LaGuardia that morning.

JIMMY DEVELLANO: [Devellano] became the assistant general manager in '81-'82 of the New York Islanders. After winning three Stanley Cups on the Island, Mike Ilitch, who had just purchased the Detroit Red Wings, hired me away to be the general manager of the Detroit Red Wings. And I'm entering my 30th year with the Detroit Red Wings this year [including a total of four Stanley Cups with the Red Wings].

Stanley Cup Finals (4-0):

New York Islanders over Vancouver Canucks

Game 1 May 8   Vancouver Canucks 5   New York Islanders 6 (OT)
Game 2 May 11   Vancouver Canucks 4 New York Islanders 6
Game 3 May 13   New York Islanders 3 Vancouver Canucks 0
Game 4 May 16   New York Islanders 3 Vancouver Canucks 1

Conn Smythe Trophy: Mike Bossy (17 G, 10 A, 27 P)

Gary "Baba Booey" Dell'Abate and Bob Nystrom, Stanley Cup
Victory Parade, 1980 [pic by Steve Donnelly]

Dell'Abate and Glenn "Chico" Resch, with Anders Kallur behind
Dell'Abate, 1980 [pic by Steve Donnelly]

Bryan Trottier, the Conn Smythe Trophy, and Jean Potvin, 1980
[pic by Steve Donnelly]

Clark Gillies and Mike Bossy, 1980 [pic by Steve Donnelly]

Duane Sutter, Denis Potvin, Steve Tambellini, and the Cup, 1980 [pic by Steve Donnelly]

Numero Uno [pic by Steve Donnelly]

THE CUP! [pic by Steve Donnelly]

Cup banners at Nassau Coliseum [pic by Kurt Christensen:
kurtchristensen.com]

Retired numbers [pic by Kurt Christensen: kurtchristensen.com]

Islanders Hall of Fame [pic by Kurt Christensen:
kurtchristensen.com]

Tribute to Mr. Torrey [pic by Kurt
Christensen: kurtchristensen.com]

Tribute to Mr. Arbour [pic by Kurt
Christensen: kurtchristensen.com]

Nassau Veterans Memorial Coliseum, 2012 [pic by Kurt Christensen: kurtchristensen.com]

CHAPTER 27:

1982-83

The Islanders struggle a bit during the regular season, leading some to wonder if their magical run is nearing the end.

DUANE SUTTER: We were very motivated, because we wanted to show everyone that we could win four straight. There was a lot of hype - the Montreal Canadiens had put together some pretty special strings of Stanley Cup wins together. But we felt - and some of us had talked about it - we could win the Cup that year. That would give us 16 consecutive playoff series wins, and it would certainly mean a lot in NHL history, towards what kind of a team we would be remembered as.

MIKE McEWEN: We started 11-2, and we were rolling. We were winning games 7-4, 6-4, or 5-3. It wasn't 2-1, 3-2, 4-2 games. Al was a great coach...but he coached defense. I heard him give a lot of good defensive compliments, I'm not sure I ever heard him give an offensive compliment the whole time I was there. So we have a team meeting, and he gives us crap about not playing defense. *Big time.* As an offensive defenseman, I was having a blast - everybody was hitting holes, it was great playing on that team when it just went offense. Getting real creative out there, it was a lot of fun to play. That night I get the puck, and everybody is diving back into their positions and I can't find anybody to pass to, and it looks like everything's defense - even when we have the puck! So we kind of went into a funk until about March. Certain guys weren't playing well. I remember I thought Dave Langevin was having the best year of anybody - just for consistency and game in and game out. Everybody [else], it was either injuries or this or that.

So Al has a meeting, I want to say March 1st - the first week of March. He was like, "OK. I'm at my wits end. Everybody is going to say their piece." So he went around the room, and everybody said their piece. He kind of had to take some stuff from us, and he took it. He said, "OK. Nothing's going to leave this room, and we're going to go on from here." So from that point on, Al didn't coach too much - Lorne Henning did a lot of it. Al just sort of…I mean, *he coached,* but as far as during practice, he just sort of let us do our thing. And I don't think we lost but two games the rest of the year. You could just see it through March - we're getting better and better and better. By the time the playoffs rolled around, we knew we were going to win. I think that was almost the easiest year. We lost very few games. But we had it all back - it just took about a year to get it all back. That's what I remember - we had some adversity off ice, and we worked it out. I think Al, by kind of admitting he had a role in it, too…as well as the players, they admitted it, too. But that meeting was really, really good. Brent Sutter was big, and Tomas Jonsson was big. Our team, we knew it was maybe better than before.

JIGGS McDONALD: It was a team that come the middle of March, boy, you would have to be super special in order to beat that team.

DUANE SUTTER: Again, that year, Bob Bourne, Brent, and I played together, and were able to put together - probably for all three of us - our best playoff season that we would experience in our careers.

BOB BOURNE: Clark Gillies, Brent Sutter, and Duane Sutter played together all year, and they had a heck of a season. And then Clarkie got hurt - I think it was the last game of the regular season - and he was going to be out for the whole playoffs. That was going to hurt us. I got to play with Brent and Duane, and from the first game we played together, everything clicked for us. We had a heck of a playoff series, all four rounds. We just played really well.

MIKE McEWEN: By the time April rolled around, and I think we went 9-2 in March [10-4-1]. We did really well. *We were ready.*

PATRICK DIVISION STANDINGS: 1982-83

TEAMS	W	L	T	POINTS
Philadelphia Flyers	49	23	8	106
New York Islanders	42	26	12	96
Washington Capitals	39	25	16	94
New York Rangers	35	35	10	80
New Jersey Devils	17	49	14	48
Pittsburgh Penguins	18	53	9	45

CHAPTER 28:

PLAYOFFS '83

The Capitals, Rangers, and Bruins are no match for the mighty Islanders in the playoffs.

DUANE SUTTER: Well, Washington scared the hell out of us. They were a team that was always knocking on the door. They had worked their way into being one of the better teams in the league. That was a tough series [the Islanders would persevere however, winning 3-1]. And then the second round was the Rangers. That was the series that Brent, Bobby Bourne, and I emerged as a pretty darn good line. I had a hat trick one of those games, so it was big. From that point on, we felt - as a line - that if we contributed a couple of goals a night, that we were going to win the Cup.

MIKE McEWEN: I didn't play much that year - I separated my shoulder and tore ligaments in my ankle. I think I only played in 42 games, and in the playoffs, I don't think I dressed for about six or seven. So I didn't make a big contribution on the ice. Tomas Jonsson was playing really well, and he was going to play. And Paul Boutilier, they were giving him a chance to play. So there were two offensive defensemen, and I was kind of "the odd man out." I remember watching from the press box. [Laughs]

BOB BOURNE: I've seen it enough times [a classic goal that Bourne scored against the Rangers, when he went from one end of the rink to the other to score] - I probably haven't watched it in 15 years now, but I just remember coming back to our end, and Tommy Jonsson was tied up to the left of Billy Smith. He was fighting for the puck, and he got free. I just yelled at him, and he dumped me the puck. By that time, I had a bit of speed built up from going around the net. When I came around the net, the Rangers were on a change. I just remember Ron Greschner coming off the bench, and I knew I was going to beat him. Then I was going down against Reijo Ruotsalainen and Barry Beck, and most of the time I would go wide on Ruotsalainen. He just anticipated that and took a step outside, and I pulled the puck back in. When I looked up, I only saw a couple of inches from the net, and luckily, it went in [the Islanders would defeat the Rangers in the series, 4-2].

DUANE SUTTER: Not quite the same series as it was in 1980 [when the Islanders faced the Boston Bruins in the Conference Finals]. I don't think it was as physical. They were a little bit younger team, probably a more skilled team than they were in '80. But again, we felt that we could get to their goaltending, and put some pressure on their younger team. And that's how it turned out [the Islanders won the series, 4-2].

Division Semi-Finals (3-1):

New York Islanders over Washington Capitals

Game 1	April 6	Washington Capitals 2	New York Islanders 5
Game 2	April 7	Washington Capitals 4	New York Islanders 2
Game 3	April 9	New York Islanders 6	Washington Capitals 2
Game 4	April 10	New York Islanders 6	Washington Capitals 3

Division Finals (4-2):

New York Islanders over New York Rangers

Game 1	April 14	New York Rangers 1	New York Islanders 4
Game 2	April 15	New York Rangers 0	New York Islanders 5
Game 3	April 17	New York Islanders 6	New York Rangers 7
Game 4	April 18	New York Islanders 1	New York Rangers 3
Game 5	April 20	New York Rangers 2	New York Islanders 7
Game 6	April 22	New York Islanders 5	New York Rangers 2

Conference Finals (4-2):

New York Islanders over Boston Bruins

Game 1	April 26	New York Islanders 5	Boston Bruins 2
Game 2	April 28	New York Islanders 1	Boston Bruins 4
Game 3	April 30	Boston Bruins 3	New York Islanders 7
Game 4	May 3	Boston Bruins 3	New York Islanders 8
Game 5	May 5	New York Islanders 1	Boston Bruins 5
Game 6	May 7	Boston Bruins 4	New York Islanders 8

CHAPTER 29:

STANLEY CUP '83

Can the Oilers dethrone the Islanders as reigning Stanley Cup champs?

GARY "BABA BOOEY" DELL'ABATE: I do remember that Edmonton series, like, "Yeah, Gretzky's great...*but we're the Islanders."* Edmonton was heavily favored.

CLARK GILLIES: The stories going into that were, "The Islanders have won three. They're a little long in the tooth, and they're coming up against the high power Gretzky-led Edmonton Oilers."

DUANE SUTTER: Edmonton, as they were for two years, had been knocking on the door, and putting up some pretty incredible offensive numbers. They had a couple of good, young goalies in Andy Moog and Grant Fuhr. So obviously, they were a very confident group. Again, a team out of Canada back to the Finals - a lot of hype through Canada.

STAN FISCHLER: As soon as the Canadian writers said that [that the Oilers were favored to win the Cup], you knew the Islanders were going to win, because the Canadian writers don't know what the hell they're talking about 95% of the time. So that was a nice thing for the Islanders, to get that blessing from these clowns.

LORNE HENNING: It's a big challenge - the Oilers were "the team." They were young and cocky. They talked a pretty good game, and we took that as a challenge. Gretzky, Messier - they had a lot of outstanding players. Again, maybe the fear factor - we didn't want to lose, and wanted to keep it going.

BOB BOURNE: Before the season even started, we got all the quotes out of Edmonton, and how cocky they were. We laugh about it now, because I'm friends with a lot of those guys - I play a lot of old timers games with Glenn Anderson and Dave Semenko, and you run into Messier and those guys. They're just all good guys. But I remember them being so cocky, and they'll be the first ones to admit it. But it kind of got us going - the old story of hanging newspaper clippings in the dressing room. And they didn't have a lot of respect for us - they really didn't. We just felt it was another challenge. We were certainly worried about them though.

GORD LANE: We had so much experience with the media regarding the Rangers. The New York press, whenever we went to play the Rangers, we could be in first place and they could be in last place, and as far as the media was concerned, we were the underdogs every time. So never even thought of it. We just understood that we had a very good hockey team, and although we understood their potential with Gretzky, Messier, Fuhr, and Coffey, we had a sense of confidence. And we had this "workmanship attitude" that Arbour instilled in us. Arbour would always say, "I don't care if the building catches on fire or if the clock falls - just keep on going." And I think that's what pushed us forward. We knew that if we did what we were able and capable of, we would win.

BRYAN TROTTIER: For us, headlines and whatever the press was saying, it meant very little to us as a group. We were more concentrating on the other team. And we knew the firepower they had, we knew the kind of season they had. They were a team that felt that was their time. So we knew we had our hands full. We weren't worried about getting respect or disrespected or anything like that. We were just concentrating on the job at hand. I don't remember what was said in the press.

I do remember there seemed like there was more attention given to Billy Smith at that time. Guys would crease-crash him, and Smitty was defending his crease - as he always does. Probably he went over the line here and there, but they should know that Smitty, like we knew you don't keep your head down against some of their defense. It was just one of those things, and there was a lot of attention to that. And Smitty rose to the occasion, and said, "You guys can say what you want. I'm just going to be a goalie." And for us to rally around it as a group I thought was pretty cool.

It seemed like we got a huge contribution from a lot of guys. I say that because I remember Bobby Bourne's line - they were on fire. I remember Clark Gillies scoring some huge goals on the power play. I think Mike Bossy had missed the first game in Edmonton, if I'm not mistaken. He had the flu. Al came out with a crazy line - "We went to plan B. Well, *we had no plan B!*" Again, it was neat how everybody made that a point, and deflected a lot of stuff that was trying to be controversial. I didn't think we were a very controversial team. Other people may say differently. But we just wanted to find a way to win. But we knew it was kind of like a keg of dynamite, and if we lit off the dynamite, it was going to be a hell of a lot harder.

CLARK GILLIES: Just before I left to go to Edmonton, I called a buddy of mine in Moose Jaw, where I grew up. My friend was actually my midget coach when I was twelve or thirteen years old. His name is John Hunter. And I said, "John, am I going to see you up in Edmonton?" He goes, "Nope. Not coming to Edmonton. I'm coming to New York - *I'm going to watch you win it at home in game four.*" And I go, "OK. I like the way you think!"

STAN FISCHLER: It all came down to the first game. And the first game in Edmonton, Bossy was ill, he didn't play. The Oilers so overwhelmed the Islanders in the first period, it looked like it was going to be a 9-0 win for Edmonton. It was the best period of goaltending I'd ever seen. I forget if it was Duane Sutter who scored the first goal…it was a 2-0 game. But the point is that they won that game, and that was huge. And they won the second game [6-3].

BOB BOURNE: Played a really good game the first one. And then the second game, that really set the stage for us was we scored a lot goals. Just really took over the series. And they never played well in New York. For some reason, they always put a lot of pressure on themselves.

JIGGS McDONALD: That was the year that Billy Smith's face was on the front page of the Edmonton Sun, with a bulls eye - done like a target - and he was "public enemy #1."

DUANE SUTTER: It was a huge controversy [over a play in which Billy Smith whacked Wayne Gretzky in the leg with his goalie stick, in game two], but Smitty thrived on situations like that. As much as they thought they were getting under his skin, it was just making him a better goalie. It kind of worked against them.

GORD LANE: That series goes right back onto Billy Smith. That was the year he won the Conn Smythe. Billy made saves with his bare hands and just stoned them. Another thing that I noticed about the Oilers is that they never would really change their style, and I think we kind of figured out after a while the way to actually play them. But Billy just flat out stoned them.

CLARK GILLIES: That was the series where he slashed Gretzky. He chopped him coming around the net. And nailed Glenn Anderson too, I think. That was the year the headline after the game where he slashed Gretzky, they had Smitty holding a hatchet in his hand on the front page of the paper, or something like that! None of that stuff ever phased Smitty. You'd think that some guys, if they hurt the star player on the other team that they'd get upset, and a little bit hesitant to go out the next night. That didn't bother Smitty at all. He kinda told them, "They all learned their lesson - don't get close to my net." I think that was actually the message that was taken - "We better not get too close to him. He doesn't really give a shit who he hurts on this team."

But those first two games were *totally* Smitty. He just stood on his head. And then came back home. I don't remember the scores, but I do remember that we beat them quite handily at home [5-1 and 4-2]. That was a real feather in our cap - there weren't a lot of teams that were picking us to beat Edmonton. Never mind four straight, but to beat them at home. We just really stuck to business. I don't think there was anybody in the locker room going, "Let's shove it up their ass. These young guys, they're going to beat us old guys?" Al always kept us pretty even-keeled. He said, "Let's not get caught up in all the bullshit here. We'll just go out and play, and if we play as well as we can, it should be good enough." We always believed that.

STAN FISCHLER: I would have never imagined a sweep. Out of the question.

AL ARBOUR: I thought that they would put up a better fight. They had a good club, too.

DUANE SUTTER: We knew we'd have to be a disciplined group, and play a real smart, defensive game. Kind of "out experience" them. And we did. We played a very calm and collected game, a very disciplined game. They were a little bit more of a gung ho group, as far as "offense offense." We played through a lot of injuries and there were a handful of teammates that were having a few personal concerns at home. But hey, we persevered and showed we were a team that should go down in NHL history as one of the best ever.

STAN FISCHLER: This was a very, very strong Edmonton team. I remember after the third win, there was a luncheon across the street, at the Marriott, and Glen Sather was there, and I was very impressed by his confidence. The guy *oozed* confidence. It was almost as if he was defiant. And I said to myself, "Boy, the Islanders better not lose game four. Otherwise, this could be big trouble." And of course, it wasn't until the very end, because the Islanders jumped ahead, and Edmonton came within a goal. It wasn't until Kenny Morrow put it away [with an empty net goal at the end of game four]. It was a four game series that felt like seven games.

BOB NYSTROM: The Oilers were an amazing, amazing team. They had everything - they had fire power, they had a group of stars that was just absolutely incredible. The Kurris, the Coffeys, the Messiers, the Fuhrs. It goes on and on and on. And we were able to really shut them down - they scored *six goals* that series. That was playing our system to a T, and really shutting down one of the greatest hockey teams that was ever assembled. That was my favorite Cup of all. It was a tribute to how good we were at that time - certainly from a goaltender's standpoint, and personnel like Bossy, Clark, Denis, and all the guys. It was a hell of a tribute to the type of team we had.

BOB BOURNE: They weren't quite ready to win - it was almost like us in '78-'79. They just didn't know how to win. They came out and tried to play their big offensive game, and we were too good for them.

LORNE HENNING: I think [the Oilers] learned from us. But at the time, maybe they weren't quite ready to pay the price to win.

BOB BOURNE: If you read Wayne Gretzky's book, he said after we won the fourth game and he walked by our dressing room door, we were all sitting there with ice packs on our heads, our elbows, and our knees. He said that's when they said, "Holy cow. *This* is what you've got to do to win." So it kind of showed them what it took.

RON WASKE: I just remember [during the early '80s] we had to go through Pittsburgh, Philadelphia, Boston, and Montreal, and the west coast teams got to play some of the lighter teams in the schedule. And they get to the Stanley Cup, and they're not very beat up - but the Islanders were. I think that was the sign of a great team that went through some very difficult series to get to a four game sweep of Vancouver and Edmonton.

KEN MORROW: At the time I didn't [realize how special it was to win four Cups in a row]. Truly, the way that I approached it was that was what I was getting paid to do. Not to take anything away from it, but I really wasn't getting caught up in…we won our fourth cup, and automatically, we were talking about winning a fifth. That's just the way it was. When you're in that environment and you're winning - and winning championships - you just want to keep it going. For me, I was so fortunate that I happened to step into the team at the right time, and got caught up in the wave. So I didn't know any better up until then. I just thought this was going to happen, and wanted to keep it going.

AL ARBOUR: We had a pretty good team that year. It didn't surprise me one bit. The following year did surprise me.

Stanley Cup Finals (4-0):

New York Islanders over Edmonton Oilers

Game 1	May 10	New York Islanders 2	Edmonton Oilers 0
Game 2	May 12	New York Islanders 6	Edmonton Oilers 3
Game 3	May 14	Edmonton Oilers 1	New York Islanders 5
Game 4	May 17	Edmonton Oilers 2	New York Islanders 4

Conn Smythe Trophy: Billy Smith (13-3, 2.68 GAA)

CHAPTER 30:

1983-84

It's business as usual, as the Islanders put together a strong regular season and welcome the arrival of two young players fresh out of the Olympics.

KEN MORROW: Maybe a few chinks in our armor were starting to show at that time. Guys were beaten up a little bit.

STAN FISCHLER: What happens is a natural attrition. You have to understand something - these guys have been having long springs and short summers. It's wear and tear. It's also wear and tear on the brain. So what happened was perfectly natural. If you look at the records, the first team that ever won three Cups in a row was the Maple Leafs. They won four Cups in five years - '45, '47, '48, '49. And '49, I think they were barely a .500 team. But, they went on and they got hot in the playoffs. So what happened to the Islanders was perfectly natural.

DUANE SUTTER: You play a lot of hockey. And going into the Finals each year, you're basically adding a quarter of a season more than what a lot of teams are playing. It was starting to catch up to us, and we had a tremendous amount of injuries. Some guys had some personal crisis in their family with their parents getting up in age and getting ill, and a couple of guys lost their fathers that season. We were a tight group, and it affected all of us.

CLARK GILLIES: Most of that stuff was taken care of by the press. It was always, you win one, the next year, can you win two? The next year, can you win three? That was pretty much talked about. After the fourth one, we went to "The Drive for Five." I forget what we had for the [fourth one], "Score for Four"? I don't know what the hell that one was. Obviously, "The Hat Trick" for the third one, "Repeat" for the second one. I don't know, "Let's Get One More for Four"? It got kind of, "How long can this go on?" But we still had a very young team. The old veterans…when I say old, shit, I was only 30 when we won the fourth one. So I wasn't old by any stretch. And then we had added some young guys, so we had some young legs. We went into training camp feeling that "We've still got the team that can do it." We didn't have to make any changes between three and four, that I can remember. It was really just a matter of, "Hey, we know what it takes, that's not a mystery to us. We've just got to apply ourselves, take care of ourselves, and hopefully, we stay healthy and we can go on and win another one."

MIKE McEWEN: In November [McEwen was traded from the Islanders to the Kings]. They had Tomas Jonsson and they were giving Paul Boutilier a real chance. I wasn't dressing. I think I called my agent or my agent called me, y'know, "How are things going?" And I said, "I think I want to be traded." Somebody got wind of that, because we had a team meeting, and Trottier gets up, and goes, "I hear some guys want to get traded. If you don't want to be here, then get the…" I'm like, "Hey Trots, if you weren't playing, you'd want to get out of here, too!" My agent called me back, and said, "They agree. They're going to trade you." And I think it was two or three weeks later, I was traded to LA. But I got treated fairly by [the Islanders] - they treated the players well. It was a great organization. They treated the players "first class," as far as everything else. I know Arbour and Torrey kind of got on the superstars, making them take responsibility and giving them shit all the time. But I think it's just the way they worked it.

DUANE SUTTER: We felt that we were a confident group. We knew we were getting older, and there had been some whispers that perhaps some younger guys were going to come in and knock some of us out of the line-up. We had Patrick Flatley and Pat LaFontaine knocking on the door, and they were going to come in.

CLARK GILLIES: And at the same time, we were getting two pretty good players from the Olympics - Pat LaFontaine and Pat Flatley.

Patty came in and this kid was so talented, it was unbelievable. The center position, we already had Trottier, Goring, Merrick, Brent Sutter, and now, we added Pat LaFontaine to the mix. It was just amazing. And then we had a feisty young winger in Pat Flatley. We added two sets of young legs to a little bit of an older group.

PAT FLATLEY [The Islanders' right winger from 1984-1996]: My parents both emigrated from Ireland, and I had two older brothers that played. When my dad got here, everybody was playing hockey, so my brothers played. I took their hand-me-downs and followed suit. I went to Henry Carr High School [in Etobicoke, Ontario], and from there, I got a scholarship to the University of Wisconsin, and was fortunate to have Badger Bob [Bob Johnson] as a coach, followed by David King with the Olympic team, and then Al Arbour with the Islanders. I had really good fortune with my coaching early in my career. And then after my first year with Wisconsin, I was drafted by Bill Torrey and Jimmy Devellano. I was the last pick in the first round, and that was at the Montreal Forum - my dad and I went together. They called my name, went to meet everybody, got in the train, went home, and went back to work.

The Olympics were the end of seven/eight months of extreme travel. Back and forth from Russia, I think two or three times. Back and forth from Europe probably six or seven times. Living in a hotel with your teammates for the entire time. A very strong bond with our own team, and then getting into the Olympics, and to the opening ceremonies, and seeing this greater team, the *entire* Canadian Olympic team - skiers, bobsledders, and figure skaters, and all the other athletes. It was an overwhelming feeling of pride to be part of such an amazing event.

I had just flown back from Paris [when Flatley joined the Islanders in 1984], so I was exhausted. Meeting everybody in the dressing room, my initial impression was Clark Gillies was really big. [Laughs] He was one of the first guys I met. Basically, you're in a room filled with men that have won four Stanley Cups. So I was obviously in awe. A combination of awe and very nervous. I remember that first practice; I couldn't even take a pass. It was just a bad moment - jet lag or whatever, it was like an out of body experience, that first practice. I remember afterwards saying to Al Arbour, "Listen Al, *I'm not that bad.*" And he responded by saying,

"Let's hope not. Because if you are, you're not going to be here that long." [Laughs] The first game was in Winnipeg [on February 29th], and I was fortunate to score my first goal.

DUANE SUTTER: The team started to evolve into a little bit different identity. Getting a little bit younger. There were a handful of players - myself included - that didn't have very good regular seasons. I think there was a little bit of uneasiness on how some of the other guys were brought in and playing ahead of some of us more experienced players.

PAT FLATLEY: I played against Pat LaFontaine 16 times that year [LaFontaine played for the US Olympic team]. So I was very familiar with him. I didn't know him really - we'd say hi to each other. But we were kind of "enemies" at that time. My memories of him was he was an incredible hockey player. It was a pleasure to play with him, because my strengths were working the boards and freeing up the puck and getting it to my center man. And when you have a center man like Pat, when you give it to him, he's down at the other end, shooting on the net before you've left your end, he's so fast. He brought speed and electric abilities. And I think I brought more of a workman, work along the boards, blue-collar persona.

STAN FISCHLER: They worked very hard during the regular season, and all of this work, it takes an affect.

PAT FLATLEY: I just remember Al Arbour, one of his sayings was, "Don't expect to turn the tap on when the playoffs begin. *It's got to be on all the time.*" I remember we were playing hard every minute of every game, leading into the playoffs, based on that philosophy. You can't just decide, "OK, now we've got to amp up the intensity." It's always got to be there. And Al was a big promoter of that, that the tap, once it goes off, is very difficult to turn back on. So you've got to keep it on. That was a big focus, because there was a tendency to let up prior to the playoffs. And we didn't do that.

PATRICK DIVISION STANDINGS: 1983-84

TEAMS	W	L	T	POINTS
New York Islanders	50	26	4	104
Washington Capitals	48	27	5	101
Philadelphia Flyers	44	26	10	98
New York Rangers	42	29	9	93
New Jersey Devils	17	56	7	41
Pittsburgh Penguins	16	58	6	38

CHAPTER 31:

PLAYOFFS '84

After the Rangers provide a major scare in the Division Semi-Finals, the Islanders get back on track against the Capitals and Canadiens.

BOB BOURNE: I got hurt early on in that playoff year. Gordie Lane got hurt, Bobby Nystrom was hurt, Kenny Morrow was in such bad shape at that time - his knees were always getting drained. I don't think he played much during the season. I remember them draining fluid from his knee for every playoff game. It was getting to be a grind - we were playing until June every year. We started training camp earlier in those days, and we'd have to be back in New York. It got to be a real grind on us. Even though we won first place overall, there might have been too much emphasis on winning first.

STAN FISCHLER: By that time, Herbie Brooks had taken over the Rangers, and he put a tremendous stamp on the Ranger team. His personality, the Olympic win - the whole thing. The rivalry was as intense as ever.

KEN MORROW: It was a terrific series. And they had us down 2-1. Again, it was a best of five, so we had to win a game in their building, to take it back to our building. And we came up big in that one. I don't know if people remember that we were on the ropes the game before. We won that game in Madison Square Garden [4-1] to bring it back to our building, and they outplayed us in that fifth game. They really did. We were able to hang in there like a championship team, and actually had a 2-1 lead in the third period.

STAN FISCHLER: It was one of the greatest games of all-time, that's for sure. And it also had the element of controversy, with the Don Maloney goal, and the way they came back and tied it at the end.

BOB NYSTROM: That was another one where we were celebrating, and it was I think nine seconds if I'm not mistaken [The Rangers' Maloney scored the game-tying goal with 39 seconds left in regulation, in the deciding game five of the series]. We thought it was a high stick, but what are you going to do? That was a great series. But that last game, we figured that we had it locked up. And out of the blue, they score that goal, and we're scrambling again.

STAN FISCHLER: And then in the overtime, the Rangers took over and nearly won it. I think it was Bob Brooke and one of the Olympic players both looked like they had Smith beaten, and he made the save. And the ironic part of it was on the winning goal, there could have been a penalty I believe on Tonelli in the left corner, that wasn't called. And then of course, Kenny Morrow with the magic stick.

DUANE SUTTER: It always seemed to be a hero that nobody would expect, to step up and get the big goal. And that year, it was Kenny. The puck had come around the boards, and he boomed a snapshot on net, and it found its way in. It was players like Kenny that kept the team ticking through the first few four Cups, and quietly went about his business and contributing in his own way. But a very quiet way. That's why we were a good team.

KEN MORROW: I was on the ice for the tying goal, when Don Maloney scored. So I felt terrible about that. It was just a terrific hockey game - the rivalry, the drama, and everything else. A lot of people consider that one of the best games ever in the NHL. In overtime, that was up and down. Billy Smith making a huge save on Bob Brooke. Billy makes a great save, the puck turns around and goes to the other end, and I slid down, and just tried to get down one of my patented slow-moving shots through onto the net. Pat Flatley had Glen Hanlon screened. He really never saw it. I wasn't able to score a lot of goals, but that's one that I'll always remember. And people still remind me about it - all the Rangers fans!

BOB NYSTROM: Kenny Morrow came up with some pretty big goals, for a guy who only scored I think a handful. I remember that play pretty vividly, where he let a little wrist shot go. It wasn't a hard shot.

CLARK GILLIES: That's nothing more than anything everybody wanted between the Islanders and the Rangers in a great series. I believe Kenny Morrow was just off the right face-off hash mark, close to the boards, and fired something through that beat Glen Hanlon. Kenny was the sleeper of all sleepers. You talk about Bossy, Trottier, Potvin, Smitty, me, Tonelli, and Nystrom - you go down the line - it would take somebody that didn't really know that team a long time to get to Kenny Morrow.

That son of a gun, I'll tell you, he was as strong a defenseman as you'll ever find. He just played solid D. I'm sure the other players that played left wing against Kenny Morrow probably dreaded it all night long. He had like gorilla strength - *incredibly* strong. But the one thing about Kenny is you go back and you look back at the goals he scored in the Stanley Cup playoffs, they just were quietly big goals. I mean, that goal he scored against the Rangers was obviously a huge goal. But a lot of them were with games on the line, and all of a sudden, Kenny busts out of nowhere, and he's got the puck and an empty net. Just makes the big play that causes an empty net goal, because he was always on the ice when it came down to that situation.

STAN FISCHLER: I remember it very well, because we were in the studio, and the TV studio was right across from the Ranger room, so Barry Beck and Nicky Fotiu were in there watching it with us, and of course, they were rooting for the Rangers, which wasn't very nice! Then they tie it, and these guys ran out. Then when we won it. It was unbelievable.

GORD LANE: It was a classic Rangers/Islanders game. We, again, understood that we would be able to win, and I think with the Rangers, you could just see the emotion in them - they tried so hard. And be it fate or whatever it was, it just wasn't to be. In retrospect, you can kind of feel bad for some of those guys, like Maloney. You'd just see, it wasn't going to happen for them.

KEN MORROW: It wasn't weird [to play against Herb Brooks, who coached Morrow on the 1980 Olympic team] - I always wished Herb well. Unfortunately for him, his teams were coming up against the Islanders at that time. I've had people tell me that Herb had all kinds of success in college and he won the Gold Medal, and then they said, "But he never had a very good NHL career." Well, they're wrong. Herb Brooks, in the years he coached the Rangers, they set some records for points. They were getting 90/100 points a couple of those years in the standings. What happened is they kept bumping into us in the playoffs. They had us on the ropes in that series when I had the overtime goal. If it wasn't for getting knocked out by the Islanders a few of those years, they may have been in the Finals a couple of those years. Herb was a terrific coach. He had success at every level.

DAVE LANGEVIN: Being from Minnesota here, I talked to Herbie a lot, and I think the thing is the Rangers *were* good enough to win a Stanley Cup, but they just couldn't get by us. I really don't remember a lot of that series - I just know that every Rangers series was a memorable series, because they wanted to beat us. I'm sure they got tired of hearing about us winning. That was probably the best Rangers team they had since I was there, and their chance of winning a Stanley Cup was high - if they got through us. It's amazing how some of those shots go in. You're shooting four feet wide, it goes off a skate, and it goes in. I give a lot of respect to the Rangers at that time. It was tough probably for them - we had one summer of it, when the Islanders lost to them in the playoffs. And they had to put up with that *five years* with us.

BOB BOURNE: Playing the Rangers was the most fun. I think it was some of the best hockey that I've ever seen. Those games were so crazy - you'd go into the Garden, and it was such a tough place to play for the Islanders because the fans were rabid down there. We just had so many good hockey games. We were the better hockey team, and sometimes, there was almost a look of defeat on the Rangers. I remember that series about that. They just knew we had something going for us, and they weren't going to win.

PAT FLATLEY: I remember Scott Stevens and Rod Langway [of the Washington Capitals, during the Division Finals] - very tough defensemen and very physical. And in that arena, the heat. That was before they had driers for the gloves. I remember it being so hot in there, and the sweat, where you really had to hold your stick tight, and at times, you'd miss an opportunity because your stick would slide in your hands, because of the moisture. Other than that, Washington didn't have the same intensity as the Rangers series - in my mind. But they had some very dangerous players; they were a really good hockey team. I think we matched up well against them.

DUANE SUTTER: The Capitals were a team that had quietly gotten better and better. They had drafted well and were a very well-coached team with Bryan Murray. It was too bad that they were in the Patrick Division. A team like that probably would have had more playoff success if there still would have been the 1-16 playoff format. They probably would have been able to work their way into the Semis or the Finals on a more regular basis. They were a good team - a good, skilled, young team, that scored a lot of goals. Goaltending always seemed to be their thorn in their side.

JEAN POTVIN: Our father died during the second series against Washington. Dad died on April 16th [from lung cancer]. I was in Washington, I was in my room at the hotel. I got a call from about 5:00 in the morning from my older brother, Bob, who was in Ottawa. We had been getting phone calls almost daily about how dad was doing. And whenever I could - Denis couldn't - I would take off, like on a Friday afternoon, fly up to Ottawa - which was an hour and 30 minute flight - spend some time with my mother, then we'd go to the hospital to see dad. He wasn't doing well. But I got the call from Bob, who told me that dad had passed away. So we chatted a little bit, and I said, "Look, I better tell Denis." Because the game was that night [game four]. So I let him sleep a little bit, and I went knocking on his door around 6:00.

When he opened the door and saw that it was me, he knew as well. So we sat together - we cried, we reminisced. Dad was not only a great guy, but he was one of the funniest guys we had ever met. He had an unbelievable sense of humor. We'd retell some of the stories that we had together found to be very funny, and stuff like that. He asked me, "What should I do tonight?" And I said the old cliché, "What do you think dad would want you to do? That does not mean that you have to do it." He says, "No, you're absolutely right. I can't not play. Dad would be very disappointed if I didn't make the effort to go out there and play." So he decided to play [the Islanders would win, 5-2].

He played well, but throughout the rest of the playoffs, Denis was *not* "Denis Potvin." He was not playing with the edge that he always had. Played well, but again, it wasn't the same Denis Potvin. And being the captain of the team, you're trying to win five Cups, there's your leader - it affects the other guys that are watching him out there, and they feel bad for him and they feel for him.

I remember him saying something to me after the playoffs. "Subconsciously, I never realized that every time I went out to play, my subconscious was telling me that somehow, some way, my father is either listening to the game or watching the game." Because my dad was funny like that. Our mother would tell us stories about how dad over the years had probably bought like 35 different radios, and she would catch him up in the second floor bathroom, in the corner by the window, trying to tune in the game. He knew every station - whether it was in Edmonton or Calgary or Boston or Toronto. And he was trying all these radios to "See if maybe I can get the game in Toronto. I had good success last time by going in the basement and opening the basement door." So we knew that dad would always somehow find a way to know what the hell happened to a certain extent.

I remember my dad - he did it to Denis, and I didn't know he did it to him - I had told Denis, "He's a real son of a gun. He called me this afternoon at home, and he said, 'Did you play last night?' I said, 'Yeah, I played last night. Why?' He says, 'Well, I didn't see your name in the summary. You didn't get a penalty, you didn't get an assist, you didn't get a goal. You didn't make much of an impression, did you?'" All these little digs, right? That's what Denis brought up. "Y'know, I never realized how much I played for dad. And all of a sudden, when he went, I guess that's what made me not be myself anymore. Because I knew if I didn't play a good game, dad would somehow find out about it."

Dad would speak to scouts. They'd always come every year to visit us in New York - several times, on their way to Florida at the end of the year, and then on their way back they'd stop at New York. All during the playoffs - maybe one month at our house, another month at Denis' house. Christmas time, he'd say, "How has Denis been playing? I want the truth, I don't want you to bullshit me." And then my dad would come right back at us if he didn't like what he'd heard. So anyway, Denis was not the same.

But that year was a strange year, in that I think Bryan cracked ribs, and he played with cracked ribs - I think it may have even happened in the Washington series. Even though he was taped up every game, you have trouble walking and breathing when you have cracked ribs. And he's a tough son of a gun - he went out and played. But obviously, he was not the same Bryan Trottier. If I remember correctly, Bossy was hurt. I think it was a shoulder injury. The year we were going for five, I think Clark scored twelve goals, because Bossy wasn't healthy, Trottier wasn't healthy. Dave Langevin had an injured shoulder - I don't know if it was dislocated or separated - but I think he played with a harness. And if it hadn't been for the playoffs, they probably would have said, "Go get your shoulder fixed" or "You're going to take some time off until it's better." But in the playoffs, you play with injuries that you would not play during the regular season with [despite the injuries, the Islanders would beat the Capitals, 4-1].

CLARK GILLIES: Guys would go out and play keep-away. They'd throw one puck on the ice, and five or six guys would try and keep it away from one another. And Patty wounded up getting fallen on by somebody, and twisted his ankle, before we played the Montreal Canadiens in the third round. So it put a lot of extra work on Trottier and Goring…it put extra work on everybody. Just little things that started to happen.

PAT FLATLEY: The main thing would be [goaltender] Steve Penney was kind of a phenom - like an up-and-comer. He was playing really well, and sure enough, he beats us the first two games [3-0 and 4-2]. And I think it was Mike Bossy who said, "Everything at him has to be high. Just keep pounding it." And sure enough, that's what everybody did. Eventually, it worked.

I remember getting in the bus [after the Islanders were down 2-0 in the series], and I was almost in tears - I was really upset about our position in the series. I remember John Tonelli sitting down next to me, and saying, "What's your problem?" I said, "This sucks." He said, "These guys are nothing. They're done - *we've got them right where we want them.* We're good now. We've got them figured out." And sure enough, we won four straight. They figured out Steve Penney. They were so confident about beating them - even though they were down two games to nothing - it was just a great feeling for me, to have somebody sit down next to me, and say, "Relax. We're going to get them." And I believed him.

DUANE SUTTER: A lot of these series, we had the quiet confidence in us, even though there was some new blood in the line-up, there was enough veteran leadership to persevere through some adversity in the series. I remember Al coming in and said, "I don't care if the roof caves in! We don't change! We keep playing the same way!" And you know what? He really drilled that into us. That was one of the reasons why there was never a lot of panic in our game. There was adversity and pressure put on us by other teams, but really, deep down, there wasn't a lot of panic in our game [the Islanders would come back to beat the Canadiens, 4-2].

GARY "BABA BOOEY" DELL'ABATE: What do they say, "Once is a fluke, twice could be luck, but three times means you belong there." The fourth Cup was amazing, but the fifth Cup was the one you really wanted, because you wanted to tie the Canadiens [who won five Cups from 1956-1960], because the Canadiens were the ones that kept you down so long from getting there. It really was that you wanted to tie greatness.

Division Semi-Finals (3-2):

New York Islanders over New York Rangers

Game 1	April 4	New York Rangers 1	New York Islanders 4
Game 2	April 5	New York Rangers 3	New York Islanders 0
Game 3	April 7	New York Islanders 2	New York Rangers 7
Game 4	April 8	New York Islanders 4	New York Rangers 1
Game 5	April 10	New York Rangers 2	New York Islanders 3 (OT)

Division Finals (4-1):

New York Islanders over Washington Capitals

Game 1 April 12 Washington Capitals 3 New York Islanders 2
Game 2 April 13 Washington Capitals 4 New York Islanders 5 (OT)
Game 3 April 15 New York Islanders 3 Washington Capitals 1
Game 4 April 16 New York Islanders 5 Washington Capitals 2
Game 5 April 18 Washington Capitals 3 New York Islanders 5

Conference Finals (4-2):

New York Islanders over Montreal Canadiens

Game 1 April 24 New York Islanders 0 Montreal Canadiens 3
Game 2 April 26 New York Islanders 2 Montreal Canadiens 4
Game 3 April 28 Montreal Canadiens 2 New York Islanders 5
Game 4 May 1   Montreal Canadiens 1 New York Islanders 3
Game 5 May 3   New York Islanders 3 Montreal Canadiens 1
Game 6 May 5   Montreal Canadiens 1 New York Islanders 4

CHAPTER 32:

STANLEY CUP '84

Can the Oilers dethrone the Islanders as reigning Stanley Cup champs, on their second try?

STAN FISCHLER: Again, the attrition multiples - we're talking about the same guys. So you had the core, and it looked encouraging. But how many teams have won five Cups in a row? Only one. And when the Canadiens won it, it was only two rounds. So realistically, we were hopeful, but not that it was in the bag.

DUANE SUTTER: Getting to the Finals was a huge accomplishment - based on the number of injuries we had. We were a really banged up team that year.

CLARK GILLIES: When we got to the Finals, Smitty had groin problems, Denis Potvin had knee problems, Bobby Bourne had knee problems, Nystrom had shoulder problems. It just took us a lot longer to get to the Finals. And the wear and tear along the way really hurt us.

GORD LANE: Shoulder - old age started to catch up to us. I think I played against Montreal [but did not play in the Stanley Cup Finals].

BOB NYSTROM: We were pretty confident. But we were pretty banged up, too. I would have to say a couple of our star players were definitely hurting. I think Trots and Boss were hurting. You're not going to survive in a series like that without your big guns.

JIGGS McDONALD: I think a little bit of that [the Oilers being media darlings] was generated by the league office. I think the National Hockey League itself was tired of the New York Islanders winning the Stanley Cup year after year, being a contender. They weren't the New York Rangers, they weren't "the big market team." Yeah, they played not all that far from Manhattan, and the team - to their credit - didn't go looking for the back page of the sports pages. Didn't really make that a priority with them. They just went about their job quietly. Endorsements, - ads for a car dealer in one particular case - were frowned on. "No outside distractions. Just keep this thing going." That was the only time that the Stanley Cup Finals had been decided on the basis of 2-3-2 [instead of the usual 2-2-1-1-1]. That speaks volumes. The league did everything in their power to knock the Islanders off the stand. But you could see it coming. In the back of our minds, the league was trying to "throw sand on the ice" - anything to slow the Islanders down, and get this momentum under control.

BILL TORREY: We were ganged up on in a number of ways, and one of them was the way they changed the series format. And that worked very much against us. We had a tough Semi-Finals series in order to get there, and Edmonton had a seven-day hiatus out west [actually an eight-day hiatus, whereas the Islanders had a four-day hiatus]. They swept through everybody, so they had a nice rest period before we went against them. And we lost the first game in our building, 1-0 - on a shot from a bad angle that went in on the short side of the net. We did not play well in that game...actually, Edmonton wasn't that great, either.

DAVE LANGEVIN: I didn't play that game [the first game], but I was up watching it. I can't remember who scored it, but someone went around Denis, then he deeked out Smitty.

CLARK GILLIES: It was a goal scored by Kevin McClelland, basically from the red line, shot it at the net, towards the net, hit the back of Smitty's pads, and went in.

STAN FISCHLER: The deciding game was that 1-0 game. It was a cheap goal, angle shot - I can still set it - and Smitty blew it. It was one of those things. At the other end, Fuhr was playing out of his mind. And that's hockey, what are you going to do?

BILL TORREY: And then the next game, Clark Gillies got three goals and we dominated them in our building, and beat them 6-1.

CLARK GILLIES: They come out and we beat them 6-1, and it was like they didn't even show up. They said, "We came here to do what we wanted to do. Now we can go home and win it at home."

BOB BOURNE: Once they got a little taste of that, they got the first one out of the way, and then we went up to their building, it was going to be pretty tough to stop them three straight games. They didn't win easily, but there was a sense of them taking it over. They had the momentum and they had a team that could play any way, too - they were a real tough team.

BILL TORREY: And then we went to Edmonton, where we had to play the next three games. We couldn't get a hotel room downtown - we had to stay at a hotel out on the outskirts of town. Mike Bossy was hurt, Stefan Persson couldn't play, Denis Potvin had just lost his father. Our team, we couldn't match them - they were better than we were. There's no ifs, ands, or buts. But like I say, the guys even to this day, when everybody talks about how Edmonton was the best team - we played them three series and we beat them two out of three series. I have a tough time selling Bobby Nystrom on that...

BRYAN TROTTIER: Lots of things. It was Edmonton's time as a group. Hats off to them, more than anything else. I think if we would have stayed together as a group...I don't know if "the kids" were ready. This is no slight to them - the kids that were inserted played extremely well. Again, not that it was their fault, but there's chemistry involved in this whole thing. Had we stayed together as a group, maybe something different would have happened. Who knows? Not taking anything away from Edmonton, because it was their time, they played extremely well. Messier by himself was just a menace. Their goaltender played phenomenal - we out-shot them I think in three of the five games we played. And probably the biggest reason I always think, I have no clue why this happened - the 2-3-2. It was an extreme disadvantage. For whatever reason, the league or committee decided to change it to 2-3-2, and it never happened before. It was just one of those things - maybe it was psychological, maybe we didn't handle it right. Maybe it is just a tremendous advantage, or too huge of a disadvantage to overcome. But again, no slight to Edmonton, because they were just a powerhouse.

STAN FISCHLER: I think they had the idea that it would be cheaper, it would be worth experimenting for one year [with the 2-3-2 format]. The travel - Edmonton and back - is very difficult. I don't think they have even to this day that you can go from New York to Edmonton non-stop. I think you have to change in Minnesota. They figured, "Why should we spend all this dough?" So they got away with it for one year [actually one more year - 1985 - before returning to the 2-2-1-1-1 format]. It was set up in Edmonton's favor - I think they put the Islanders at some crummy hotel and it was all kinds of behind-the-scenes shenanigans. But what the heck, they won. Their time had come. And alibis are out the window - forget about it.

EDDIE WESTFALL: Wasn't that silly? It was something that had been part of hockey forever - the four out of seven series. If you're looking for an excuse, it's like golf - you can always find one. But I don't think that is an excuse for why the Islanders didn't make it. I just couldn't figure out - it was kind of disconcerting to the fans and the players. "What the hell is this all about?" And I don't know if anybody ever had an answer to it, other than people in the NHL front office decided to try it. I never could figure out…the only thing I can think is a little less traveling. Because it's east to west, it's a long trip back and forth when you go 2-2-1-1-1. Maybe they thought it would be for better hockey, if the players weren't so tired from travel.

JIGGS McDONALD: The fact that it was 2-3-2, the fact that the phones in the their rooms kept ringing in the middle of the night, and they changed hotels in Edmonton.

DAVE LANGEVIN: It was kind of like they just wanted to find a way to dethrone us. And they finally did with that stupid…they went to the NBA/2-3-2, which I don't think is good for any sport, because you go to some place and you play three in a row, it's kind of hard. But still, all we had to do was win the games at home.

CLARK GILLIES: I've still never really gotten an answer for this in all the years since I've retired.

BOB BOURNE: I think Mr. Sather had a lot to do with it.

CLARK GILLIES: Somebody from the NHL offices, which were at that time, in Montreal, decided that the Finals weren't going to be 2-2-1-1.

BOB NYSTROM: It was tough going into their building for three games. No question about that.

JEAN POTVIN: We were just not the same team that we had been the previous four years in the playoffs. We had baggage with injuries. And I remember watching my brother play, and it made me sad. Because I could tell that no matter what was going on, it was like he was in somewhat of a daze. Sometimes I'd catch him out there, and I'd say, "What the fuck is he doing? Denis, *snap out of it!*" It's like, all of a sudden, he'd start staring, and he's on the ice. What are you staring at? The play is over there!

AL ARBOUR: We didn't like it at all [the switching of the game format]. And we couldn't stay in our hotel - they had the rooms rented, and we stayed way out of town. The players had nothing to do. We knew we were done, right then. We stayed way, way out. The players...I don't know, we didn't have the same thing, the same fight or something like that.

CLAIRE ARBOUR: That was difficult. We were in Edmonton, and when all is said and done, what happened there, the only time they had us there for three games, that was not the set-up that hockey was used to. And that was an awfully long time [to be there]. And then what they did in Edmonton, because they had some convention or some darn thing there, they had no rooms for the Islanders, and they put us out in the boonies, away from everything. The thing with the playoffs, you almost have to be kept in the groove of things, in order to not come down from it. And they were away from the hotel where they had the trophies and all the stuff you keep yourself all wound up and thinking about it. I was there, and I could just see it. It was just like, "Wow. *Why are we here?*" There was nowhere to shop, nothing to do, nothing to look at. And you could just see the team was really exhausted.

We just talked to Zdeno Chára the other day, he called before the season started - he always likes to connect with Al. He has a place down here in Florida, just down the road from us. And he didn't have time. He said, "This was a short summer." And that's what happens when you win the Stanley Cup - you have very short summers. So when you think of it, we had *four* short summers. To keep athletes that geared and at their best all those many years, it had taken its toll physically and emotionally. And they really thought they could do it. It would have been nice, but I don't think they had the energy to do it again. It had been a long, long time. You barely have time to come down from that, and then you have to get yourself ready for the next season. It was like a wound-up machine. It was a different time in our lives.

KEN MORROW: We just never were able to change the momentum once they got going up there. Give them all the credit in the world - they won three straight on home ice, and we just couldn't stop it. Looking back, if we'd have been able to win just one game and get it back to home ice, they still might have beaten us in our building, but it would have been nice just to get it back to Long Island, just to give it one last shot. And we weren't able to do that. Looking back, if the series was the old way, we would have at least gotten back to our building to try and win and change the momentum. But we weren't able to do that, and they were the champions. They deserved it.

PAT FLATLEY: We would have had a much better chance to win if we got to come back to Long Island for game five. That still annoys me, because Edmonton had a huge advantage at home - with that super-fast ice, and that type of team that they had. I thought it was a big edge for them. And we were a different team in our building, and Edmonton would be a different team in our building, too. If they go up three games to one, and they come home, and then it's three games to two and we've got to go back there, they might get a little tight, and "Here we go again." But when they get that three games at home, that's a tough scenario. I'm glad they stopped that. They won two Cups with it, in the exact same fashion - they split in Philadelphia, and then they won at home [in 1985].

JIMMY DEVELLANO: Oh sure, absolutely [Devellano continued to follow the Islanders]. I was with the Red Wings, and I missed out on "Stanley Cup #4," because I was with the Red Wings, and then of course, they had a chance to win five. I was looking up at the scoreboard and watching. Oh sure [in response to if Jimmy was pulling for the Islanders to win a fifth Cup], because a lot of those players I drafted, so a lot of those players were mine. You always want them to do well.

MIKE McEWEN: I was following that pretty close. The year before, Edmonton would take a lot of chances in their end with the puck. And it cost them a goal or two a game in the Finals before. And the next year, Roger Neilson came on board, and I'd known Roger from when I was a kid - he grew up in the same community that I did. He's all about defense and taking care of the puck. In their own end, they were unbelievably responsible - they played like any other team in their own end for the first time I ever saw. They just played good defense and they took care of the puck. Once they got outside the blue line, they opened up their offense. I've got a feeling that was all Roger Nielson. They got smart. They learned not to give up bad goals. And then Messier took it over.

PAT FLATLEY: This team just never stopped believing. After the fourth game, we all went out and had a team dinner, and everyone said, "No worries - *the next one's ours."* And it turned out not to be ours, and it was devastating. The most devastating part was I thought we were going to be right back there the following season, but as I've learned, it's not quite so easy to get there. I guess the thing that stands out in the series was Messier and Gretzky - they were very difficult to counter. They were on fire. Even though it was a 2-3-2, could we have contained that pair, along with Grant Fuhr and Paul Coffey? I don't know. I think it might have been their time.

DUANE SUTTER: I know I was in the penalty box for a couple of goals in the final game up there, and that still doesn't sit well with me. But you know what? I was an agitating player, and I prided myself on getting under the opponent's skin and contributing on the scoreboard when I could through the playoffs. When it was all said and done, our injuries and the challenges that we had faced through that first three rounds had caught up with us. Edmonton had matured and learned through their previous two-plus seasons. They were ready to raise the Cup - much to our disliking.

AL ARBOUR: What stands out was the last game, that we lost. We should have lost to Montreal in the playoffs - we were lucky to get by them. We didn't have anything left. The players were all dead. We knew darn well that we were finished that year.

BOB NYSTROM: You're just destroyed [after losing the Stanley Cup Finals]. A lot of the guys were really, really destroyed. Because you're there and you're so close. We were all getting a little older. It was just a very, very tough series.

DUANE SUTTER: It was probably more devastating because at that time, we realized that we had a significant run, a huge impact on NHL history. You sat there and looked around the room, and you think back to the first Stanley Cup, and see how guys had matured and aged. Just by sitting there after the last game, you had come to realize that there was going to be some changes going forward.

BOB BOURNE: I think the hardest thing in sports is going to the last game and losing. Certainly, no one remembers who finished second. I can't even go back to last year and figure out who finished second. Very somber. I think we were so tired, but we had guys in the stands that played a regular role in the four Cups. When you get some of the key players out, and we had to bring up some guys from the minors - and nothing against them, but it wasn't the same hockey team in that last series. I'm not giving any excuses or anything, but we weren't the same team as we were the year before.

AL ARBOUR: It was a very crushing loss. At that point I couldn't really think straight. It was very, very disappointing.

GARY "BABA BOOEY" DELL'ABATE: Just what a bummer it was. You really wanted it. It was going to be history. I mean, already, that team has to be remembered as one of the greatest teams of all time, but it would have put them in that "upper-echelon."

DAVE LANGEVIN: I didn't like the way we lost. That's all. Because I think the team gave up. That's just my feeling. I think everybody just had enough. And maybe it was different for me, because my dad died during the playoffs…it was a tough time for everybody. Denis' dad died during the playoffs, too. It was just the way everything fell apart at the end. You could hear guys saying, "I think I've had enough" and "We had a good run." Stuff like that. I just never give up.

BILL TORREY: We played Edmonton in the Quarter-Finals in 1981 and beat them. It's an interesting thing that I raise every once in a while I'm around Glen Sather - we played the Oilers three series in the Stanley Cup and playoffs and we only lost to them once. And unfortunately, it was the year we lost to them in the Finals. The year before, we beat them four straight, and Smitty was the Conn Smythe winner - and deservedly so. And hey, they were a great, scary, fabulous team. Take nothing away from them. But when you beat somebody four straight, I think it sends a message. And all I know that since then, every time I see Gretz, Messier, or any of those guys, they all say the same thing - they learned an awful lot in losing that series. And we weren't 100%. We had a lot of guys hurting. So, to lose in your 20th, after winning 19 consecutive series - and I don't know of any sports team yet [that accomplished that feat]. Montreal won five Cups in a row, but they only played twelve series in those days. We had to play 19 series to win four, and almost get a fifth. I know that the guys, whenever I'm around them, they all quietly say, "Let somebody else try and beat that record."

EDDIE WESTFALL: The Islanders and Edmonton were the only teams to win the Stanley Cup in the '80s…Montreal won it once [as did the Calgary Flames], they interrupted the string that Edmonton was in. But primarily, those two teams won the Cups in the '80s.

STAN FISCHLER: Bottom line is the law of averages caught up with the Islanders in every way. Fatigue. You just don't win them all. Like the Penguins in the '90s, they won two in a row, and the Islanders torpedoed them [in 1993].

DAVE LANGEVIN: I kind of figure the Stanley Cups as the first one, you're just glad because you never won one. The second one was to prove that the first one wasn't a fluke. And the third one to me was we were the best team and we deserved it. And the fourth one we won, I was just glad, because my dad died after that. It was nice because he was there to enjoy the Stanley Cups, and he got to drink out of the Cup. The fifth one, it's still tough for me to watch, because I still think that's our Cup. You hate to lose it. It was just a sad ending.

CLARK GILLIES: It took a while, but we realized that all good things come to an end. It was very disappointing - I can't tell you how upset I was. I don't cry very often...well, I cry at Hallmark commercials, if you ask my kids. But I was very, very disappointed when we lost that fifth Cup. Nobody liked to lose, but if we could have mustered up enough strength to win that...the interviews after that were tough to do. You've got to give a lot of credit, I'm sure the phrase "Passing the torch" was used a lot in the post-game interviews.

I really thought that after they beat us that that was a team that could go on and win at least five or six [in a row] - they were just kids when they beat us. They won the next two, and if not for an errant pass in '86 against Calgary - Steve Smith, who is kind of like "the Bill Buckner" of the Edmonton Oilers - who knows? I really thought that they would win as many as us and Montreal and maybe more. But as it turns out, they won five out of seven.

It was difficult to face the press and face people after we lost, I can't tell you...it was very emotional, and we were all very upset. It took a couple of days to get over it. At the end of the day, you look back and go, "Man, that was some tremendous run." You just can't draw that up on paper. I've always said those 20 or 23 guys, they're pals, my buddies, and we went through hell together to get those four - and almost five - Cups. You never forget that.

DUANE SUTTER: When it was all said and done, *19 consecutive playoff series wins.* That record will never, never, never be broken.

Stanley Cup Finals (4-1):

Edmonton Oilers over New York Islanders

Game 1	May 10	Edmonton Oilers 1	New York Islanders 0
Game 2	May 12	Edmonton Oilers 1	New York Islanders 6
Game 3	May 15	New York Islanders 2	Edmonton Oilers 7
Game 4	May 17	New York Islanders 2	Edmonton Oilers 7
Game 5	May 19	New York Islanders 2	Edmonton Oilers 5

CHAPTER 33:

AFTERMATH

So close to winning a fifth consecutive Cup, some question why the NHL suddenly opted to change the format in 1984. Sabotage, perhaps?

GORD LANE: It boils down to our success for so many years before. When you end up at the top of the league year after year, you end up with lower and lower draft picks. Their franchise was built initially by getting that number one pick, and they were very fortunate they were able to get some guys like Bryan, Boss, etc. But I think as the guys started to get a little bit older, the new guys who came in - other than say, Pat LaFontaine - there wasn't that same kind of chemistry. And the chemistry had as much to do with it as the ability. We won because it was such a close-knit group, of guys like Wayne Merrick, who centered the Banana Line, to Chico, to Boss and Trots, and Hector Marini, and Dave Langevin. There was this chemistry there. It was kind of like the spokes of a bike. Then when they started to replace guys - which that's the nature of the beast - after a certain stage, you have to rejuvenate. I think that culture, the guys that came in were good guys and good hockey players, but there was just that culture thing that wasn't quite…it started to change a bit.

DAVE LANGEVIN: That was a strange atmosphere on the team that year. That's when we had LaFontaine and Flatley come in, and it seemed like they wanted to make those two guys "the marquee players," and Trots and Boss were supposed to be "third and fourth players" now. It started right before the playoffs, when Boss was trying to get his 50 goals, and he was kind of taken off the power play and things like that. If it wasn't for the last game of the season…I think what, did he get three goals? So to put him in that situation, it just shows what kind of a great player he is, but I think before we got to the playoffs that year, the team was starting to lose…it was just that mental or that feeling of that things are changing. It's hard for me to say things like that, but I don't think you use the playoffs to groom players for the future. I think Trots and Boss and a lot of the players that got the four before should have been the ones that got the chance, and the other guys should earn their keep.

The thing was they were trying to change the image of the team to LaFontaine and Flatley. Maybe getting away from us being…at that time with the Oilers coming up, they could see maybe they were going more with weaving and speed. And I think we didn't stick with our style of play in the playoffs. We tried to change our style to try and meet the Oilers, which wasn't the style of team we had. I think if we would have stuck with what got us the other four Cups, I think we would have won five. Because in the Finals that year, we won the year before by putting Butch Goring on Wayne Gretzky. We never did that in that one. It doesn't go on forever. We were getting beat up, we were getting old. Not old, it was just physically starting to get to us. We went to the Finals five years in a row, and we had two Canada Cup series in that time. We played probably about 500 games. Say, you play over 100 games a year, five years in a row. Maybe it was just Edmonton's time.

AL ARBOUR: I don't agree with that standpoint [that the Islanders focused too much on the younger players during that fifth Stanley Cup run]. The players were hurt, and that's why they played so much in the playoffs. The players were hurting, and Denis wasn't "Denis" at all. He lost somebody in his family and he wasn't the same. So I knew right away we were in trouble.

PAT FLATLEY: I'm still friends with a lot of guys on that team, and they feel bad that we didn't win the fifth one. They've told me, "It would have been great for you to get one." I think there were probably some people that thought that Pat and I might have hurt their "Drive for Five," and other people would say they might not have made it to the Finals without us. As a hockey player, I don't think those are decisions or perspectives that I'm entitled to have, really. My job is to play hockey, and it's the coach's job to decide who should play, and the manager's job. So that's how I always looked at my career and the circumstances around it. I really don't want to have an opinion on that, because I don't think I'm entitled to, really.

BRYAN TROTTIER: I thought we got disbanded too quick. I think the playoffs, 2-3-2, never happened again. No one ever presses that issue - we don't scream it from the rooftop, either, we just recognize it for what it is, because it certainly wasn't traditional hockey. Maybe a little bit the timing of everything, and how evolution is. The coaching evolution, the player evolution - it worked against the Islander tradition of the late '70s/early '80s. Although we were a core group that grew up together, the core group seemed to get disbanded pretty quickly.

JP PARISÉ: Mr. Torrey kept most of those guys too long, and that's what [caused] the demise eventually. It took a long time, but he was very loyal to his players and to the good guys. He never got the draft picks that he should have got, and trade some of those guys. That's a hard business. But how do you replace a guy like Trottier, and a guy like Bossy, who had to retire early [in 1987, at the age of 30], and Potvin? You don't replace guys like that. It took him a long time to recover from that.

BRUCE BENNETT: You would see teams that would change up one or two parts from year to year, and bring in one or two players or three players. A younger guy in their organization would be able to be brought up, and supplement the mix of veterans and guys with the experience. And what happened is - as what happens in a lot of the dynasty situations, especially through the '60s, '70s, '80s, and early '90s - it's a very fragile chemistry to mess with when you change bodies in and out. The Islanders were very good at maintaining those veterans and bringing up one or two guys, or trading one or two guys. They didn't really mess with the chemistry. But more so, what was the biggest problem was when they got to that year five against the Edmonton Oilers - Edmonton had lost the year before, and you always need to lose to understand how close you were. So they were more motivated in that year five, when they went up against the Islanders.

JIGGS McDONALD: Loyalty…and this is not meant as a knock against Bill Torrey - Bill did a tremendous job in building that team, replacing parts as he went along. But maybe some people got a little long in the tooth. And I go back to the fact that now you've gone five consecutive years - you've won 19 consecutive series of a different level of the game over those years. And that number of games takes a toll on the body and the mind. Maybe more so on the mind than a lot of people recognize. I think they were tired. They maybe missed the opportunity to move some players earlier, only because of loyalty and what they had done for the franchise. That's one aspect of it.

But then you move on a couple of years and you go through the ownership change [Pickett sold the team in 1992], the philosophy change. Bill Torrey was no longer "a smart man," he got "dumb" very quickly in the minds of the new owners. Garth Snow has been there quite a while now, but prior to that, you saw almost a "general manager of the year" kind of thing going down the pike. The four gentlemen that owned the team [Robert Rosenthal, Stephen Walsh, Ralph Palleschi, and Paul R. Greenwood], I think they had different outlooks as to what it took to win and how to go about it. One would say, "We need to get a defenseman," the other would say, "If we don't get a big right winger, we're not going anywhere."

The draft, the lack of patience in developing players and letting them stay at the junior level until they had matured a little more - a byproduct of the 18-year-old draft. Not having the experience in the minors, just being rushed into situations that they weren't ready for. Todd Bertuzzi comes to mind. Then you look at the situation with Brett Lindros and the concussion [Lindros was forced to retire in 1996 due to post-concussion syndrome, after playing only 51 NHL games]. Draft picks that didn't pan out.

I think when Jimmy Devellano left the team, the scouting didn't produce the type of individual that he had the good fortune of adding to the franchise, to the roster over the years. I think that was a huge loss to the overall Islander organization. But opportunities, you can't stop an individual that comes along so often - in Jimmy's case, to move to Detroit. And look what he's done there over the years. And then, you come forward to the Mike Milbury years - just general lack of common sense, or hockey sense. I'm sure he had a game plan, but going through that period of time, where if you were an Islander alumni, you had no part to play in the organization. It was the dark ages. We're still paying the price for that.

RON WASKE: It comes down to their drafting position. When you start to draft 23rd, 24th, 28th, you're not getting the top draft choices in the league. I think that was one thing. Jimmy Devellano's departure, Al Arbour's departure [Arbour retired in 1986, before returning as the Islanders' head coach from 1988-1994], and Bill Torrey departing [in 1992] - those were all reasons for the change. And I think they've had a difficult time with the whole picture of hockey. I'm sure that's why they're mired in a difficult situation now.

GLENN "CHICO" RESCH: It's been said that probably Bill Torrey held on to the guys longer than he should have years later, but nobody wanted to leave Long Island, and Torrey didn't want to trade guys that had gone to war for him. It was probably a little of the problem of going into the late '80s and early '90s, where the Islanders had the dip. But remember this, and I'm trying to tell people in New Jersey, when Denis Potvin is not in his prime anymore, Billy Smith, Mike Bossy, Butch Goring, Trots, Boss, Gillies, when these guys get older, you can't replace those guys. You try, like Pat LaFontaine, he came along and he was a great player. But was he Bryan Trottier? No, not quite at that level. Other guys that came along that they drafted were really good players, but...I just say this - a lot of times, you talk about the intangibles. That's sort of the fun part of writing books and stories and making it sound like, "Wow, if that hadn't of happened, they wouldn't have won."

But I've got tell you, from my experience around the NHL, the team that wins, 95% of the time had the best players. When the two buses for the two teams playing for the Cup pulled up to the arena, the team that wins the Cup, generally, the players getting off their bus were just a little bit better than the guys getting off the other bus. No one will convince me otherwise. Nowadays, a little bit different again, because free agency and all the things you can do at the trading deadline. So that's why that team won. Again, that's not to take anything away from anyone. Coaches and managers, they can screw things up - there's no question.

PAT FLATLEY: I was shocked [that the Islanders didn't return to the Finals again sometime in the mid-late '80s]. But if you're looking at us in a microscope, you can't just look at our team. Yeah, we were good. But you look at some of the other teams in the league, they were pretty damn good, too. So the competition I think may have gotten better. I think the league got better, and the different types of players. If you go back and compare the Vancouver Canuck team [that the Islanders played in the 1982 Stanley Cup] to the Edmonton Oilers, I think the Oilers were a much better team than the Canucks. And I think that continued through the '80s. The Islanders set the bar for everyone to catch, and "How are you going to beat the Islanders?" And then, I think people figured it out. Then we had ownership changes, management changes, players retiring, players getting traded. It wasn't the same team that won the Cups.

JIMMY DEVELLANO: It's unfortunate - the team has deteriorated, they've had all kinds of goofy owners come in. They really haven't had much stability. It's been a rough go for them. And those of us that are alumni are a little saddened by it. I've got my fingers crossed that maybe they're going in the right direction now. I've met Garth Snow on a few occasions, I like him. He's been on the job a while, so I'd like to think he's gathering experience and getting better. They did work to sign a couple of their younger players, I'm happy about that. But saying all that at the end of the day, you've got to be a playoff team in order to sell tickets. And I don't know if they are...I hope they're closer to that.

CHAPTER 34:

THE ARCHITECT

The Islanders' general manager from 1972-1992, Bill Torrey [inducted into the Hockey Hall of Fame in 1995].

STAN FISCHLER: Bill Torrey was one of the smartest executives in history. He - along with Jimmy Devellano - built the team that is unique. The only American team to win four Cups in a row. No team ever won 19 straight playoff series. [Torrey is] a lot of fun. Great sense of humor. And had the wisdom to hire Al Arbour.

JIMMY DEVELLANO: My mentor, a guy that gave me an opportunity to flap my wings. A good person, a good boss.

BOB NYSTROM: He was just such an expert at reading people. I think he, Jimmy Devellano, and Al worked in conjunction with each other, just to try and bring the cogs to the team. But Bill Torrey was really the engineer of it all. I think he pulled together an incredible group of people to assist them.

AL ARBOUR: He brought stability, and let me tell you, he knew what he was doing all the time.

CLAIRE ARBOUR: [Torrey and Arbour] had the best working relationship going. That's why it worked so well. They understood each other. They could yell at each other - I heard it once, and I thought, "Oh my gosh! They're having a fight!" Well, they weren't. They were just having "loud words." [Laughs] A line that I often used [that Torrey said] - "Arbour, there's no pleasing you. I could be trading *the whole team!*" But it was the heat of the moment after the game, and then the next morning, everything was fine. They would just move on.

LORNE HENNING: They called him "the Architect," but Bill and Al were obviously the two guys. Bill put the front office together - the scouting. He did all the trading. And the pieces, obviously, Al and Bill talked, and they knew what they needed. But Bill was the one that put it together, had a plan, and right from day one, wanted to save his draft picks. He knew we weren't going to be very good, but he knew drafting was a big part of it. He got Billy Harris, who turned into Butch Goring. And then he gets Denis Potvin, Trots, and Bossy. He basically built the team through the draft. You don't see that anymore, either. But he was the one that really had the plan, put it together, and gave Al the players.

BOB BOURNE: Bill Torrey was the most calming influence. He was a wonderful man. He and Al Arbour really became confidants of mine. Al was a little bit more closed, but he was a coach, and he had to be. But he was a funny guy. He wouldn't say a word to you for a month, and then he'd tell you that you were the best player on the team! He made you fly high, is what he did. He was a great motivator. We had so much respect for him. Even as a coach, he pissed you off a lot. And of course, when you're kids, you think you know everything. Especially when we're winning, we're thinking, "Well, what does he know?" But he knew everything, and he was the guiding force of it.

   Bill was a guy that…no, I didn't go into his office very much, but you could just walk down there and walk into his office. He had the time for you. And very professional, very introspective - if you asked him a question, he didn't give you an answer for a minute or two. But I always felt good around Bill. Every time I saw him, it was just a warm feeling. Very bright guy. You knew he really cared, and he cared about the players. I think with Bill and Al, that's what we really knew - they had our backs all the time.

EDDIE WESTFALL: Best at reading people. He hired all of the right people…I mean, it took him a while, but he got all the right people in the right jobs. And as a general manger, you're not supposed to know who the best hockey player is. Judging talent, I don't know if he could judge talent, but he hired the people that *could.* And when he hired Al Arbour, I mean, Al Arbour didn't have a lot of experience coaching, if he had any. But Torrey knew him as a person, and also, Jimmy Devellano worked at St. Louis the same time as Al Arbour was there. I have to think that Devellano had something to do with Torrey hiring Al Arbour.

BILLY HARRIS: He created it. He was able to put the whole cast of characters together, and weed out the ones that didn't fit in, and then bring other people in. He was a pretty smart guy, and he had good people skills. I never heard too many bad things said about Al Arbour or Bill Torrey. *Ever.*

CLARK GILLIES: He was the one who had to make the final decision on which players came in, who stayed, and who left. And I've got to say, made so many great decisions. He was the builder, he was the architect behind that whole franchise.

BRYAN TROTTIER: I always felt Bill was very organized. I always thought he had terrific motives. I thought he was a planner. There was no "knee jerk" with Bill. I liked the way he communicated to us. I always liked his demeanor - I thought he had a terrific composure about himself. He and Al, I thought we were a pretty good reflection of management.

DUANE SUTTER: Bill had an air about him where he could walk in the room, and all he had to say was a couple of words, and he'd get your attention. For myself, personally, he was a lot like a father to me, coming in as a 19-year-old kid and moving pretty much across Canada to the US to play.

JIGGS McDONALD: Again, a father figure. I think Bill has a huge, huge space in the heart of every guy that played for that franchise. I think he was as honest and straightforward with everybody. Good, solid negotiator when it came to contracts. But he had innate ability to recognize who would compliment whom on the forward line. He and Al worked together so closely, and had his rapport with his coach, where they trusted one another. He could say, "If you put so and so with Trottier and Bossy..." - if you think back, they alternated a lot of left wingers there. Gillies, Tonelli, Bourne - they all got a shot on that line. But Bill had that ability to be able to judge the talent and who would compliment whom.

NELSON DOUBLEDAY, JR: There's nobody better. He was a fabulous man - he knew his players, he knew his management, he knew his coaches, he knew what he was going to try and do. And he did it.

CLAIRE ARBOUR: He was the one that decided on player movement and all that. He would discuss with his staff, but he was pretty shrewd on his selection of players, and who would fit in nicely. They were on the same page for that.

JP PARISÉ: Just so clever and such a good general manger. And said the right things. [Laughs] When the general manager with the North Stars said, "Mr. Torrey would like to talk to you," I want to say it was a Sunday morning. And I think they were playing the following night. He says, "JP, we'd like to have you fly to New York right away." I said, "Jesus Christ. Bill, I've got to go to the bank!" I had a shitty attitude, because I didn't want to go to Long Island. I said, "I'll go there when I'm friggin' ready." I was obnoxious. And he didn't lose his cool, he said, "We got you because we need you. We think you can help the young kids, and with your leadership." He sold me a bill of goods. I was like, *"I'll be there right away!"* [Laughs]

DAVE LANGEVIN: Bill Torrey is the guy who put it all together. It all starts with the general manager, or more importantly, it starts with the owner. The owner gave Bill full reign and I think Bill hired some great people. If people are looking to win a Stanley Cup, I think they should look back at the '80s, and see how it was done.

MIKE McEWEN: I don't know how much luck there is in building a team like that. Trottier was drafted 22nd, and Bossy I want to say late first round - 15th or something. And they ended up being two superstars. Back then, it was so much simpler. Between him and Arbour, I played on a lot of organizations, and maybe David Poile and Bryan Murray had it, but those two guys were like *glue.* If you were talking to one, you were talking to the other. A lot of organizations, you can kind of feel the differences between the coach and general manager. But those two guys were on the same page all the way. I think that as kind of the strength of that deal. Torrey is an affable guy - you can talk to him. He was easy to talk to. I remember after the fourth Stanley Cup, I was in the press box, and we were going down the elevator together, me and him. He turns to me, and goes, "Well Mike, I know it's not the way you wanted it to work out." I just looked at him, and went, "Hey, *four Stanley Cups*. Who gives a fuck?!"

RON WASKE: Bill was a great executive. He let us do our job. He didn't micro-manage us. He had high expectations for us, but he wasn't a micro-manager. That allowed me a lot of freedom to do the things that I could do.

JIM PICKARD: Mastermind. Loyal. Very knowledgeable and very fair to everybody.

PAT FLATLEY: Accountability and stability.

KEN MORROW: Bill Torrey was "the Architect." That's what he's called, but that's an appropriate word for him. I've told people that in any sport - and this rings true today - you've got to have stability and leadership, starting from the top on down. And that's what the Islanders had. They had great leadership with Bill Torrey. Patience. And then it went down to Al Arbour, with just the strong presence of Al Arbour. You knew what was expected of you. You didn't have a turnover of general managers and coaches through those years. The players knew what to expect, they knew what was expected of them. They were the face of the New York Islanders, and they were the reason why those teams did what they did. And no more classier guy than Bill Torrey. He was fair with everyone.

CHAPTER 35:

RADAR

*The Islanders' head coach from 1973-1986 and 1988-1994,
Al Arbour [inducted into the Hockey Hall of Fame in 1996].*

EDDIE WESTFALL: Al Arbour wore glasses - he couldn't play without wearing glasses. He had the strap around the back of his head, to keep his glasses on. I think this was "pre-contact lens days." He had a sight problem, particularly without his glasses. So they nicknamed him "Radar," because he could operate pretty good without seeing as well as he needed to.

CLAIRE ARBOUR: New York was a tough market. We had been in St. Louis, where they adored their players. They just *idolized* their players. There's not the pressure you would ever, ever get in New York. I had two of my older kids working, and two of my younger kids still in school, so I had a foot in both worlds. And there was a lot of pressure in New York - the kids would come home and say what was said to them. And I'd always say, "Oh, don't say anything. We're just laughing all the way to the Stanley Cup." And Joanne, the one that was in the working force, would say, "Yeah, but we could win 15, and they'd always say, 'You're not as good as the Rangers'." There was always that element there. It was hard on the kids. Even the first year when we won the Stanley Cup, there were banners everywhere - "FIRE ARBOUR," "GET RID OF ARBOUR." Our youngest daughter, who grew up at the rink, would say, "Oh look, there's a sign about daddy up there." And I'd say, "Oh yeah. Don't pay attention to it." [Laughs] It was a tough year, until we won it. It was like, "Wow...*in spite of.*"

JIMMY DEVELLANO: Terrific guy, wonderful coach. Knew how to deal with people. Got screwed in St. Louis by the Blues when he coached. Came to the Islanders, and showed the Blues that he was maybe the best coach in hockey.

BILL TORREY: There's just no question that of all the decisions that I made while I worked for the Islanders for 23/24 years, whatever it was, that was the most important decision that I made. All the reasons that I wanted to hire him, and obviously, I had no idea he would remain our coach for 19 years. You don't see that very often. He was a special person, his family is special to me. We had a great relationship. Not always did we agree - we had a lot of "dandies." But we had one thing that we always did - when we had a difference of opinion, we would close the door, and we would come to a decision one way or another. He won some, and I won some. But in the end, when we reopened the door, we were 100% together. That doesn't happen in pressure and high stakes in pro sports very often. But I give him credit - he was competitive, he had a fire in him. Winning and making your mark and proving a point. No one would battle harder than Al.

GLENN "CHICO" RESCH: I think that the '80s Islanders teams certainly deserved the rewards they got, because it wasn't an easy journey. And certainly, I think Al Arbour and Billy Torrey really, really need recognition. A lot of the players are really happy that those two guys were rewarded, because they're both terrific gentlemen. They didn't play a lot of games, they didn't try and put this unnatural fear into you. There weren't threats. There wasn't crazy, angry speeches by Al or Torrey. It was straight up - "Here's the situation, boys."

Like, Al, if he's telling you something, he'll give you the chance to go out and see if you can make a change. If you don't, you sit for a while during the game. And then he'd say, "OK, go up to the press box and have a look, and see if you can find what you need to find by watching up there." If those three things didn't get your attention or you couldn't make the change over, then Bill was very good about saying, "OK Al, we're going to find someone who can." It was a secure but edgy...whatever that edge is - I don't know if it's peer pressure or never wanting to look like you're going to fail - that team had it.

LORNE HENNING: We had a couple of coaches before, but Al came in and gave us a system and discipline. I think discipline is probably the biggest thing for me. But the leadership part, too - his will and determination for me, he was a pretty impressive guy. Guys would go through the wall for him. But he was hard-nosed. He made you work and made you pay. If you didn't toe the line, you weren't going to play. It was his team - his leadership and his character built the team. The guys were sort of a reflection of him, basically.

GORD LANE: He was the core. On any successful sports franchise or even business, you mirror the leadership. And Arbour, he set the whole tone and everybody had the utmost respect for him.

BOB LORIMER: Al was such a great coach, and so good for me. Al was very good at making sure players did their job, so he didn't want you to do too much or too less. And that was illustrated one night in Vancouver, when I scored two goals, which is very unusual for me, because I typically only scored one a year. But I was feeling pretty good about myself after the game, and all the reporters were around your cubicle. And then Al came over to me, and said, "Can I see you in my office?" I thought he was going to say to me, "What a great game." And he proceeded to blast me, and said, "What the hell were you doing tonight? You're up the ice all night. I don't want you to do that." That really told me that Al didn't want you to do too much and he didn't want you to do too little. He was the best coach I ever had, in setting those parameters and figuring out what every player's strength was, and making sure that they played to their strengths, and not tried to do too much that would put them outside their comfort zone.

EDDIE WESTFALL: Al Arbour's on-the-job training is as good as it gets. I give him all of the credit he deserves. He was so good at coaching. He knew each player individually - what made them tick. He knew their moods, he knew when to push, when to lay off. And it was recognized by the players, because his idea was that, "Yeah, this guy might be a lot better player. But he's not going to get treated any better because he's a better player." And he never varied from it. *Ever*. If anything, he would go overboard, because he was going to be critical - privately, out on the ice when we stood around at times or in the dressing room, where it wasn't going to be evident to anybody but the players. I don't think you could say that he criticized any player in public, which is amazing when you think of what they went through together as coach and players. And not everybody was happy with each other all the time. But he managed to make it all work. There's some stories - particularly with a guy like Denis Potvin, who always felt that he should be treated special. [Laughs] The two of them, they wouldn't be going to each other's house for dinner, I can guarantee you.

CLAIRE ARBOUR: His work ethic rubbed off on them. A good coach sets the tempo. And I think they just read into him, what his expectations were. And he always drew the best out of every player. In fact, some reached more than they thought they could do. He had that gift of teaching them to dig deep. The biggest philosophy they had was that they had to care for one another - that it was a team effort at all time. That was what he projected.

BOB NYSTROM: Al is probably the best motivator that I've ever met. I think he has to be rated as one of the top coaches in the National Hockey League. There is no one who could push buttons better. He just had a way about him. And he really took it to heart, where he analyzed how he would deal with each individual on the team. There was no one that was the same. He just knew how to pat them on the back or kick them in the ass. Some guys, he would even embarrass in the room. But he knew which guys could take it. We looked at Al like a father figure. Many of us were like 19 years old when we first came there, and were with Al for the entire time.

KEN MORROW: You didn't always know what you were going to get, but that was what kept you off balance a little bit. I am stating the obvious, but he's one of the all-time great coaches in the history of the game. His record speaks for itself. His teams were a reflection of him. It was the way the team played - mentally strong, disciplined, real good fundamentally, strong defensive presence. But what a lot of people don't know about him was he was an innovator. A lot of the things that teams are doing nowadays, Al was in on the ground floor - the video taping, the off-ice conditioning. What are so important to teams nowadays, Al was on the ground floor of all that stuff. And the way he was able to handle so many diverse personalities on the team. We did have a team that had a lot of diverse personalities, and he was able to handle all of those better than any coach I've ever seen.

DUANE SUTTER: Al would take you in on one-on-one situations in his office and talk to you about your game and your life, and life in general. Again, he was very much like Bill - both were the same age as my parents and I really respect them and look up to them. And listened to whatever they could offer me - both on the ice and off the ice.

JIGGS McDONALD: Again, preparation. The way Al could break down video. One of the things that really stood out, Al was "a sports psychologist," before we ever heard the terminology. Al knew what buttons to push. Al, I think a lot of guys would tell you would be their father figure. He knew what he could get out of his players - if it took an arm around the shoulder, a pat on the back, or a "Good job" or "That a boy." Or if he had to bark at them. He knew what buttons to push, but he also knew what was going on at home. He had two wonderful sources - one being Lorne Henning, who was a playing assistant coach, and then later on he had Butch Goring as a playing assistant coach. So he had a pipeline in the dressing room.

But he also had a pipeline in the wives room, in Claire. And I'm not telling anything out of school here, but Claire had a great rapport with the wives and the girlfriends. And she knew if there was a sick child, if there was a problem, if something wasn't going right at home, if there was family visiting. And Al could translate that into performance on the ice. "Oh, spending too much time either going to the City, going to Broadway, going out to dinner. Just not concentrating 100% on hockey." He could pick that up and straighten the guy out - either with the arm around the shoulder or a kick in the pants. He just kept that team clicking. It was like well-oiled machine, but a lot of it was due to the knowledge he picked up either from the room or from the wives' room.

GLENN "CHICO" RESCH: You know when you say, "He's a player's coach"? It can mean a lot of things. But in Al's regard, if there's a line - and every coach would know it or have it in there in their repertoire, where they think that line is, where you can be friendly with the players, but not *too* friendly. Al pushed the line a little farther towards being friendly with the players. But never ever, only one time did you ever hear...Pat Price broke an egg over his head, when he was trying to make a point. That was the only time that I think the player - Pat Price, although maybe he wasn't alone - thought he could have more fun with Al than you could. And when Al was making the point with the eggs that each of us were going to take home with us, he quickly - after chastising Pat - he came back and explained, "Hey, there's times to have fun, but this is a serious moment. I'm trying to make a point here. You just can't cross that line." And Pat was traded a couple of weeks later.

That's "the egg story." We got smoked in Chicago, 8-0 or something. So we came back to practice at the Coliseum. But remember, at that time, there's no charter, so we have to be in our suit jackets, because we're traveling with the public. We had our suits when we went to practice, because we went to the Coliseum as soon as we got off the commercial flight back from Chicago. And then the eggs were there, and we didn't know what they were for. Al said, "Just get dressed and I'll fill you in." As we're sitting there, he's telling the story about, "I want each of you to take that egg, keep your sports jacket on the rest of the night - even when you get home. Put that egg in your coat pocket, so it's on the outside, so if you bump into anything, it will break. But I guarantee you, if you walk around and conduct the rest of this evening the way you did last night in Chicago, none of you will break them. Because you don't bump into *anything.*"

He was making the point of being physical and taking the body. So as he's finishing up, I'm watching Pat Price sneak up on him, and I'm thinking, "Pat...*I wouldn't do that.*" Of course, in retrospect, I would have jumped up, and said, "Hey Pat!", or something to save him. But once he did that, he put Al in a position. Al had to show that line had been crossed, and he did. But Al did it in a real classy way.

BILLY HARRIS: He made it all work. Without him, they would have floundered forever. He was that good. I've played for a lot of coaches, and he learned from a lot of different styles of coaching, and he made it work. The team was so fundamentally poor - I'm not saying I was a great hockey player, but I could pass the puck, I could do a lot of things. I had good coaching growing up. But we had guys that I'm sure didn't have *any* coaching. So in practice, it was almost like a mini hockey school. He'd bring 2x4's out on the rink, and we had to practice passing the puck over the 2x4's. Stuff like that. Just fundamental stuff. But he realized that the guys needed it. And he worked on that. And then we had systems - he would change systems halfway through a game, and they worked. And you can always talk to Al, too. He used to call me sometimes in the middle of the night, and I'd go over to his house and drink beer with him. "What am I going to do with these bunch of clowns? These wives are fighting in the stands!" I go, "Now you know why I'm single, Radar."

BRYAN TROTTIER: Discipline. Fair. A great, great motivator. Really terrific preparation drills, terrific team systems. Accountability was huge, really felt that accountability came from the players and not from him. I thought that was probably the best thing that happened to our team. Al was not a screamer. He was a father figure to a lot of us - how he treated us like a parent. Just, "I need this, demand that, and this is our family. And we work together." It was a really good reflection on all of us.

CLAIRE ARBOUR: He was all-consumed by it. Totally all-consumed. Even the kids would say, "Dad's here, but he's not really *here*, is he? He's kind of thinking somewhere else." In fact, our daughter was married on October 2nd - they've been married 30 years. There was an exhibition game at Madison Square Garden, and Lorne Henning [who was the assistant coach then] had to take over. I guess there was a real bru-ha-ha, everybody fought. But anyways, now we're at church, and we're having the rehearsal, and I don't know how many times I told Al, "This is what you have to do. You're not listening, are you?" And he'd say, "They're stepping on the ice right now. I wonder how the players are doing?" He couldn't focus on the wedding ceremony, because he was thinking about what the team was doing! He was all-consumed.

RON WASKE: Al Arbour was just a true gentleman. He was a great man to work for. He was funny, he was focused. Certainly one of the hardest working people I had ever met. He was just a great man.

DAVE LANGEVIN: He made it clear that the team is more important than any individual. We had a great system for the players we had. And it made everybody feel important.

CLARK GILLIES: A lot of guys felt differently about Al, and that was because sometimes he drove them a little hard. I always considered Al like a second father. He would always be there when you needed a little pick-me-up. He always knew what buttons to push and how to get you going when you weren't playing your best. He was at the wheel of a very high powered car, and he knew how to keep it going in a straight line, that's for sure.

JIM PICKARD: A mastermind. Fair. Just a tremendous human being.

PAT FLATLEY: Mentorship, perseverance. You knew he cared about you as a human being more than he cared about you as a hockey player.

JP PARISÉ: Al Arbour is by far the best coach I've ever had. And at the age of 33, I learned how to play hockey. Just a great, great motivator. Clever. Ahead of his time as a coach. Good guy.

CLAIRE ARBOUR: He was close to all of them. They all became very special to him, in all different ways. They all had different needs. I think Clark Gillies was definitely right up there [as a favorite player of Al's]. All of those young men. Jean Potvin still calls up - he keeps in touch with Al. He was almost their "father image," in a sense. Bobby Nystrom, very close, and Bryan and Mike Bossy. These guys grew up with Al, really. [Jean] is sincerely interested, and loves to chat with Al. I think that's wonderful.

JIGGS McDONALD: Al, such a student of the game. The x's and o's. Good at teaching the game and the breakout - how to get out of your own end, how to get out of trouble, how to take a man out without taking a penalty. Just genius when it came to coaching. And how to get into the heads [of players] - what it took with individuals.

Al was always all over Denis. Oh, Denis was "the whipping boy." What that puts into the other guys in the room is, "If he can treat Denis - who's our star - like that, what the hell is he going to say to me?" It kept them on edge. It kept them being better than maybe they were, in some cases. Al is just the all-time great.

STAN FISCHLER: Arbour could qualify as the greatest coach in history. Even though he didn't win as many games as Scotty Bowman, he had less talent to work with for a long time. Every player I know loved him, and that's a basic difference between Arbour and Bowman. Al was a lovable guy as well as a brilliant guy, and that's why they were able to win so much for him. Very special. Never met a coach I liked more than Al.

GLENN "CHICO" RESCH: When we had our reunion [of the 1980 Cup-winning team], it would have been in 2000 - we had a player, coaches, and family-only dinner. And I've got to tell you, we're there and we're having a good time. Guys are getting up and speaking, and of course, Al, he's just so humble. And then the boys started going, *"ARBOUR! ARBOUR! ARBOUR!"* And he was so sincerely moved, but didn't want to get up. He shook his hand like, "Come on guys," and we just wouldn't let up until he got up there. It still makes me teary eyed - guys were crying. He gave an awesome speech. You talk about a guy who you would almost do anything for, would be Al. And of course, his wife Claire - you can't really talk about Al without injecting Claire's influence in his life. She was the perfect coach's wife, as well.

DUANE SUTTER: There's no doubt [that Arbour is one of the greatest NHL coaches of all time]. You go back in history, and Toe Blake, Al Arbour, Scotty Bowman - from those Stanley Cup eras, from the mid '80s going all the way back into history, there's no question that he was, and probably still is, one of the best.

CHAPTER 36:

JIMMY D

The Islanders' Eastern Canada Scout from 1972-1974, Director of Scouting from 1974-1982, and Assistant General Manager from 1981-1982, Jimmy Devellano [inducted into the Hockey Hall of Fame in 2010].

STAN FISCHLER: Jimmy Devellano is the unsung hero of the franchise. He did as much as Bill Torrey. And to Torrey's credit, he brought Jimmy along. He got a lot of the guys, he did tremendous scouting. He's responsible for getting a player like John Tonelli, who could have wound up in the WHA or with another NHL team. And Jimmy was sort of "the silent partner" for Torrey. And his genius was proven when he went to the Red Wings [after the 1981-82 season] and built championship teams there.

AL ARBOUR: Jimmy was a great scout and a great guy to have around. He was an honest guy, he worked, and he really knew the players. He knew what we needed, and he was drafting correctly. He knew exactly what we needed, and we were all on the same page - all of us.

BILL TORREY: Jimmy Devellano was a part-time scout for the St. Louis Blues. He worked for the Blues their first year or two of expansion on a part-time basis - he was born and raised in Toronto, he was involved with minor hockey there. I didn't know him personally, until I got a phone call from Scotty Bowman, advising me that because the St. Louis franchise was having some financial difficulties, that he was having to let people go, and he was letting Jimmy Devellano go. He wanted to know if I could do him a favor, and at least interview Jimmy. He had heard that I might be adding to the Islanders scouting staff, which at that time, was comprised of just three people. So anyway, we were in Toronto for a game, and I invited him to come up to my hotel. I met him officially then - I had seen him before, but I didn't know him personally. I met him there, and we had several meetings. I decided that we did need more scouting - particularly in the junior ranks in Ontario. Jimmy, being a Toronto guy, I hired him as a part-time scout, and then eventually, made him our full-time junior scout in that area. He was very industrious, very hard working. His whole life revolved around hockey and his interest in the sport.

EDDIE WESTFALL: Jimmy Devellano drafted all of the nucleus of the New York Islanders Stanley Cup teams. He started in 1972, when they drafted Billy Harris - he was the first player that he picked. I was so happy for him when they put him in the Hall of Fame. I don't think the Islanders wouldn't have been the Islanders if it wasn't for him. For Christ sake, he was like a *deluxe* sniper. He was the guy that dug through all the wheat fields and swamps, finding all these hockey players! He knew everybody - the mother, the brother, the father. He was the deluxe scout. God, he would go and see hockey games in places that most people didn't know there was hockey.

JP PARISÉ: Jimmy Devellano, eventually I got to know him, because I did some scouting with the Minnesota North Stars. But he's the guy who put those guys together, and got some of those guys with late drafts - guys like Bobby Bourne. Even Bryan Trottier, he was a second round pick. Knew how to organize a team - just knew how to put a team together. And being that they were so awful the first couple of years, it allowed them to draft high. But you've got to make sure you pick the right guy. Obviously, Denis Potvin, you didn't have to be a rocket scientist to figure out you have to draft him. But Jimmy Devellano knew how to put a team together - with defense, center, and goaltending.

PAT FLATLEY: The same persona as Mr. Torrey - someone who looked at you to deliver. Jimmy drafted a lot of the players - him and Bill. You didn't want to let him down. He held you accountable, and you wanted to do well on his behalf.

JEAN POTVIN: Jimmy D, to me, is probably the most underrated hockey person in the whole league. This guy was an amazing talent, in terms of recognizing talent. If you look at his track record, he was there with the Islanders at the beginning, so he had a lot of say in the players the Islanders drafted. If you look at the Islanders and who they drafted every year, every year they drafted another person who would become a big piece to that puzzle. He started off with Denis Potvin, Billy Smith they picked up in the interleague draft from the LA Kings. And then Gillies, Bourne, Nystrom, Howatt, Trottier, Bossy, Tonelli, the Sutter brothers - I mean, it was never-ending! There was always another great player that they would draft. And Jimmy had a say in every single one of them.

After our third Cup, the opportunity came for him to go to Detroit. Detroit were bottom feeders at that time - they were just the worst team in the league, year after year after year after year. But he had a chance to go there and be the GM, and almost immediately, that team started to become respectable. And look at that franchise since he's been there [the Red Wings have won four Stanley Cups since Devellano has been on board]. I mean, he doesn't play the role that he used to, but I'll guarantee you, Jimmy Devellano still has his say. And when he talks, people listen.

He's one of the greatest identifiers of hockey talent that the NHL has ever seen. I mean, you look at the draft choices that he's made in Detroit, oh my god. You've got Zetterberg, Franzén, Datsyuk, and there's another guy - four absolutely outstanding hockey players over the last seven/eight years. If you look at where these guys are drafted, they were all drafted around 200th or higher. *That's amazing.* To recognize that this guy - with some work in the minor leagues, paying his dues for one or two years, and being coached properly by a minor league coach, who teaches him the Detroit Red Wings system - by the time he's 25/26 will be a very good hockey player. Nobody else saw that. They'd send these kids to the minors, and they all came back when they were in their mid to late twenties, and for the next four or five years, they won something like three Cups in five years or six years. And again, it's Jimmy D.

CHAPTER 37:

SMITTY

The Islanders' goaltender from 1972-1989, Billy Smith [inducted into the Hockey Hall of Fame in 1993, and his #31 was retired by the Islanders the same year].

GARY "BABA BOOEY" DELL'ABATE: Billy Smith was a nut job - I love that guy! He was fuckin' nuts. The year that I interned for them [1980-81], a lot of times I would be there when those guys came on and off the ice. You would be behind a gate. And I remember there were people that were allowed to be there in the back area, and Billy would come off the ice and swing his stick at them! He would swing his stick at *civilians!* I would think, "What is your problem, bro?"

BILL TORREY: Billy Smith is one of the great characters of our sport. A lot of people that rooted for our opponents didn't like him. They thought he was at times crazy or goofy or you can use whatever word. But he had a burning desire to succeed. I first saw him as a goalie for Springfield in the American League - the year they won the Calder Cup. Butch Goring also played on that team. They were not to be the best team in the American League, but those two guys carried that team to a championship. Once the lights were turned out and the game was, no one had better intensity or competitive fire than Billy Smith. He was not technically the best goalie, but you had to go some to beat him. And I'll tell you something, if there's ever another war and I'm in a foxhole, I'd like to have Smitty right beside me.

BRYAN TROTTIER: True to his nickname - "The Greatest Money Goalie in the History of the Game." The bigger the game, the better he played. He demanded that of himself. I would say just one of those guys, again, a warrior. Absolute greatest teammate you could ask for. Dependable beyond dependable. He gave us a level of confidence because of his confidence. He rose to every occasion and was unmovable. He was like "the battleship" of our team. He was one of those immovable objects that you couldn't deter. He was just constant, constant, constant.

CLARK GILLIES: Smitty is somebody I'll never forget. He had an attitude which he still has to this day. Smitty went out there and played tough every night. The thing that stands out the most about Smitty - his personality, the way he played the game - he said to us in the locker room one night, "The code of ethics is if somebody hits your goaltender, you take care of them. Listen, if I get in a fight with someone, it's probably because I started it. So unlike other goalies, if I'm in a fight, don't jump in and get thrown out of the game - I'll take care of it." And he did. And there were times when we got a bit of a knock on our players, because we didn't protect Smitty. He wasn't afraid of anything, and he wanted to make sure people should be afraid of him.

EDDIE WESTFALL: Billy Smith was a different cat. He was great. When he learned how to play the game the right way…you could tell he was a little awkward when they traded for him out of LA. But again, Devellano, I'm going to give him the credit, he saw something in Billy Smith. He was the epitome of a contrarian. Everybody's going to do this, he's going to do that. It's black? No, it's white. Everybody's going to go sign autographs to help out a charity? He's not. He'd irk the guys a little bit too that way, but Billy was…you knew what you got. I didn't have any trouble with him.

When I was broadcasting, that was the good thing about working for the station, not the team, was that I could keep my objectivity. So Bryan Trottier, Billy Smith, and some of them were pretty upset with me at times. But I couldn't cheat the fans by ignoring something that I thought was an absolute violation of the rules of hockey. But Billy used to make it known that he was not too happy with me. But you expect that. On their side, they were winning Stanley Cups and they were "kings of the hill." For somebody to criticize them, it's like, *"Wait a minute.* You're not supposed to be doing that!" But we worked it out.

GORD LANE: Billy Smith was "the x factor." In the regular season, he was an OK goaltender. When there was money on the line, there was nobody better.

STAN FISCHLER: Billy Smith is the top money goalie of all-time. Not stylish, but certainly, the most combative. It's all there in what he did. He was as pivotal as anybody - particularly in the series against Edmonton in '83. That Rangers series in '84, that phenomenal series when the Rangers tied it on that Maloney goal that sent it into overtime. I mean, Smitty saved them in overtime. Smitty saved them in Edmonton in game one, in '83, when he was the whole thing. But en route to the Cup, I would say Smitty in the third period, after Philly tied it [in 1980].

JIMMY DEVELLANO: Billy Smith was a battler. Hard-nosed, tough, and come playoff time, he would ratchet his game up to a whole new level. He was better in the playoffs than he was in the regular season - not that he was bad in the regular season, but he was "lights out" in the playoffs.

MIKE McEWEN: Concentration-wise, he had his whole routine, and he basically didn't talk to anybody 24 hours before a game. What I remember is back in a two on one in a game, you're backing up as a defenseman, and they're coming down two on one on you, and you're hearing the goalie behind you go, "I've got this guy!" I never heard that before, I'm like, *"He's* got a guy? What's going on here? You've got to stay in the net!" And he would. If you took the shooter and angled the shooter off to a good point, if the pass was made, he had the pass.

JP PARISÉ: Billy Smith was kind of a unique player. When it was time to play, the day of a game, you couldn't talk to him. I don't know if it was some kind of a "fog" that he was in. So competitive and not intimidated by anything. Nothing bothered him. He just felt that this team here could beat anybody.

LORNE HENNING: As soon as we had practice, as soon as you put five dollars on the game - everybody [put in] five dollars - Smitty was a different player. He loved to win and he loved to compete. He obviously kept his crease pretty clean. He was pretty talented too, but it was his will and determination that for me, you'd look at him and see the intensity on his face. Game days, guys stayed away from him, because he was pretty intense. Ready to go.

PAT FLATLEY: Great teammate. Intensity, preparation. For games, his preparation started at the pre-game meal. You left him alone. That was his way of getting ready. But it also sent a clear message to the rest of the team - everybody else better be ready, as well.

JIM PICKARD: Shitty Smitty! Very focused. I know that on any game day that he was playing, in the morning and at night of the games, he had made it clear that you don't talk to him. You don't even look at him. You just left him alone, and he prepared his own way. When Ronnie Waske left, his replacement was Craig Smith. I guess we had "Pretty Smitty" which was Craig, and "Shitty Smitty" which was Billy.

RON WASKE: He would come into the locker room for each game, and he would have to have a glass of ice and a can of Coke. He'd change into his hockey gear, and he would never say a word. Nobody would talk to him, he wouldn't talk to anybody. You just knew to stay away from him. He was getting focused. That was his style, and it worked very well for us.

AL ARBOUR: Billy Smith is the toughest goaltender that I knew of. Billy Smith, the day of the game, you couldn't put him in practice. You didn't have him practice, we'd tell him to stay home and sleep, because he'd come in and he was just a fighter. He'd kill anybody. And there's enough fighting at night - there's no fighting in the morning. So I told him to stay home.

CLAIRE ARBOUR: Billy Smith was quite a competitor. Al knew that when the crunch came, and when it was the big games, Billy would be there. He knew how to deal with his temperament. He understood him, and he knew just when to push with Billy.

JIGGS McDONALD: Battlin' Billy. Bill and I had been together in LA, when he first arrived in NHL training camp. Just a fun-loving, out-going, devil-may-care kind of guy. By the time I got to Long Island, they had established themselves, and Smitty would be the first to tell you that his overall career numbers maybe aren't all that good. But he didn't play that many games. He shared, he swapped with Chico, instead of playing, say, 60 or 65 of the 80/82 games, he played 42/44. It was pretty evenly split between the two goaltenders. But when push came to shove, and if I had a game to win today, the goalie I would want? Billy Smith. He would do whatever it took to win. You just didn't get in his face, you didn't get anywhere near him on game day, and that would even be in the middle of the season. He was just *so* focused. As I said, if I had a game to win, I'd want Smitty in the net.

BOB NYSTROM: No better playoff goalie than Billy Smith. He just got into a zone and was absolutely fantastic. A really interesting character. Funny, mean at times. But you know what? Without Smitty, we wouldn't have won the Stanley Cups.

BILLY HARRIS: A complete cement head. Raw talent, much better than Chico, but Chico was probably a better "strategist" - he wasn't big and strong. Smitty was a big, strong guy. He just had that natural ability, and he was fearless. But I just don't like the way he would try and cheap shot guys. That was the big thing. He came in after one period, and he almost took some guy's head off. And then he had this butt end sticking out about six inches, and he hit some guy - broke his cheekbone. And he snorted when he laughed. He says, "I almost took that fucking guy's eye out!" I said, "Yeah, that's really great Smitty. You almost just blinded a guy." And he thought that was really cool. The guys just shook their heads. He's a good goalie, came up big when you needed to.

MIKE McEWEN: He was a tough guy, and he wasn't going to let anybody take any privileges around the crease. I wasn't all that great at clearing guys in front of the net, and there were about four times when I was kind of with a guy and we're about two feet apart, pushing and shoving. Smitty yells, "Get the fuck out of here! Get him out of here!" And his stick comes up right between the two of us. The goalie stick - which is really heavy - comes about a foot between our faces. *Whoa!* A different kind of attitude, a great goalie.

The game by game part, any time they shot the puck in our end, he was yelling at the defenseman where to put it. If you just listened to Smitty, he always had the best play available. He was your eyes and ears back there. You're turning back to get the puck and getting pressure, and he would let you know what to do with the puck. Some goalies did that some of the time. He did it all the time, and he was always right.

BOB BOURNE: The greatest thing about Billy is I guess he got his dues now - he's in the Hall of Fame. But we knew going into every game that Billy was playing, he was going to give us his best. He was so intense before a game, and it kind of made us become more intense. Because the greatest thing about a lot of our guys was they demanded that, "This is the way I'm going to be, so this is the way you have to play." We were so intense because of guys like Billy, and Duane Sutter was intense, and Bobby Nystrom was intense, and John Tonelli was intense. There was just an atmosphere around that team that you'd better come and be intense, and you better be in shape, and you better want to win. We heard about it in the locker room. If you weren't the same weight as these guys, then you heard about it. And Smitty was the first one to tell us, "You'd better protect me, or else you're going to hear about it." That's the way Billy was.

DUANE SUTTER: Smitty was a pressure goalie. Could intimidate the opponents with big saves - some showmanship saves at times - with his intense and confident demeanor. He played with confidence and it was something that rubbed off on the rest of us.

KEN MORROW: Billy Smith…*the money goalie.* I know he's been called that in the past, but that's what he was. Maybe no fiercer battler than Billy. He was unique. There was never anybody like him, and I don't think there ever will be. He got the job done, and he did whatever it took to get it done. He's one of the all-time great playoff goalies.

DAVE LANGEVIN: Billy and I were very close. Just a lot of confidence. What I liked about Bill Smith was no matter if you made a mistake in front of him, he would never say anything. Because the thing is, at one point, we all bail each other out. Even if I made a mistake and made him look bad, he didn't try and embarrass me in front of the crowd. Some goalies, you see them raise their gloves in the air. He was another feisty, battling, hated-to-lose type character. He was probably the first enforcer on the Islanders. He used to fight more than the players they had at the beginning! I'm just glad that when he got his chance, he proved that he was the goalie that could bring them to a championship.

RON WASKE: Billy was a different sort. He was very focused on his job, funny sense of humor. But when he came into the room to play hockey, it was all hockey.

CHAPTER 38:

MR. ISLANDER

The Islanders' right winger from 1972-1986, Bobby Nystrom [his #23 was retired by the Islanders in 1995].

JEAN POTVIN: Bobby Nystrom...what can you say? Probably the most popular Islander in the history of the New York Islanders. And this is their 40th season. Bobby was not only popular, I don't think I've seen too many players that wanted to win more than he did. And Bobby did not exactly have superstar talent, but he came up huge in so many games for us throughout the years.

JIGGS McDONALD: Bobby Ny...this game, yeah, it's changed a little. There's the group out there that would like to take fighting out of the game. Bobby Nystrom, not a goon by any means. But if he was called upon, *look out.* He would take a man apart. But came with talent and a scoring ability, and a defensive ability. He was the kind of guy that every team in the league was looking for, and it wasn't just the overtime goal or goals - he was strong, kept the opposition honest. Just brought an element to that team...very few teams had a guy like that.

BRYAN TROTTIER: Probably he and Clark were the greatest two things that ever happened to the Islanders - as far as "big brothers," as far as stand-up guys that wore the Islanders' crest on their heart and their fists. Nobody was going to push us around because of those guys. I think Bobby Nystrom was the thunder of a lot of that. Bobby was a huge presence because of that. And to this day, has scored the biggest goal in the history of my life - the overtime goal against

Philadelphia. It's still the greatest moment I will ever have in the game of hockey. And I had nothing to do with the play.

My love of the guy goes way beyond that goal. But that goal is just the highlight of a Bobby Nystrom career, because I've seen him do that play…if I've seen it a hundred times, I've seen it a thousand times in practice. Where he'd drive the net, the pass would go across, he'd tip it, and make something great come out of it. *Clutch.* He was just one of those guys that always seemed to have more energy than anybody else. It didn't matter if the game was first period, overtime - there was nobody that was going to out-grind him or out-work him. And I think he took every loss to heart. He took every win to heart. And I liked that about Bobby, because he wore victory on his face and he wore defeat on his face. There wasn't an ounce of energy left in his body because of it. I like warriors like that.

CLARK GILLIES: Great friend, great room mate. A real leader. Bobby came to play every single night. I can't ever remember him taking a night off. He was so intense for every game. One of the great leaders on that team. Never wore a "C," never wore an "A," but you knew that if you had to look to somebody to get something started and go out there and fire the team up, Bobby was the going to be the one.

PAT FLATLEY: I was afraid of him! [Laughs] Intensity - his intensity in practice. He was intense all of the time, and it was infectious. He was a big part of that team. Big leadership.

MIKE McEWEN: Good guy, good team guy. When I got traded [to the Islanders], I was over at his house the first week. He was welcoming me to the team. He didn't swear - one of the guys that never swore. Never used bad language. Again, another guy that would probably get on the bench - I don't know if it was once a month, but certainly three or four times a year - and just gave everybody shit for the effort we were putting out there. I remember talking to him after playing, they wanted him to coach. I guess he tried it, and I talked to him again, and he only lasted about three or four months. And I was like, "What happened?" He goes, "I couldn't do it. I'm too emotionally involved. It's like I'm playing, but I've got no outlet - I just get crazy. I can't coach!"

DAVE LANGEVIN: Like a lot of players, Bob Nystrom was a great character player. He was a player that I think you could say had the same characteristics as every player on that team. Came hard every game. Gave 100%. Bob worked hard. He knew his role, and I think everybody knew their roles. He was a great guy. I sat next to him, and it was interesting times. [Laughs] He didn't say much - he just went out and did it.

STAN FISCHLER: Symbolized the tenacity, the hard work that went into winning. He made the most of what he had, and he really is the eternal hero for that one goal.

GARY "BABA BOOEY" DELL'ABATE: Everybody loved him. He lived on Long Island, I think he married a Long Island girl. You'd always hear, "Oh, Bobby Nystrom's wife was at Roosevelt Field [Mall]." They were pretty visible on Long Island. And he was a good, solid player. But after he scored that goal, he can live the rest of his life on Long Island like a hero.

BOB BOURNE: Bobby Ny. I give him and Garry Howatt the credit for turning that team around. And then of course, Clarkie came in the next year and *really* turned it around. But when you're playing the Philadelphia Flyers after they've won two Cups in a row - they talk tough, they have the strut and everything - Bobby Ny and Garry Howatt were the first two guys to ever really stand up to that team. They fought everybody and they told everybody on that team, "The Islanders weren't going to be pushed around." And to me, those two guys became the face of our hockey team. There was a lot of talent involved at the time, obviously - Bryan Trottier, Denis Potvin, and of course when Mike Bossy came in. But those two guys set a standard for us.

Everyone says, "Oh, no one got in shape in those days." Well, I remember going back after my first year, and I went down a couple of weeks early. They had a gym set up in the Islanders dressing room long before gyms became the standard. And you better be in shape, because if you didn't go back in shape, those two guys let you know it. They were always in great shape. We just knew going in that we had to be in shape. Those were the years we started to really work out. I was in excellent shape, even in '75-'76, going back to those days. *We had to be in shape.*

BILL TORREY: He was a third round draft pick out of Kamloops. I saw him play as a junior out there. He was obviously tough. Wasn't afraid of anybody. Had a pretty good shot, wasn't a good skater. It was very questionable whether his skating was going to be good enough to play in the NHL. The first summer after we drafted him, his agent lived on Long Island, and when Bobby was there during the summer, I told his agent, "I want to send Bobby to a skating coach." At first, Bobby [didn't like the idea]. Little did he know that the one that I sent him to was going to be a woman, because that was the first time that's ever happened. But we had a lady, Laura Stamm, on Long Island.

I had seen her work with kids and bantams and juniors, and she really knew her stuff. She was a figure skater, and one thing I learned early on from the days I worked for John Harris, when he owned Ice Capades - figure skaters, from the standpoint of balance and power out of their legs and their thighs and their lower trunk had much better technique at that time than hockey players did. Much to Bobby's chagrin, when I said, "You are going to go," at first, he said he wouldn't do it. It took me a little convincing. But it made a difference in him. What really made a difference in him was his determination to be a player and not only to be just a player and make the NHL - but to be *a real good player.* Great team man. Still on Long Island.

BILLY HARRIS: Bobby's a great guy. A tough son of a bitch. But you just have to respect him on how he worked on his skating. He made himself a good hockey player. Hard worker, tough, intense. *Very intense.*

JP PARISÉ: Bobby Nystrom, we became really close friends. His wife and mine became really good friends. He was a good, young guy, who was kind of raw at the time, and made himself one fine player, by just hard work and doing extra things to make himself much better. His skating suffered, he worked on that - he took skating lessons. He'd do anything for the team. Everything for him is "team." A great teammate and nice man.

CLAIRE ARBOUR: Bob Nystrom was such a hard-working individual, that Al could count on him always going 110% out there. His effort was always there, and he came to play every night. He didn't need to be pushed or anything - he was always there and ready.

AL ARBOUR: A great guy, a tough guy, and a great player.

RON WASKE: Bobby was one of the hardest workers we ever had in the ten years that I was involved. His work ethic was just unbelievable.

JIM PICKARD: Bob Nystrom never took a second off practice and games.

LORNE HENNING: Bobby's a big-time player. Bobby played both ways - he was really tough, a great fighter, and played hard. He hated to lose. Even playing charity games, he hates to lose. Just a competitive, competitive guy. A lot of guys are like that, but guys who hate to lose, it wears off on other guys. And he made sure other guys were ready to play and other guys were giving 110%. Nobody took any shortcuts when Bobby was around. If you were playing on his line, you'd better work.

DUANE SUTTER: Clutch guy. Always was playing with his sticks. Wanted to be the guy to contribute that big goal, and he certainly proved that he could. Great teammate.

JIMMY DEVELLANO: Heart, soul, learned how to skate, good guy. Clutch, clutch player. Hard-nose competitor.

EDDIE WESTFALL: That's heart, personified. He's living proof that what you may not have in raw talent, you can make up for with hard work and dedication. And again, another one of the guys from the time he got here to today, he's never wavered - he's the same guy. You're happy to be in his company. He's the kind of guy that he never has to say anything about himself - leave that to me and the other people he's been friends with all his life, because we all brag about Bobby Nystrom. He's got a lot of depth. I often remind him, "Bobby Ny, they talk about guys making 20 goals today, and they want two or three million bucks. Think of it this way, I think it was our second year, when he and Garry Howatt were brought over from New Haven, and Howatt, Nystrom, and Westfall played most of that year together. And we averaged 20 goals a piece on a really bad team, with all three of us not really being goal scorers. Warren Buffett would want our autograph!" [Laughs]

KEN MORROW: Pound for pound, maybe the toughest player of that era. You can ask any of the guys that played against him, and they'd tell you the same thing. "Mr. Islander." He was "Mr. Clutch." I scout now for the Islanders, and there just aren't those kind of players around. It's rare to find a guy that can fight, that can score, can hit, and have character. That was Bobby Nystrom.

CHAPTER 39:

THE CAPTAIN

The Islanders' defenseman from 1973-1988, Denis Potvin [inducted into the Hockey Hall of Fame in 1991, and his #5 was retired by the Islanders in 1992].

AL ARBOUR: He was a great player, an outstanding player. Just a marvelous player - the best. He was one of the best defensive players, and one of the best offensive players, too. He was good all-around. He was just a smart guy, period. But you had to be on his case all the time - he loved "the good life." [Laughs]

CLAIRE ARBOUR: Denis came with this absolute incredible background of being a very great, super junior hockey player. And Al wanted to make sure he continued that way. And he pushed Denis *incredibly*. There were times that Denis wasn't always too happy with his coach. [Laughs] And Al was always, always watching him. He was kind of stern and tough on Denis. And Denis knew it after his career was over, it was for his benefit. I remember the time where he missed the team bus, and he went back home - he didn't know what to do. The bus left and didn't wait for him. He said, "They didn't wait for me?" They gave him an alarm clock for Christmas. [Laughs] With Denis, he would get him almost angry at times, and Denis would go out there and play his extreme best, because he'd be "getting back" at Al. But the talent was always there. Gosh, he was quite an asset. And he stayed with the Islanders - those were the days where players stayed with the team. They grew together.

EDDIE WESTFALL: A talent, a real talent. He was not only a talented hockey player, he was a physical force - particularly his first years in the league. My observation is when he came into the league, it felt like he had to prove something. And he did. And then after he was in the league for a while, he had proven that, but he was a very talented puck handler and shooter - along with when he started, he could hit. He was a very good body checker. And that's a talent in itself that is disappearing out of the league. But he had the talent to do that, and I knew exactly where that came from, because he had that ability to throw a really good hip check. A guy named Leo Boivin was his junior coach up in Ottawa, the 67's. And when I joined the NHL in '61, who was my defense partner? Leo Boivin. He taught me how to do that, too.

But Denis was a superior player. He was picked number one, and he proved that he was an NHL player immediately. He just had to fine tune. He had to do things maybe a little quicker, and he would have guys that would pound him - he wasn't just pounding other players, he would get hit back. Like a lot of us, we decide we don't want to do the pounding any more, we'll rely on the finesse game. [Laughs] You last longer. But he had a Hall of Fame career.

I don't think he really gave himself a chance to be as good a teammate and as good a friend to his teammates. I think he was a little standoffish. He was bilingual - he spoke French Canadian and English very well. And he was wonderful in interviews. He was well-spoken and had good ideas. He had a good mind. But I think at times, he felt that he was better than other people, and that hurt him as he went along. I would be only honest with the fact that if you ask Denis, "If you could go back and change something, what would you change?" I would not be surprised if he said, "I would have much sooner had a relationship with my teammates."

JIMMY DEVELLANO: The biggest, most important ingredient in getting the Islanders off and running in year two. Superstar.

JP PARISÉ: Denis Potvin was just a great player. When I was there, he had been a superstar all his life. Extreme confidence. Worked hard, and would never admit he had things to learn in the National Hockey League, as an 18 or 19-year-old kid. Certainly, nobody's complete at that age. But he worked, observed, and made himself a great player. He was tough.

BILLY HARRIS: Denis was another guy that marched to his own drummer. But not like Smitty - Denis was a smart guy. We had a lot of Western Canadian guys - a lot of farm boys, ranchers, dirt farmers. Y'know, they weren't going into the Metropolitan Museum of Art. Denis Potvin would. So there was always a gap there. But I liked Denis - I got along well with Denis. I had no issues with Denis at all. I'm from Toronto, I wasn't a westerner, but I wasn't French. But I was from a big city, so I could deal with all the different goings-on, because I got along with everybody. But there were definitely guys that didn't get along with certain guys on that team, or didn't think the same way. We all *got along,* but on road trips, there were just certain guys you wouldn't go out to dinner with. Which I think is bad - I don't think that's good for a team. Whether it was a cultural, or a French, or…who knows what it was. But there were certain people that hung out together, and that was it.

BOB BOURNE: Denis was so solid. I remember for a player like myself, if I'm on the ice with Denis Potvin and Bryan Trottier, I knew I had a good chance to not be "a minus player." He was so smart and steady. He was one of the first defensemen ever to when there was a shot at the point, he'd step up and block that shot and away we'd go. Somehow, he had an uncanny knack of blocking shots with his stick. He always had his head up, and certainly, one of the best passers ever in the game of hockey. I used to get a lot of breakaways, because Denis could pass so smooth and right on your stick. Very calming influence. And man, the guy could *score.*

RON WASKE: One of the most skilled players that I ever saw play the game. His passing skills were unbelievable. He'd make passes that you would just go, "Wow. How did he do that?"

MIKE McEWEN: Arguably, one of the top five defensemen of all-time. He was a complete defenseman. Defensively, we talked about Stefan Persson and Dave Langevin, and he didn't give up anything to them. Probably the strongest guy in the NHL. Maybe the meanest. If you beat him, he would get pretty dirty with the stick - he'd make the guys pay. So you didn't really want to beat him. Offensively, a great passer. Really intelligent and smart passes. Played the point, a great point man on the power play. If he was fast, he probably would have been the best defenseman of all-time. But certainly, up there with Orr or anybody you want to mention.

CLARK GILLIES: Great defenseman. Knew what he was capable of doing. He's been compared with Orr and Coffey - I think he was a combination of Bobby Orr and Paul Coffey. Hardest shot I've ever seen. I'm not talking slap shot, I'm talking wrist shot. And one of the greatest passers I've ever seen.

BILL TORREY: Denis Potvin, in my opinion, outside of maybe only Bobby Orr, no one ever had better all-around skills - defensively, offensively, physically, scoring-wise. He could pass the puck as well as anybody that's played the game. Coming out of our end, no one laid a pass better than he did. His presence, for a very young team, what he was asked to do - not that he was perfect. But Denis, without him, we don't have four Stanley Cups.

BRYAN TROTTIER: Denis sat next to me for 15 years, and to this day, is one of my best friends. I just consider him probably the anchor of all anchors when it comes to defense, the power play. Putting the perfect breakout pass - he never put you in a situation where you were in trouble. He always had the right pace on the pass, he always had the right pace on his shot that you could deflect. Whether it was a half-slapper or a full-slapper. And he was strong like a bull. There was probably nobody in the league that had a meaner streak, that hit harder with intent to hurt - to put a little sting on you. And I liked that about Denis. He was just a great teammate, I love the guy.

There were moments I think even for Denis where he'd kind of surprise himself. I used to like that, because he'd come in and he'd have that little look on his face, and I was like, "That was totally awesome!" He'd say, "I don't know where that came from." It was kind of neat to see that in a guy that I thought was an extremely confident guy. And another thing about Denis, I liked "the little boy" in him. He always had a youthful enthusiasm about him - even though he tried to be a solid kind of leader, he was one of those guys that had a little "imp" about him. And I loved that, I loved to see that side of him. When you're the captain, you always have to have a certain demeanor, and Denis always had that little youthful enthusiasm on the side.

BOB LORIMER: A great leader, a tremendous talent. Very demanding, as far as demanding excellence from guys. If you made a bad pass, you'd hear about it. And I think that's important from your leadership. If you want to be a championship team, you can't be sloppy. Everything has to be played to your ability and to a certain standard. And Denis was very much a leader in that respect, because he was so talented and he demanded the best from everybody. I think it brought up the overall skill level of the team.

JIGGS McDONALD: There's just so much I could say about Denis - his leadership. He came out of junior with all the accolades; everybody knew he was going to be "consensus #1 pick overall." He had to make the adjustment, number one, to Al. But number two, he wasn't your typical hockey player, in that he had interests outside of hockey. And that maybe upset some of his teammates at the outset. But he had the ability to combine the two, and not be entirely different from his teammates, or not a team player - he was every bit the team player. He could control the hockey game, the pace of the game. He controlled the room. And he had a lot of room there, you got guys like Gillies and Trottier, and even Langevin. Some outspoken guys. You can factor Smitty into that too, when it comes to dressing room, from what I was told by the guys back then. No, Denis was just solid. His nickname was "The Bear." When he hit, guys knew it. He read the play so well. His shot from the point. The ability to jump into the play, from in and off the blue line. He gambled a little bit, but he read - he knew where the puck was going. Just splendid.

JIM PICKARD: He played it mean...*tough* I guess is a better way of putting it. He always said the right thing at the right time, and followed it up by his actions on the ice. He was a great captain also, like Eddie Westfall was, and Clarkie too.

DAVE LANGEVIN: Denis was probably the premier defenseman in the league. He was a great captain in regards to he could handle the media. Nobody else liked doing that, and he loved it. I think he'll go down as one of the best defensemen. He could play it both ways - he was one of the best wrist shots ever in hockey. He was a strong defenseman - strong mentally. And favorite of the Rangers!

LORNE HENNING: Certainly, Denis ran the power play, and was the leadership of defense. When you needed a big play, he was there - whether it was a hit, a power play goal, or a set up. He could do anything. When you have the leadership and depth that we had on defense, Denis was certainly the one that generated everything back there. Him and Stef were quite a twosome on the power play.

GARY "BABA BOOEY" DELL'ABATE: I always thought he was one of the great, all-around players. Even as a defenseman - a great scorer, soft-spoken, and a key to those teams.

DUANE SUTTER: Denis was always just "Mr. Steady" back there. He could contribute in any way. Crunching hip checks, huge shot from the point. He's one of the best there ever was.

BOB NYSTROM: "The General" on the power play. The type of guy that controlled it all - just an incredible force on the blue line. A dominant player. Really, the best thing I can say about him is he's a true Hall of Famer.

GORD LANE: Likely the most complete defenseman. Look at guys like Scott Stevens who played a little bit later - he was "the tough/physical defenseman," as Denis was, but he never had the offensive sensibility. And Denis was mean, but he was also a very good hockey player. I think of all the defensemen that I have seen play, he was probably the most complete.

PAT FLATLEY: Strength and character. Led by example, and confidence.

KEN MORROW: Denis Potvin probably doesn't get the recognition he deserves, for being one of the best defensemen in the history of the NHL. And I know he's considered to be one of the best, but having played with him and watched him over the years - I was his partner for many years - I'll tell you that there was maybe no better all-around defenseman than Denis Potvin. The guy did it all. There were other players that were better in certain aspects of the game, but the total package, I would put Denis up against anybody in the history of hockey. He scored, he intimidated physically, he led, he was a captain, he was a leader. He was a captain of Stanley Cup teams. The guy was incredible.

STAN FISCHLER: Of the three or four greatest defensemen of all-time, he's there with Eddie Shaw, Doug Harvey, and Bobby Orr. I'd put him ahead of Orr - he did more than Bobby Orr. Great captain.

CHAPTER 40:

JETHRO

The Islanders' left winger from 1974-1986, Clark Gillies [inducted into the Hockey Hall of Fame in 2002, and his #9 was retired by the Islanders in 1996].

EDDIE WESTFALL: I gave Clark the nickname "Jethro," because he enjoyed 'The Beverly Hillbillies.' He reminded me of a big character in the Clampett family, Jethro Clampett!

JP PARISÉ: Clark Gillies, again, he was just a young kid. A gentle giant. I'm not sure that he really liked the role of being an enforcer. Probably the clown of the locker room - always coming up with funny things and jokes. So kind, and smart enough that he refined his game and made himself a pretty tough player. By doing that, he made the line of Bryan Trottier and Mike Bossy one fine line.

JIGGS McDONALD: Here's another guy - talk about Bobby Ny - that you didn't want to tangle with. *At all.* And fortunately, for a lot of people, he was slow to anger. He would cut you some slack. But geez, if you stepped over that line, he'd put you in place in a hurry. Great hands, great scoring ability. Kept everybody loose. His singing, his ability to sound like Kenny Rogers - Clarkie would get singing. Clarkie would be telling stories - he loved to tell stories. He just kept the bus, the dressing room, or around the hotel…everything loose. He was an amazing man - still is.

BILLY HARRIS: I roomed with him, so we always had a lot of fun on the road trips. He was a good buddy. He had a long fuse, but if you pissed him off, boy, you wouldn't want to be that other guy on the other end. I mean, there were some big heavyweights, but no one really wanted to mess with Clarkie if he was mad.

JIMMY DEVELLANO: Big, strong, intimidating, good hands, terrific on the line with Trottier and Bossy as their protector.

DAVE LANGEVIN: Clark was a force on the ice. When they had that line together - Clark, Trots, and Boss - nobody was going to goof around with our top players. He was a great guy in the locker room. He was a tough guy that could play hockey.

GARY "BABA BOOEY" DELL'ABATE: Man, long before they had championships, Clark Gillies made the Islanders a team not to be fucked with. That's a contribution that cannot be overlooked, because it was a time when everyone had an enforcer, and the Islanders had Mike Bossy, a skinny little guy and a goal scorer. But everybody needed a protector. I always say the day that everything changed for the Islanders was when Clark Gillies beat the living shit out of Dave Schultz. It was a "Ding dong the witch is dead" [moment]. I thought that changed the attitude of the Islanders. That day was as important as winning the Rangers series, and changing the perception of who the Islanders were, and, "You're not going to fuck with us." He was an important part of that. I was really happy when he got into the Hall of Fame, even though it was much later. I think even he was a little surprised by it, but a little happy about it. He was on a line with two Hall of Famers, and he made a wonderful contribution.

BILL TORREY: Jethro is one of a kind. The players are all big today. Not all, but when you're talking about a big man today, you're talking about 6'5" and 250/260. I think when we drafted Clarkie, he was 6'3" and he weighed probably 200/210. But he was a large, ominous looking guy. He wasn't one to go out and start trouble, but when he was provoked, he did an awful lot of damage to a lot of people. He was a good, all-around player. But he would always subjugate himself to who he was playing with. For Clarkie, winning and having a good time because of that was more important than self-promotion. But he was a dominating, strong player. When we played the Russians in Madison Square Garden ["The Challenge Cup" in 1979], he was the best player on Team NHL. He was very good in the playoffs. He was always a good scorer. But he had a great sense of humor, and was a very popular player in our dressing room. And very well-respected.

PAT FLATLEY: He's close to Al Arbour in mentoring and caring about his teammates. Obviously a great hockey player, but more than that, he was a great teammate, and he really cared about us all - in every aspect of our lives.

AL ARBOUR: I liked Clark Gillies - he was one of my favorites. He is the type of the guy that you couldn't give hell to. I found out that you couldn't give him hell at all. He was a captain for two years, and that was it. He couldn't be the captain, because he took everything to heart. He was funny - certain things he did very well, and other things he didn't do so well. And he didn't do so well when he was pressured. When there was no pressure on him, he'd just go like crazy. And there's enough pressure to play the game, you didn't want to add pressure to him.

EDDIE WESTFALL: Just the best. He - like Bobby Nystrom - they don't get any better. When he came in, he was another force, physically. He didn't like fighting, but he would, because people were going to test him. And they made that mistake. But from the time that he arrived, he improved *so* much. His game elevated. I suppose playing on that line - he played so much with Bossy and Trottier - that he got so involved with making the plays, improving his shot, his positional play, and learning how to play particularly with Bossy. You weren't forced into it, but you had to learn there were certain places to be, so you can get the puck to him. He's "the supreme finisher." He worked very hard on his game, and became a much better player than most people thought he would be.

BOB NYSTROM: He meant a lot to our team in so many different ways. From comic relief - best joke teller - knew the right time to maybe barb Al or prod him a little bit. And then, when we needed him on the ice, he was there for us. Toughness, ability, scoring - anything you can ask from the guy. But he was one of the funniest guys - he was my roommate for a lot of the years. There is no better guy than Clark Gillies.

CLAIRE ARBOUR: Clarkie was very meaningful to the team - both on the ice and in the locker room, because of his personality and his way of joking. I can tell you this one incident that happened. Right after they won the first Stanley Cup, in training camp, they were playing a farm team. And it turns out that after the first period, it was such a lopsided shots on goal - the farm team players had 20 shots, and there was only one shot by the Islanders. And Al went in there and had a tirade in the locker room, saying, *"20 to one? You're playing awful!"* And yelled everything he could have at them, slams the door, and walks out. He's standing out in the hallway, and you could hear a pin drop in the locker room. And all of a sudden, Clarkie said, "OK...*who's the wise guy that took the shot?"* They all burst out laughing. Al said he broke out laughing, too. That's where his personality was such [an asset]. And he was like that in every incident - he could just break them up and relax them. He was another one that worked very hard out there. He came to play.

LORNE HENNING: Clarkie was "the beat" of the dressing room. He was a fun-loving guy and guys loved him, and loved to be around him. He had the toughness, but he was an easygoing, fun guy, joking around. He made a lot of guys laugh and relax. But the big thing, on the ice, he was the first real power forward. He could do it all out there. He was a good player, plus he was tough. I think the coming out party for us was when we beat the Bruins, and Clarkie and O'Reilly had all those fights - game after game. That's what set the tone for us.

BRYAN TROTTIER: I don't have any success without Clarkie. He had my back all the time. I felt like there was a guardian angel, a big brother, a guy who could do it all on the ice. Ask him to score a goal, ask him to get the puck out of the corner, ask him to drive the net, ask him to do the stuff in his own zone. There wasn't anything that Clarkie couldn't do. I thought that was just a huge reason for any kind of success that I had. There was a guy that I could depend on, who kind of thought like me, felt like I had the same kind of qualities and work ethics. Family mentality. Just really a kind of guy I could turn to, depend on, and was always there. You need that kind of a teammate. And a guy that never lacked any confidence. I never, ever felt, "Uh oh, Clarkie's out of his comfort zone." He'd find a way to make me feel a lot more comfortable about my comfort zone. I needed that. Even through it, because this is not "reflection" for me, this is not "20 years later." I played three years of junior hockey against Clark Gillies. And when I went to the Islanders, here's Clark Gillies, who is now my teammate. I'm like, *"The hockey gods are smiling on me,"* because I don't know if I could have a better guy that I want as a teammate. And then to play all those years with him on my left side, I'm the luckiest man in the world.

MIKE McEWEN: Probably the best tough guy of all-time. In my book, him and John Ferguson. But Fergie wasn't the hockey player Clarkie was. A tough guy who gets 30/40 goals a year and is a legitimate all-star - that's hard to beat. Fighting...he was probably the nicest guy you'd ever want to meet. But challenge him to a fight, and his eyes would turn. But at the same time, a real honest hockey player. When I played against Clarkie, he wasn't dirty. He was a good, honest hockey player - but was tough. A good offensive player.

JIM PICKARD: For whatever reason, Clarkie was probably my all-time favorite player I ever had, and I've been on like four teams in this league. Al used to always say, "Get into the game, Clarkie. Because if you don't get a hit or get going, it's like letting a sleeping dog lie."

KEN MORROW: Clark Gillies was one of the leaders on the team. The true definition of a power forward through the ages. He was maybe the most feared fighter at that time in the game, although Clark probably wouldn't talk about that. In talking to all the other players that I played against throughout the years, they feared him. He scored 30+ goals.

DUANE SUTTER: Clarkie had a demeanor on the ice and a presence on the ice that was unmatched by any player that I played with our against through my eleven year career. Excellent teammate. Somebody I really looked up to.

STAN FISCHLER: Gillies was sort of minimized by some. I was on the Hockey Hall of Fame selection committee for two years and I tried to get him in, and they rejected him. But Gillies was the perfect winger for Trottier and Bossy, in that they had a chemistry - one guy could do one thing very well, the other guy could do the other thing very well. And Gillies did a lot of different things well. Plus, he was adaptable - he could play on other lines as well. One of the best fighters in the league, while having the talent.

BOB BOURNE: Well, Clarkie's my best buddy. His daughter, Brianna, is marrying my son, Justin, in September of this year [2011]. We lived beside each other for a few years in New York, and we were always going to the games together, and we went to all the playoff games together. Clarkie was so much fun - he was a great player, great teammate. He was one of the guys that kept us loose. One of the funniest men you'll ever meet in your life. Just a great, great teammate.

BOB LORIMER: Hockey Central in Toronto, a couple of years ago, when Clark was put in the Hockey Hall of Fame, the guys were saying, "Look at his stats, he can't be in the Hockey Hall of Fame." But I just know back when Clarkie played, every GM in the league would have traded - in a heartbeat - almost any player on their team for Clarkie. Because he was *the* dominant power forward during his era. He was tough, he was a great team guy, scored goals, responsible defensively. Tell me one team that wouldn't have traded for him? He was just the most dominant guy. It was a no-brainer for guys that played with Clarkie. Fans that didn't see him play all the time, they tend to just look at stats. Stats are important, but there are so many more aspects to the game. During that era especially, the toughness that Clarkie brought allowed everybody to play a lot more comfortably. And you can't underrate that.

CHAPTER 41:

TROTS

The Islanders' centerman from 1975-1990, Bryan Trottier [inducted into the Hockey Hall of Fame in 1997, and his #19 was retired by the Islanders in 2001].

CLARK GILLIES: Bryan is the best overall player I've ever played with or against. You hear, "Who was better, Gretzky or Lemieux?" Well, they were both great. But they didn't do the things that Bryan Trottier did. He could do it all - kill penalties, power play, great guy in the locker room. But I think one of the things that gets bypassed with Bryan is they forget how physical he was, and how intimidating he was. There isn't a single guy around the league who would be afraid to step on the ice with Wayne Gretzky, or for that matter, Mario Lemieux. I'll tell you what, there were guys out there that were very, very wary of Bryan Trottier when he was on the ice. I think Bryan was the total package when it comes to a hockey player. If you could clone six other Bryan Trottiers, you'd have some NHL!

CLAIRE ARBOUR: When Bryan Trottier came, he was very young. He was only 18 years old I think, or 19. They had to nurture those kids. And the playoffs were hard on these guys, because so much was expected of them. They were just like all [Al Arbour's] kids, and he understood Bryan in his personal behavior and everything. It was just something very special.

BILL TORREY: He came under different circumstances, because the draft was different. And who knows what would have happened if the draft had stayed at 20 years of age - we probably would have never had the opportunity to get him, because of our success we had had, we would not be drafting where we were drafting. But when the rules were changed and my scouts out west kept telling me, "You've got to see this kid" - particularly our part-time scout that lived in Lethbridge, Alberta. He traveled to all the little western towns, and spent a lot of time in Swift Current, and knew that team inside and out. Bryan, because he's part Native American, is so determined, had an inner-fire - even as a young man.

And when I told him that I was sending him back to junior, he looked at me and his eyes...I was a little nervous. He was mad. His father - who is a very big, strong man, and broke horses and had a horse ranch out in western Canada - didn't like it. His agents were mad. But for Bryan Trottier at age 17 going 18 to come into New York and try and compete with bigger, stronger men at that time, although not much, I just felt was a mistake. I also sent him to Lethbridge in the Western League, and Lethbridge was coached by Earl Ingarfield.

A very, very good, all-around player. Knew the game, understood the game, was a westerner. Sending Bryan back to Earl was the right move. The next year, when he came back to training camp and signed him, he was just 18 years of age, and he was pure and simply the best player in training camp. Even at that age, I was a little worried about, really, a quiet western boy. Because he was not yet a man - he was physically, but not in maturity. I was concerned. But it worked out, and he became a very, very special talent. Right from once you saw him in training camp that year, you just knew he was going to be there. The thing about Bryan, he could hit you, and it was like getting hit by a Mack Truck. But he didn't look that big, and he didn't look that strong. But ask anybody that ever played against him head-to-head. And then of course, the relationship he formed with Mike Bossy was very special and very unique. They became close friends - on and off the ice.

JIGGS McDONALD: Bryan brought a talent to that team, coming out of that 18-year-old draft. He's special. Special today, special back then. He would go through the wall for Al. He loves to tell a story about Al calling him in, and asking him what was wrong with Boss. "You've got to get Boss going." And he would go, "But Al, Boss had a goal and two assists last night. We won, didn't we?" "Yeah, but he's not going. You've got to get him going, Bryan. Get him going."

The next guy in the room was Boss. And Al would say to Bossy, "What's wrong with Trots?" "What do you mean what's wrong?" "He's not going. You've got to get him going." "But Al, he had a couple of goals last night. We won, didn't we?" "Yeah, but he can play a lot better than that." He played the two, and Bryan told me he didn't realize at the time what Al was doing! But again, it was the mind games - *"You can be better, you can be better."* And Bryan had a leadership. Bryan brought something - he could hit and hurt as well. But just a great playmaker. Unbelievable passing ability and ability to read the play. That bump pass of him off the boards, Bossy skating into it, even Potvin - some of the things they did together. But Bryan brought a lot to that team.

AL ARBOUR: Bryan Trottier was just a great all-around player. He brought a lot of leadership and smarts to the team. He was a great playmaker. He saw the ice very, very well. He *made* Bossy, with perfect passes right to him.

BILLY HARRIS: He was a class act. A very soft-spoken guy. A very home body-ish type guy. Didn't drink or go out much. But he could skate, he could shoot. No one could knock him off the puck. He was quality - great player.

LORNE HENNING: Trots was probably the top two-way player in the league. He played hard, and a real competitive guy - hated to lose. He was tough to play against. I mean, he *hammered* guys. Plus, that line…when you're the center iceman, with Boss and Clarkie, they had a phenomenal line. He could play both ends of the rink and play hard. He was really hard to play against. You talk about [the best] two-way players in the game that ever played, his name always comes up, for sure.

BOB NYSTROM: The best two-way center in hockey. In my mind, I just don't think there is any comparison, because he played both ends of the ice, and he played them well. I don't think they gave him enough credit for how he dominated other centermen from the strength standpoint. But he could hit. He did basically everything in both ends. Incredible passer and another Hall of Famer. The best in the league.

GARY "BABA BOOEY" DELL'ABATE: Trottier and Bossy were my favorite players. They were the perfect compliment to each other. Bossy was a big goal scorer - not to say Trottier wasn't. Trottier could score the goals and make the assists. Bossy was one of my favorite players, but if I had to pick one favorite from that era, it would have to be Trottier, because I thought he was the all-around, unselfish player. He could score, he could dish it off, he hustled like nobody's business. He just seemed like a stabilizing force on the ice.

STAN FISCHLER: If there's a better two-way center, than I don't know who it can be. He could do things that Gretzky never could do - play the body, play smart, score. He got an overtime goal in one of the playoff series against the Rangers in the early '80s, which was the turning point in that series. Tremendous body checker, and of course, could put up the points - which he did.

DUANE SUTTER: Trotter had a quiet demeanor to him. When he spoke in the dressing room, everyone listened. It wasn't very often, but everyone listened. That was just the way he handled himself. He was quiet, extremely professional. Somebody who I can lean on in different ways - going back to we played for the same junior team. Not with each other, but the same team. We had a unique relationship.

RON WASKE: He was probably the one that supported us most, as far as my staff was concerned - Jim Pickard and I. He respected us, he helped us immensely.

JIM PICKARD: On the Islanders team when I was there, he was the best two-way player. He was built like a fire hydrant. Just a fantastic two-way player.

JP PARISÉ: He never bragged, just humble. Fearless - not only physical, but in terms of, *"We're going to win this."* Worked on being a face-off man, and eventually became one of the best face-off men in the National Hockey League. Al Arbour had him on the ice most of the time for face-offs in our own zone. When they won their second Cup, they beat the North Stars - Bryan Trottier played that whole series with a separated shoulder, and nobody knew it. Just a nice, young man.

DAVE LANGEVIN: Bryan was a good player that worked hard. He had skill - he could play tough, he could play clean. He really complimented Boss. Those two worked together, they knew where each other were, they made each other better. He was a great leader - he came up with a lot of big goals for us. He was one of the better hitters on the team. He'd get in there and rock people. He stood his ground. And that's what I think was great about those top players - they could give it out as much as they could take it.

MIKE McEWEN: I played with a lot of good players and I played with a lot of different teams, and he'd be my number one pick for any team of all-time. Probably the best pure hitter I ever saw in hockey. He was a middle linebacker hunting for guys. Defensively, he was better than half the defensemen in the league. In your own end, the centerman helps out the two defensemen down low. Really strong defensively, and always there to bail you out. If you had the puck, he was open. Offensively, I don't know where he stands on the all-time goal scorers [Trottier is 32nd all-time, with 524 goals], but 30/40 goals a year, 70/80 assists a year. Not bad.

PAT FLATLEY: I would put Al, Bryan, and Clark...a lot of these guys fall in the same category - their character traits. Trots moved me out of a hotel, moved me in with a family, Pat and Warren Ammendola, who were fantastic people in their own right, my first year. And that's Bryan not just caring about "Pat Flatley the hockey player," but "Pat Flatley the person." Trots lived there too [when he first arrived to the Islanders].

EDDIE WESTFALL: As a player, just tremendous play-making ability. And he had a stamina, where a lot of players, after a minute or a minute and a half, would wear down, he never looked like he was "chugging," as we would say. He just went on. He never had a real fast, and he never had a real slow. He just was very steady. He had tremendous stamina and could stay out there shift after shift if you let him. He'd almost have to get the hook to get off the ice. He loved to play and it showed. And he had that ability to make wonderful plays.

A student of the game - he studied the game and he worked on it. His face-offs I think were one of the things when he went from junior to the NHL, he soon caught on how to be a good face-off person.

JIMMY DEVELLANO: Superstar, great talent. Great on-ice presence. Terrific number one all star centerman.

KEN MORROW: The best two-way center for my money of that era, and maybe of all time. I don't think you'll get any arguments about that. Again, in talking about all these guys, maybe it was a part of what the Islanders were, because all these guys were just tremendous two-way players. And that's what Bryan was. There was no better two-way player in the game. He scored, he was always up there in NHL scoring. The magic that he and Mike Bossy had together was unmatched. Bryan hit, blocked shots, won face-offs, killed penalties...he was great at every aspect of the game. Again, those kind of players are like gold.

EDDIE WESTFALL: I saw him a few weeks ago at Pat LaFontaine's golf outing, and he's the same enthusiastic, wonderful guy. He had some very difficult times, so I admire him for not only taking his stamina and getting through that personal stuff, but he's still just the nicest guy.

BOB BOURNE: It's pretty easy to say if I had a brand new NHL team today, and I had to pick one player that you would start a team with, it would always be Bryan Trottier. So I can't say much better than that. Just a fantastic leader, fantastic player, and a treat to be around. The thing with Bryan is he didn't say a whole lot in the dressing room, but when he said it, it's like the old saying, "Everyone listened." Bryan led by example. We had so many leaders on that team that if you weren't working yourself, you were going to hear about it. The thing with Bryan, he would take you aside, he never yelled and screamed or anything. He'd let you know, "Hey, *it's time to get going.*" He'd want to find out what's going on in your head. He was just a great, great teammate. I love the man like a brother. A quiet leader, but he was always the hardest worker on our team. And when your best player is your hardest worker, it's pretty easy to follow.

CHAPTER 42:

BOSS

The Islanders' right winger from 1977-1987, Mike Bossy [inducted into the Hockey Hall of Fame in 1991, and his #22 was retired by the Islanders in 1992].

BRYAN TROTTIER: Probably the number one reason that I had any kind of success offensively was Mike Bossy. To have the kind of success and put up the numbers was having Mike on my right side, having him as a roommate, a line-mate, a teammate. He helped me see the game through a different set of eyes. Something I never thought of before. I was always kind of one of these guys, like, "I have to contribute offensively" or "I have to do this defensively." Mike had another paradigm that I thought was refreshing for me, because I thought selfish was bad. But there's a *good* selfish, and Mike had the good selfish. I really appreciated that. I thought that was healthy for us. I liked that there was a healthy competition with us, too. It wasn't that we were trying to out-do each other, but there was a competition to help each other achieve the best that could possibly be. And I thought that was just a terrific friendship. A friendship that maintains today. That's qualities that help players achieve not just a certain level, but to another level. He's one of the biggest guys that I can ever thank for that.

BILLY HARRIS: He was always a little bit different. He was from Quebec, and he sort of kept to himself - with Trots. Boss was like "a Denis Potvin" - he was a mystery man. He stuck to himself, him and his wife just hung out with Trots and that was it. Never went out after the games, ever - on the road or at home. So a lot of the western guys didn't understand all that. I sat next to Boss and I knew him real well.

I've got no problems with him. But a lot of times, you get that Western Canadian/French Canadian kind of a rift. Where you would never know it was there, but we had a few little flare-ups with these guys. They'd start speaking French in the locker room, because we had Jude Drouin and JP Parisé. I didn't know what the hell they were saying, but I didn't care. But a lot of these western guys would get pissed off - "You can speak English but we can't speak French. So what the hell are you talking about?" It was petty bullshit. Who cares? But Boss kept to himself. Unbelievable shot, very deceptively fast skater.

EDDIE WESTFALL: Mike Bossy was a very quiet guy. And he and Bryan Trottier - almost to the disdain of certain players - went everywhere together. They didn't always go with the team. I don't know that they ever drank beer like the rest of the guys. And Mike Bossy smoked - there were a few of them on the team that smoked, that in today's world seems unusual. It didn't seem that unusual back then. Bobby Nystrom, Clark Gillies, Denis Potvin, Mike Bossy - they used to duck into the facilities of the dressing room and have a cigarette between periods. It certainly didn't do any damage to him, the way he could play.

He was…how would I say it? His difference was he was not a macho kind of guy by any means. I don't want to say he was effeminate - that's why I try to describe him as "a Nureyev on skates." Giving him the strength. If you didn't ask him and didn't know, you wouldn't know he was a hockey player. I don't know that he swore much or anything, like the most of us. If you didn't know him…he's not a nerd, but you'd almost think he's nerdy if you met him somewhere and didn't know what he did or who he was. But I guess that's part of his quietness. He and his wife Lucy really enjoyed their quiet time.

JIMMY DEVELLANO: From the time that he joined the Islanders as a 20-year-old, he scored goals right away. He did it consistently. Was the greatest goal scorer I ever was involved with - even today. He was a scoring machine.

BOB NYSTROM: Just a prolific scorer. A lot goes to Trots for getting him the puck, because Trottier laid it right on him all the time.

No one I've seen could shoot it and hit the five hole like Boss. Just a real sniper in every sense of the word.

AL ARBOUR: Mike Bossy was very special. He was the type of goal scorer that could score goals from anywhere. His shot was unbelievable. He had a great shot - he could score from a flying position, on one leg, in the air. He had the knack to put the puck in the net. And he did that very well.

BILL TORREY: Six hundred and some odd goals in nine years! [573 to be exact] Find somebody that could ever match that record. Just an extraordinarily gifted talent. His vision and his hands were extraordinary. He scored goals like lightning - I mean, out of nowhere, all of a sudden, it was just a bolt of lightning. *Bang!* It was in the back of the net. There was something special about Mike, and there were a lot of games it took him a while to get warmed up, and hardly noticed him. But then by the end of the night, two goals, an assist, or whatever. And you've got to remember, it didn't take very long before the league started to gang up on him. And while he wouldn't fight, he was never intimidated. Very intelligent.

CLAIRE ARBOUR: When he came to the Islanders, Mike was a very coach-able young man. He wanted to be out there. Al knew exactly how to make him want to be also a defensive player - that's where he was lacking. He couldn't check very well. That's why he wasn't picked up by the other scouts. Don't think they didn't all kicks themselves in the butt afterwards. So Al sort of slowly brought him in. That was hard on Mike at first, because he wanted to play more, and he'd say, "No. You're not ready for this." And then when he was put in, Mike was a two-way player after.

JIGGS McDONALD: Boss, very quiet. I think the world of Mike. I maintain that you can blindfold Mike, spin him around until he was dizzy and put the puck on his stick, and he could still hit the net. Boss could shoot from anywhere and very, very rarely missed the net. The quick release. But quiet - from a broadcaster's standpoint, I found that you had to be prepared. When Mike came in, you better have your questions ready, or he'll laugh at you. You'd better have good questions and know what you were talking about, or he would give you a two-word answer or just kind of chuckle, and you'd get nothing out of him. He understood the endorsement end of things. He always came in with this red Titan stick. Never did an interview in the studio without that stick in his hand, and the logo being right there, where it was on camera. That's not a knock by any means - he just knew how to promote.

JIM PICKARD: I asked Mike recently when we were at a reunion...I was with the Lightning at the time, and guys would ask me about him. So I asked, "Boss, when you were playing, did you shoot for corners, or where you shooting?" And he said, "No Pick. Mostly, I wanted to hit the net." So his shot was unbelievable. He was just a sniper.

CLARK GILLIES: Boss was the quintessential goal scorer. He was so impressive. I used to tell people that he could shoot the puck ten different ways. Gilles Meloche played goal for Minnesota when we beat them in the Cup Finals, and Meloche made a comment, that when Mike Bossy comes down on you, he's got ten different ways he can score on you. Something to that effect. So unless you guess the right one, he's going to score. I saw Mike shoot off one foot, off two, off slap shots, wrist shots, quick slap shots, on the ice, off the ice, top corner...he just kind of knew. He was very prepared when he was playing against a certain goaltender - what their weaknesses were. But it doesn't get any better when you talk about goal scorers. I may be a little bit prejudiced, but you put Mike Bossy in his prime against any of these guys that are playing today or before him, and he's tied for first in all categories, as far as goal scoring is concerned.

JP PARISÉ: He completed that line. A tremendous goal scorer, and he worked on his game so much that all of a sudden, you see him killing penalties. He's on the ice, you better watch what you're doing, because he's going to go and score goals. He was just a great goal scorer. Totally dedicated. Worked hard after practice, on shooting. He made himself a really good player.

MIKE McEWEN: The only guy to score 50 goals in each of his first nine years in the league. That kind of says it all. Around the net, the best hands I ever saw in hockey, whether it be quick and accurate, or kind of patient, or just delaying a guy or whatever. Trottier used to, every practice, they'd go out 15 minutes early, and just play around the net, passing back and forth. Sometimes hard sometimes easy, just doing their thing - back and forth - getting used to each other around the net. Get in the game, and they'd do it, just around the net. I think Bossy and Trots kind of went together. Before every game, when we were getting ready, he always gave the goalie's scouting report - he let you know what the other goalie's weaknesses were and the best way to score.

STAN FISCHLER: As good a natural scorer as there ever was. Unfortunately, overshadowed by Gretzky, otherwise, he would be for that era the top offensive talent. Withstood a lot of tough physical play. Never backed off. And his big goals were plentiful - especially during that '81 run.

PAT FLATLEY: Intensity, perfection, and again, holding his teammates accountable - holding them to perform to a higher level. He didn't push you, it was just the way he prepared, he made it clear.

DUANE SUTTER: Boss was a guy I really admired, because you wanted to score half as much as he did! [Laughs] And you watched how he carried himself - his approach very seldom wavered. He was a quiet, confident guy, that took advantage of every situation that he could get. Obviously, one of the best goal scorers in history, and a teammate that I really respected for what he brought and how he handled success. One reason why I think Boss was as prolific a goal scorer as he was - his emotions, he very rarely showed them. His game and performance was probably the most consistent of anybody on the team.

DAVE LANGEVIN: He's just a goal scorer. And I know goalies, when they saw him having the puck, they knew that he could find a spot. You look at any goaltender, there's a hole somewhere. Even if they tried to sucker him into shooting somewhere, he'd still get it by them. I was just impressed with his toughness in front of the net. He'd stand there and get chopped, hit, and crosschecked - he's still standing there, getting his rebound goals. You don't see a lot of those. Players today even, you could start seeing it decline when you had

Lemieux and Gretzky starting to whine because too many people are hitting them, and "We've got to change the way the game is, because people come to watch *us* play." You never heard that from those guys - Boss and Trots. Because that's the way the game is.

BOB BOURNE: Mike is another guy who is a bona fide superstar and obviously in the Hall of Fame, and it's the same thing - you had to work as hard as him. Mike really, really improved his game. He might not have been the best skater when he came into the NHL, but he certainly became a great skater. Mike had an inner drive in him that very few people have, and he always wanted to be the best. He always, always played in the tough games. We'd go into Philadelphia or Boston, and he knew they were coming after him, and he always showed up. I always look back, and every team that wins Stanley Cups needs that guy to score a goal when you don't think you're going to get one. And Mike was always that guy.

KEN MORROW: Mike Bossy was the best pure goal scorer I've ever seen. And I think his stats will prove that - he had a shortened career, but his goals per game might be the best in the NHL. *The guy was magic.* There was no more dangerous sniper that ever played the game than Mike Bossy. Could score goals in any fashion, in any way. The goalies will all tell you he had the quickest release and the most accurate shot of anybody they ever played against. He was worth the price of admission, watching him out there. The goal he scored in Vancouver in the Stanley Cup - and they've showed it in highlights, when he's in the air - maybe the most incredible goal I've ever seen.

GARY "BABA BOOEY" DELL'ABATE: He was a scoring machine. 50 goals in 50 games. Again, all these things that brought identity to the Islanders, that brought identity on Long Island. *On Long Island,* we had a guy that was breaking Rocket Richard's records. It was a big deal. And also, he's not just "50 goals in 50 games," some of the goals he scored - the acrobatic goals, the one where he got up-ended - he was so dependable, so good.

And I loved his low-key attitude. Some of my favorite athletes, like, Curtis Martin is probably my favorite Jet of all-time, or very close. The thing I loved about Curtis Martin was when he ran into the end zone and scored, he would just drop the ball. Like, "Look what I did. I don't need to tell you any more." There was a lot of that in Bossy. Bossy might have pumped his fist, but sometimes, he'd just skate away. Like, "I don't need to get on my stick and ride it like Tiger Williams or any of that shit. I don't need to celebrate because I just showed you what I can do." That's what I loved about him.

JIMMY DEVELLANO: Best pure goal scorer I was ever associated with in my 45 years in the NHL. *A scoring machine.*

CHAPTER 43:

UNHERALDED HEROES

In addition to their Hall of Fame players, the Islanders teams of the 1970's and 1980's contained some great - yet oft-overlooked - contributors.

STAN FISCHLER: The guy whose banner is not up, and that is John Tonelli. The only difference between Tonelli and Nystrom was that Tonelli fed Nystrom the pass, and Nystrom scored. Tonelli came up with the big one in that Pittsburgh series when they looked like they were going to fade away. He was the guy in the corner that set up that Morrow goal against the Rangers. He was just indefatigable. He faded later on, but that didn't matter - we're talking about the important years. The guy like Tonelli on defense would be Stefan Persson - tremendous, but more in the shadows.

BOB NYSTROM: [John Tonelli] came up with some of the biggest goals in Islanders history and was just the workhorse of the team. Probably could have got a lot more points playing on the front line or the second line. But he was with myself and Wayne Merrick on the third line. Just an incredible leader. If you wanted the puck, you sent him into the corner, because he would come out with it. I've never seen a guy - other than maybe JP Parisé - that played the corner better than John Tonelli. You look back in Islander history, and some of the biggest goals were scored by him or assisted by him. I've got a lot of respect for him.

PAT FLATLEY: John Tonelli to me is unheralded. He was a tremendous workhorse. He made a lot happen, and created a lot of opportunity. His intensity and work ethic, again, is second to none.

AL ARBOUR: Overlooked? I'd say Kenny Morrow. He never said a word, just very quiet, and he got the big goal in LA for us, an overtime goal. He was just a great player. A great defenseman, and a great guy, too.

CLARK GILLIES: Kenny Morrow. He just went about his business day to day. You never read too many quotes from Kenny in the paper. He's someone that came in after winning a Gold Medal, and was probably more comfortable when there was no press around than when there was press around. He just wanted to go out and play. Kenny got a little beat up. I tell people that talk about getting knees scoped and this, that, and the other thing, in the latter years, Kenny would have his knees scoped on Tuesday, and play on Wednesday. He was getting his knees drained constantly with fluid build up. But he just went out and played every night. He played in a tremendous amount of pain many nights, and did a lot of great things for that franchise. Of all the guys that never got talked about too much, I think Kenny would probably be the top one.

DUANE SUTTER: There were so many. You could say Kenny Morrow, you could say Ny, you could say Johnny. You can go right around the dressing room, and everyone contributed in a different way.

BILL TORREY: The guy that had as big an impact probably was Butchie Goring. The only other addition we made to the team, when I got Butchie, I traded Dave Lewis to LA. And Dave Lewis was a very, very solid defenseman that Al Arbour loved. Having to give him up - as well as Billy Harris - to get Butch, some people felt I really over-paid. In many respects, I probably did. But what people don't seem to remember is the only way I could make that deal was after watching Kenny Morrow play in the Olympics in Lake Placid, and when I saw him shut down the Russians, if you go back and look at the film, in all the tough games, at the end of the game, when they needed solid defense, there was just the big, tall bearded guy that was out there. Kenny Morrow was maybe the most underrated player that we had on that team. He was phenomenal. He was calm, he was cool, he was smart. Very seldom out of position. A very good passer of the puck out of the zone. Unfortunately, he injured his knee, and as the years went on, it deteriorated a little bit from the skating. But he was a good skater and a great passer of the puck. Always played his best when we were behind or when we needed a boost. A very unique athlete.

GARY "BABA BOOEY" DELL'ABATE: Goring would be one. I think Kenny Morrow would be one, also. Boy, talk about getting there right in time, huh? What did he get there, in March of the first Stanley Cup year? But also, incredibly quiet, and a really important part of the team. But there were so many - Tonelli was another guy who was such an important part of those teams.

GORD LANE: You look at a guy like Butch Goring, who played second fiddle. But I think we were not "there" until Butchie came. He was a smart little player, but he also understood what his role was. He knew Bryan was the big dog. Bryan was going to play the power play, Bryan was "the number one guy." And I think to Butchie's credit, he understood that. He understood his role. You look at all the players, and he probably had the biggest impact. Just because he made that second line what it was, nobody could focus [solely] on Bryan's line. They had to focus on both lines.

BRYAN TROTTIER: Probably the most unheralded is Gordie Lane. I never saw his name in the press, never saw his name on the score sheet outside of a penalty. Without him, we don't have half the success. He just gives us another level of mean, another level of keeping the other team off their game a little bit. I love the guy. I sat next to him - a good western boy. He had the mentality that "I'm going to find a way to make you pay the price, in order to not beat us. But you're going to pay the price, *while we beat the shit out of you, too.*" Gordie was a menace, and I just saw him with rose-colored glasses. When he came to the team, he was one of these guys that knew his role, and he played it to the max. I'd get up in the morning and say, "Boy, I'm glad I don't have to play against that guy anymore. I'm glad he was on my team." He just never got a ton of headlines. I think if you ask Billy Smith, he might say the same thing - we talk about Gordie Lane as probably our "most unheralded."

STAN FISCHLER: I did a book called 'Who's Better: Rangers, Devils, Islanders or the Flyers?' And one chapter was "The Best

Underrated Acquisition," and Gordie Lane was the best underrated acquisition that Torrey made. Guys that played will tell you. They had Denis Potvin - he was phenomenal. They had Kenny Morrow - he was terrific. They had Stefan Persson. But they didn't have a guy who put fear into the other team because you never knew what crazy thing he would do. And believe it or not, that's been an ingredient for a lot of Cup-winning teams. Gordie Lane could play, but he also played with that edge - sort of like Sean Avery today. And that sets off the opposition. Plus, he was tough. So all of these things made him special in a very low-key way. Of course, you can't compare him with Denis, because Denis is a Hall of Famer. But he had that special quality, and that was the round peg in the round hole on defense.

BOB BOURNE: I'd have to say Gordie Lane. Gordie came to us the same year Butchie did, in '80. When he came to our team, we didn't really know that much about him, but he was just one tough, intense person. I certainly wouldn't want to play against him. His stick was everywhere - he hurt people, and he let you know about it. Gordie I don't think ever got enough credit. But there were a couple of guys, like Stefan Persson - he won the four Cups, he was brilliant on the power play. And really, really good defensively. I don't think people gave him enough credit for that. A really smart player. And just one of the nicest men you'll ever meet in your life.

JIM PICKARD: One of the characters that we had was Gordie Lane. I don't know if it's ever been mentioned, that he stutters. One of the more comical things, it was probably the third or fourth year, and we had some younger guys on the team, and we were in the Finals. And I think we were going to be on 'Hockey Night in Canada.' I would imagine it might have been on a national basis in the States. Guys were a little nervous, and they were getting dressed for the game. I remember Gordie leaning over, tying up his skates, and he says, "Don't worry guys, there's 400 million Chinamen that don't give a fuck!" And that really loosened up the locker room - that brought the roof down. We went out and away we went.

JIGGS McDONALD: A guy who doesn't get a lot of credit for what he did or what he brought to that team was Gordie Lane. Gord Lane could hack and whack - he kept everybody honest. Yeah, you had

Denis and Dave Langevin, you had Persson who could move the puck. You factor in what Gordie Lane did, and maybe some of it wasn't legal - maybe there was a little spearing - but you just didn't want to get in his area of the ice. "The dirty areas" they call it now. You didn't want to get in an area that was being controlled or patrolled by Gordie Lane.

BOB LORIMER: I don't think people realize how good of a player Stefan Persson was. I know management did, but I don't think the average fan knows how good. I think he's good enough to be in the Hall of Fame. He doesn't have the stats to be there, but playing on four Stanley Cup winning teams and an integral part of the team - killed penalties, great on the power play. And a lot tougher than people think. Not physically tough, but *so* mentally tough. You couldn't intimidate him. He'd play his game no matter what people did to him, and that's a sign of toughness - the guy who doesn't change his game despite being physically abused sometimes. And he made all these little, subtle plays to make the game easier for him. So I think he's extremely underrated. He doesn't get nearly the credit that he should get.

LORNE HENNING: For all the points [Persson] got, he never had a lot of recognition.

JIM PICKARD: One guy I would like to mention who was there for two Cups was Garry Howatt. He was a little spark plug.

MIKE McEWEN: I don't know if anybody was unheralded. I think everybody got their fair share of credit. A guy like Billy Carroll - a fourth line centerman - him and Butch were our first penalty killers. And that's a big role to be that. Maybe somebody like that. Maybe Wayne Merrick - he was the third line center. Our whole third line was like 6'2", 210 pounds. All capable of getting 30 goals a year, between Nystrom, Merrick, and you put Tonelli there - he always thought he should be with Bossy and Trottier, and sometimes he got there, but that was kind of Clarkie's spot.

Maybe Anders Kallur. I'd say Anders Kallur - nobody remembers this guy. I think he played six or seven years. He was a second line penalty killer - him and it was usually Bourne or Trots.

Strong, 200 pounds, 5'10", and fast. You had Bourne, Butch, and Kallur on that second line. Anders Kallur was one hell of a hockey player, and he was only here for a while.

Did you hear the story of how they got him? He was from Sweden, he came over and was a free agent. He landed at La Guardia, and was ready to sign with the Rangers. Torrey met him at the airport - I guess he was with his agent - talked to them, and wound up signing him there at the airport. [Laughs]

DAVE LANGEVIN: I would say the "unsungs" are anybody that doesn't get the notoriety today - the guys that have been forgotten. As time goes on, all you remember is Boss, Trots, Clarkie, and Smith. But if you just put those four or five guys on any other team without the rest of us, they wouldn't have won a Stanley Cup. I watch games now, and they're talking about their top hitter averages three hits a game. I'm thinking, "Well, what is that?" We charted them for about a month with the Islanders - I averaged 12-20 hits *a game*. I think the thing is everybody brought something to the game. That's why we were so good. You stopped Boss and Trots, well, then Tonelli will score, or Merrick will score. And we had Tambellini in there. We got our goals from everybody - Nystrom scored, Henning scored. I just think that unsung...anybody after the top five. That's what made us a dynasty - the depth of everybody else.

JIMMY DEVELLANO: They had a handful of guys that were good players, really when you think back, whether it was a Stefan Persson, or a Kenny Morrow. Dave Langevin was a hard-nosed kid. Butch Goring, the trade that Bill Torrey made, gave us a strong second line center. Your John Tonellis were good, solid, all-around hockey players. Garry Howatt was a strong, feisty kid. Bob Bourne had good talent, very, very good. It was a pretty damn good all-around team. I don't even know if there was a bad player on that team. I don't think so. Most teams today, you get one or two players that really aren't that great - of course, we're living in a 30 team league now, so it's a little harder. But back then, they could *all* play, and they were *all* good contributors.

CHAPTER 44:

THE RIVALRY OF NY

There were few pro sports rivalries as fierce as the one between the New York Islanders and New York Rangers during the 1970's and 1980's.

STAN FISCHLER: There have been some tremendous rivalries in sports - the New York Yankees/Brooklyn Dodgers, the Brooklyn Dodgers/New York Giants. But the Rangers and Islanders in terms of intensity topped anything that I'd ever seen. It got mean on every single level - the fans, the players. And *intense.*

BILL TORREY: It was great going into the Garden. Fans used to spit at me and one guy tried to punch me out in the elevator one night. He hated me. [Laughs] It was good! Hey, that's what it's all about.

JIGGS McDONALD: I had never been exposed to anything like that. When I first got to the Island, I think the first game at the Garden, at the press room before the game, Eddie said, "I think we better go up now." "Go up now?" I looked at my watch. "Yeah, before they open the doors, we've got to get up there." OK, all well and good. The second time in, the same thing - "We better go." OK, up we go. We got off the elevator, and we're walking along the wall there, going to the broadcast booth, and there were two guys sitting there. They're in about the second row down in one of the sections. There isn't an usher, there isn't anybody - we're going up that early. And I overheard the one guy say to the other one, "There's Eddie now. Ask him, he'll know the answer." Well, here's a hockey question. As we got there, the guy said, *"Hey, Westfall!"* and the guy took a swing at him! From then on, somebody from security went up with us.

So if the rivalry between the Islanders and the Rangers comes right down to the broadcaster or the analyst…holy smoke, it was wild. We made sure we got there early of course, into the Garden. And we made sure we left late, and that we came out that side door and across the street to where our cars were - in a hurry. Oh boy, it wasn't fun going into the Garden. I had never seen the hatred.

It's something that you can't create, it's something that happens. The idea of more games within the division to create these rivalries, well, the things that creates rivalries are fights or injuries or playoff series. Wins and loses at playoff time, in my opinion, is what really creates the rivalry. You can't just say, "OK, we're going to play eight games against one another. Here's your rivalry." Calgary/Edmonton, the hate between the two cities and the two teams, but nothing - throughout the entire National Hockey League - compares in the way of a rivalry between those two, the Rangers and the Islanders.

BRUCE BENNETT: Islander/Ranger games in those early days were filled with stress. I'm sure for the players it was a pretty stressful situation. And to this day, I don't like going to a game where there are so many visiting team fans in the home building. It just doesn't seem fair in a way. And I think that's why the Islanders took such pride in battling the Rangers for every point in their home building. To maintain their fan base and to treat their fans, it became really important to them to play up to the Rangers every time they played in that building. And one of the reasons was just to shut the visiting fans up. The early days, going into Madison Square Garden, it was like going into the lion's den. I'm sure it was how teams felt going into Philadelphia during the Broad Street Bullies days, or going into Boston for the Big Bad Bruins. They knew the Rangers were going to try and intimidate them, they knew the fans were there to intimidate them with their taunts. It was amazing in a lot of those situations how the Islanders were able to raise the level of their game, maintain their composure, and walk out of there with a victory.

LORNE HENNING: It was always, to me, like that was the Stanley Cup. We went at each other pretty hard. A lot of times, we'd play each other in the first round. In earlier days, it was the Semi-Finals or whatever a couple of times. But we were pretty even. It was pretty intense, and the fans were into it. It was high-pressure games. But the intensity is what I remember - the City and Long Island. We used to play after the circus, a lot of games late at night. It was pretty cool, you can't beat the rivalry. It's one of the top rivalries in the game - Montreal and Boston, Rangers and Islanders.

AL ARBOUR: I think it was a great rivalry - really something. If we beat the Rangers, we knew we were going to be good, because they always had a good team. They had a very strong team - there's no question about it.

JIMMY DEVELLANO: The New York Rangers under Emile Francis really had good teams - Jean Ratelle, Brad Park, Rod Gilbert, Harry Howell, and Eddie Giacomin. They had good clubs. A little bit unlucky that they never won a Cup [from 1941 through 1993], truthfully. For us to knock them off in that short series, it was a real blow to their team, because they were such significant favorites - as they should have been. We knocked them off and that really got the Islanders on the map. Nobody made fun of us ever again.

DAVE LANGEVIN: Oh, it was fun. Driving in and having the crazy fans outside the door, y'know, driving into Madison Square Garden and having those idiots throwing crap at us, it was a great rivalry. The thing is, it wasn't brawls every game - it was just going hard at each other. I *hated* those guys. I didn't like them, I didn't want to like them. I think a lot of it was that when we played them at Nassau Coliseum, when we'd score, the fans would go nuts, and when they'd score, the fans would go nuts, too. You didn't get that in the Garden. You had a few fans, but they were probably killed by the end of the game. [Laughs]. It was a rivalry the way it should have been.

EDDIE WESTFALL: When it started out, it was "a Ranger home game" each time they played us at the Coliseum. And over two years, we started to win our own fans. And then the rivalry *really* got going. There wasn't really any rivalry the first couple of years, because we were just a doormat for most of the teams that had any kind of depth. But in that third year, we started to win as many as we lost - particularly against the Rangers. The fans were just dying to have that rivalry, that we didn't have in the first two years. So it caught on big time. And then as the Islanders got stronger, not necessarily that the

Rangers got weaker, it was just that the Islanders got so much better. And then it almost tipped the other way - the teeter-totter swung the other way now. So it wasn't much of a rivalry, because the Islanders were so strong. All of a sudden, here we were, so look out! The players were enjoying it. Don't for a minute think that that the players don't read the papers, watch the TV, or listen to the radio about the Rangers/Islanders thing, because they do. They won't admit it maybe, but they do - and they did. So they get caught up in it, and they didn't want to lose to the Rangers, whether it was in there or out here. It was a wonderful thing.

CLARK GILLIES: I wasn't there in the early stage, I got here three years later. The first game we played against the Rangers, my first experience of an Islanders/Rangers game was at the Coliseum. The Rangers scored the first goal. I was on the bench, and I go, "Holy shit...*are we at their rink or our rink?!*" The guys go, "You better get used to that. The Rangers fan that can't buy a ticket to the Garden comes here when we play the Rangers." I said, "That's bullshit. That's got to change. You're playing in your own rink, the visiting team scores, and there's a standing ovation?" I think we got many people to convert to drinking "the Islander Kool Aid" after we beat them in the spring of '75. It was intense. The games we used to play them in the playoffs and in the Garden, this whole metropolitan area was alive. It was pre-Devils, back in those days. This whole place, you couldn't open up a paper without half the paper being Rangers-Islanders/Islanders-Rangers. It was really special to play against the Rangers at that time. And it still is. You talk to the nowadays players and they can't wait for an Islander-Ranger game.

BILLY HARRIS: It got to be pretty hectic in there - to the point where that one guy came down and dumped a beer over...who was that coach that wore the track suit? Jean-Guy Talbot. I was out on the ice and saw the whole thing happen - he went over the glass and chased this guy. That was the beginning of World War III with the crowd and the fans.

BOB NYSTROM: It was intense, because what happened was families were even split. And there was such pressure put on us by the fans, because it was more important for them. I mean, we played it like a regular hockey game. The intensity of the fans, the rivalry, and the hatred was just intense, so we felt the pressure. It was a great rivalry, there's no question about it. I think what really put us over the edge and brought our fan base up dramatically was when we beat the Rangers in '75. There were so many incidences, whether it was fish coming down from the rafters to having young ladies cursing at me while I was standing at the Garden in warm up. It was absolutely incredible. When they beat us in '79, it was pretty ugly. When they came back in that one series, in '84, where they tied that game up in the fifth game, we were scrambling. It was a great, great rivalry.

BOB BOURNE: My first exhibition game was on Long Island, and we were playing the Rangers. And y'know, Jean Ratelle and guys that I grew up watching. And it was the most intense game - even exhibition games were fantastic. I thank god that I got a chance to play against the Rangers. It was just the greatest games. People talked about them three days before and people talked about them three days after. And it didn't matter if it was the eighth time we played them or the first time. It was an awful lot of fun - very intense. Playing at the Garden was tough sometimes. We weren't really welcomed there, like a lot of teams weren't. The fans are tough there. When you're warming up, they're ten people deep in our end. You had to be pretty tough mentally to go in there and play a hockey game. But all in all, I'm really thankful that I got to play the New York Rangers.

JP PARISÉ: I never realized there was such a rivalry. My first game [that Parisé played as an Islander against the Rangers], we played at Madison Square Garden, and in the warm-up before the game starts, a guy leans over the glass, and yells, "Hey Parisé, *you no-good cocksucker!*" [Laughs] I'd never heard anything so awful before in my life!

GLENN "CHICO" RESCH: And then remember Ulf Nilsson when Denis Potvin hit him [Potvin hit Nilsson on February 25th, 1979, which resulted in Nilsson breaking his ankle, and the birth of the "Potvin Sucks" chant at MSG]. And there were a lot of moments of us beating them, them beating us. Bobby Nystrom breaking Ed Hospodar's nose later. I mean, some of the fights we had...

JIGGS McDONALD: A large part of it goes back to Denis' hit on Ulfie.

JEAN POTVIN: The fact that my brother went out there and knocked Ulf Nilsson for a loop, and that started "the chant" - that only added to the rivalry, where they picked on him. And they still do, which is kind of comical.

MIKE McEWEN: It was the ice that caused the injury. It was a pretty clean hit. It's the ruts of Madison Square, and his foot was caught in one. Potvin hit him, and he got twisted. I don't remember any player being so upset by it, figuring it was vicious or cruel. It was just that he got caught in a rut. That's part of playing on Madison Square Garden's ice.

DAVE LANGEVIN: I think they still chant, don't they? They don't even know why I bet you, half of them. It probably makes it worse that it was clean. They've got nothing to bitch about.

STAN FISCHLER: Well, first of all, the hit was clean. It was said to be clean by the victim, Nilsson. Potvin was an excellent target, because he was such an outstanding player - and a tough player. It was almost like a folk legend, that has extended until today. It's an amazing thing. And of course, the fact that he knocked out a very important Ranger at an important part of the season was even more significant. So it all gelled into a huge incident that has a forever shelf life.

JEAN POTVIN: It's funny. Look, Ulf Nilsson has admitted - begrudgingly maybe a little bit at first - it was a clean hit. And he had his head down. Denis was known as "a hitter" from the time he was like ten years old. And when he was able to perfect the hip check, he could be devastating. I mean, I saw him hit some kids in junior, that it's like, "Oh my god. *He's going to kill them.*" Denis had it down to a science, and he had great, great timing. Y'know, you had your head down and you were coming up center ice...Scott Stevens would hit you high. He had great timing as well - look at that Lindros hit. But Denis would not have hit Lindros there. Denis would have hit Lindros right at the knees. Lindros would have done five pirouettes in the air, and landed maybe on his head! So it could have been even worse. Denis did not hit you standing up the way he came in with a hip check. Although, I think if there was a player that was hitting anybody like that in the NHL [today], he'd get a penalty every time, because you're going for the knees. Now, you can go for the head though, which is a whole other story. Anyways, that naturally added to the rivalry. And Billy Smith being such a meek, mild-mannered goaltender - never swinging his stick at anybody. [Laughs] That added to the legend as well. It was just a great rivalry - I loved playing the Rangers. And I'm sure they loved playing against us, because you don't have to motivate yourself to put on your uniform to go play against them.

GLENN "CHICO" RESCH: That was like...you started to chuckle. And you'd think, "Can you really believe this is happening?" Every aspect of it, when a Rangers game was coming up, at practice, you started to hear about it, or you'd hear Rangers fans at your practice. Before the game, the day before, of course, with the press. And then, the noticeable competition between the fans once the game started was also what made it special. You can say Leafs/Canadiens, but the difference is in those buildings, it's not 50/50. When it was Rangers/Islanders - especially when it was in our building - the fans were 50/50. It wasn't like Islanders fans with a sprinkling of Rangers fans. You had just an incredible burst of energy every time you walked into the Coliseum or you walked up the ramp at the Garden.

Everyone knew that this was a game that was going to be a special night - the fans, players, everybody. I've got to tell you, I don't want to say we didn't play them enough, because we did, we played them just the right amount. But oh my goodness, the truth was I didn't dislike the Rangers fans as much as some players. You wanted to beat the Rangers only because of the rewards you'd get - not because you disliked their team. But the rewards were tremendous if you could beat them.

I think they'll say '94 is the golden year of modern day hockey in the Garden - and I guess you have to, because they won the Cup. But for what, ten to twelve years, from '74/75 to the late '80s, there wasn't a more intense hockey rivalry ever. And it just kept going on and on, and kept getting more and more intense. Finally, we drove the Rangers off Long Island - not really - but they moved over to

Westchester [to practice]. That was another thing, in the early years, they were in Long Beach, so that also added to it. Living that was one of the big highs of my life - that rivalry with the Rangers.

GARY "BABA BOOEY" DELL'ABATE: We had a leg up - we won it four years in a row, especially after that '78-'79 series. It was great to win the Stanley Cup, and it was extra great to know you had to beat the Rangers on the way there.

CLAIRE ARBOUR: My kids didn't want to talk about it, so they didn't. Most of their friends were Islanders fans. I remember my grandson went to school with Darcy Regier's son, and both of them were being maligned all the time about the Ranger/Islander thing. And my grandson, Jesse, I'd say, "Well Jesse, what do you say to them?" And he said, "Oh, I only say *'1940!'*" [Laughs] That was a great "out" for the Islanders fans then. I was so sorry to see it go! Because you didn't have to say much. I know that Jesse would never have started a fight, and my son is the same way.

    My son…I have three daughters and one son - I had a very wise principal, who called me in, and he said, "I want to point out that your son gets a lot of attention because of his father. I'm concerned with how he handles it." And I said, "Oh my god, what does he do?" He said, "He does nothing, and that's what concerns me. He internalizes. That's very dangerous. He will need an outlet. Whether it's negative or positive, to show something. He doesn't show anything."

    I got to see that when he would come to the some of the Islander/Ranger games, and I'd say, "Why don't you just stay home?" Because they were hard to take, because you heard so much. He never knew how to express it and let it out, he said nothing. That's what was hard. Now, the girls, well, Janis enjoyed it. Janis - the youngest one - grew up there.

MIKE McEWEN: I think for the Islanders, it might have been a bit bigger deal, because they were trying to get more recognition in the New York area. We won four Stanley Cups in a row, and we were still…I don't want to say we were playing second fiddle to the Rangers, but if it had been the Rangers winning four Stanley Cups in a row, it just would have been a whole lot different deal. And the players were aware of that. To me, it didn't matter. But it was hard to take advantage of it in the whole New York area - it was kind of strictly to Long Island.

DUANE SUTTER: That was certainly the top rival that we had. Washington and Pittsburgh came into it, and Edmonton.

PAT FLATLEY: I remember at the end of the games, just being completely exhausted. Such a high level of intensity, so physical. The fans, the emotion - it was an unbelievable experience. Each game was like the Olympic Gold Medal game basically, because of the intensity of MSG, the Coliseum, and the fans. Their intensity transcends itself onto the ice, and it just carries.

MIKE McEWEN: Possibly [in response to being asked "Could the Rangers have won the Stanley Cup in the '80s if not for the Islanders?"]. We played them in the Semi-Finals that year [1981]. That team was really talented. I think Herb Brooks had them playing the European system. I remember that year, we beat them four games to nothing, but every game was kind of touch and go. We played Minnesota in the Finals that year, and they would have given Minnesota a run, for sure.

STAN FISCHLER: The Rangers had a good team with an excellent coach. The reason why the Islanders have to be rated with two or three of the greatest teams of all time is that en route to the Cups, they had to go through the Rangers a few times. And if the Rangers beat them, who knows? It's one of those things. Shakespeare said, "There's much virtue in 'if'." You can "if" until the cows come home, it doesn't mean anything.

BRYAN TROTTIER: Extreme, but highly motivating. I think their group was very skilled. It seemed like they were constantly in a state of regrouping. For the '70s, they had a certain style and a certain group of players, and all of a sudden, Herb Brooks comes along and brings another style and level of play. It was really all really dynamic. For New York, it always had a flair. There were no "gimmies." Going into a game, it didn't matter if there were injuries on either side, players found that other level, because of the intensity, the focus, and the hype that went with the Islander/Ranger rivalry. I thought it was really unique. We certainly embraced it, because it brought out the best in our guys. And we knew that we generally got the best out of the Rangers - we had a lot of respect for them.

KEN MORROW: I hated them, they probably hated me, and it didn't matter who it was - it was whoever was wearing a Rangers jersey. They could have been somebody you knew or played with or against, in the true sense of the word, you hated them more than you hated the other teams. So all those games, whether it was the regular season or the playoffs, had a special significance. You just didn't want to lose to them, no matter what. We could have been in first place, they could have been in first place, and the other team in last, it didn't matter. It was who won that night. A lot of great memories of those series that we played against them.

BILL TORREY: It was great. It was something that unfortunately, hasn't quite continued. We were the only two-team market. They were the big guys - they had all the money, they had all the press. All everything. We were just those "little guys from out on the Island," y'know?

PAT FLATLEY: I think what makes the rivalry is the fans. It's everywhere. It's in the air the day of a Ranger/Islander game. It starts with your coffee at the deli, with the guys talking about it. You go get gas, the gas station gentleman is talking about it. You get to the rink, the people that work at the rink...*it's everywhere*. It's like a viral contagion - you can't get away from it! It's in you for that 24 hours. Again, the fans really make that rivalry happen, and that transcends itself into us, and then onto the ice and into the game.

BOB BOURNE: I've always thanked the New York Rangers for being who they were, because they were always good teams in those days and we had such a great rivalry. Just hated each other. There were a lot of times during the summer you'd run into those guys - playing charity softball games and things like that - and we got to know them so well. Ron Greschner and all those guys. We ended up all being friends, it was kind of funny. There was so much pride in New York about winning. You'd go to the deli the next morning, and if you lost, you felt like a piece of crap, and you'd hear about it everywhere you went. I think we were a little bit lucky, too. We were a different hockey team. Most of us were married when we were young - not a lot of partying. I think the Rangers were a little bit different in those days. It was just a different atmosphere. But boy, it was a lot of fun playing those guys.

CHAPTER 45:

PREPARATION AND CELEBRATION

Behind the scenes in the training room, and after the game.

RON WASKE: I think that it's become much more sophisticated, with the technologies that have developed in sports medicine. When I think back to when I was working there, we were right on the edge of some of the newer things. That really helped the Islanders organization, as we tried new things. Got into fitness a little bit more. But I think back in the late '60s/early '70s, fitness was a huge issue with the guys. As technology increased, the fitness end of it - and with my knowledge in physical education - I think it worked out really well. And we started doing some different things. And I think it was successful, as you can see with the Stanley Cup run.

JIGGS McDONALD: What impressed me more than anything was the way they prepared. That was due largely to the training staff - to Ron Waske. The two teams that I had been with before; I guess the attention paid to fitness wasn't the top priority the way it was with Ron. The testing that he put them through, I think it was three times a year. First it would be at training camp, then at mid-season, and then there was a testing program he put them through at the beginning of March. That gave Al all the information he needed, as to who had to be in better condition and who needed to work harder. And they did. The fact that there were no public appearances; everything was geared toward April and May hockey. And it started at the beginning of March - they just bought right into it.

RON WASKE: We did that a couple of years, just to see where our players were and their level of fitness. We did some cardiovascular testing, and developed some off-ice cardiovascular training programs to enhance their fitness level, so that later in the season, when everybody else was fatiguing a little bit, we were still maintaining a high level of cardiovascular efficiency. And it showed with our third period performances and our playoff performances. I think our teams were in better physical condition than our opponents.

EDDIE WESTFALL: [Waske and Pickard] approached it the same way that most of the players approached playing the game - they were very serious when they had to be, and very prompt and very good. I don't think they ever said no to anybody.

RON WASKE: Wayne Merrick suffered a serious shoulder and lung injury in the Garden, and he came back really strong after that, and succeeded. Duane Sutter came back from a serious knee injury, and playing very well for us. So we had some of those types of injuries. Fortunately, most of the injury situations were pretty easily managed by the medical staff.

JIM PICKARD: Never heard a thing about it [if there was any talk of steroid use in hockey in the '70s or '80s]. Never saw, nor heard - not even a sniff of anything about that. I'm not saying it didn't go on, but I don't think it did. Again, I never heard anything about that.

RON WASKE: I think back then, it wasn't an item that we had to deal with. Size wasn't a huge factor in the game. Now, people see that bigger people are being drafted in the first and second rounds, so the bigger people kind of gravitate towards hockey now, whereas before, they may have played football or basketball. Now, the bigger players are saying, "I can make a nice living developing hockey skills if I have them." I think that's made the game - the bigger players necessarily gravitate towards hockey. Whereas before, they wouldn't have. But steroids, we never saw any tendency towards anybody on our team. The bigger people on our team - like Clark Gillies and Dave Langevin - were just naturally big and strong men. And they worked at their strength training.

EDDIE WESTFALL: I don't think people realize how important [Waske and Pickard] were to helping develop that team and maintaining it. They were such a part of the team. When the games were over, they were working their tails off back in the dressing room. We'd go out for a beer and a sandwich or something, and in a lot of cases, they wouldn't get a chance to go with us. When we were on the road, it was the same thing - we'd come into town and they would have to go hang up the equipment and get the stuff ready for the next day. So they didn't get to sit down - not as much as you'd like to have them. They were "the missing cog" when we were traveling, particularly. There were only two of them, and there was a lot of work.

RON WASKE: They did a "day of the game skate," so that would take them 35/40 minutes to get there from there they lived on Long Island. Many lived on the north shore. So it was down for an hour skate, back home, they'd show up at the rink anywhere around 6:00 or so. And they would just get prepared. We'd play the game, and depending on what we were doing the next day, we'd maybe fly out. Most of them got in, did their job, and got out.

MIKE McEWEN: Preparing for a game with the Islanders was always a highlight. It was quiet, you could always hear a pin drop. For 20 minutes between warm-up and the game, there would be ten or fifteen guys - depending upon the day - that would throw out something that we had to do. Some people always had the same thing to say. I always tried to come up with something different. But it was quiet, and you would hear these things we gotta do. Sometimes Trottier would get up in front of the room and go nuts for about a minute - yell and scream. It wasn't business-like, it was absolute controlled emotion.

CLARK GILLIES: It was electric. I said to Pam, my wife, one night when I came home, "I've got to learn to control myself. I get too hyped up and I get too excited. I went out there tonight, and I start preparing early for the night game. I got on the ice for warm-up, and the fans were all out there and things were on fire. I just burned myself out in the warm-up! I've got to control my emotions during the day."

So I would just put my mind on other things the first half of the day, and then after I woke up from my pre-game nap at like 3:30/4:00, that's when I would really start to let my emotions get going. It happened to me at the Coliseum - very big game, and I went out there and I was a young kid. I was so fired up that I just really burnt myself out in the warm up. I took advice from some other people and was able to control it to the point that when I started the game, that's when I was peaking - not in the warm up.

BILLY HARRIS: We couldn't do much [partying] with Al Arbour - he kept a pretty close watch on you. On Long Island, we had our little places we all hung in after the games, we all had local joints then. But that wasn't Manhattan. I knew guys [on the Rangers] that were going to Studio 54. This is what Freddie "The Fog" Shero wanted, from what I understand. It was a different atmosphere. They never practiced at the Garden, they lived in Long Beach or moved up to West Chester. I guess they wanted guys to get more "in tune" with the City. But we didn't party that much. We had nice restaurants on Long Island, nice little villages - it was nice to go out.

RON WASKE: They were social. I don't think it was a big part of their success. But they did enjoy each other's company. And we had the typical team parties on the holidays. I don't think they were a "go out to the bars and hang out every night" kind of a situation. But they were social - I don't think they were overly social.

MIKE McEWEN: It was fun to be a part of that group. It was a fun team. Just being around those guys, I think on that team, there's 20 guys, 16 were married with kids, and I was married but didn't have kids. It was the kind of guys that knew responsibility, and they get out of the house and away from the kids, so they're ready to have fun. [Laughs]

BILLY HARRIS: There were times on certain road trips, depending on where we were and where we were playing...I don't want to say too much, because I don't know what you're going to put in the book! All I can say, I'd go on road trips, I enjoyed staying in the hotels and ordering room service. I'm single, right? But the married guys, holy shit - you couldn't find them! [Laughs] A lot of the married guys were gone. I didn't need to go out on road trips to party. It happened, let me put it that way. Some players more than others - not Bossy and Trottier.

EDDIE WESTFALL: Probably not any more than anybody else [when asked if the Islanders were partiers]. I would say that we held our own, when you have the kinds of characters that were on that team. But as we went along, everybody realized that going into the season and playing the games were very important - you weren't here just to party. Listen, I'd been on a team in Boston that was supposed to be well known for that, too. But when it comes to playing the games, they were ready.

CHAPTER 46:

THE BROADCAST BOOTH

Welcome to the broadcast booth, with Eddie, Jiggs, and Stan.

STAN FISCHLER: It's like working with two legends - Jiggs was as good a play-by-play man that I've ever worked with, and Eddie was a tremendous player who some believed should have been in the Hall of Fame. And they were terrific guys. It was a once-in-a-lifetime thing. The chemistry was really good. Fun guys. Jiggs was "the jolly fellow" - he had a Santa Claus personality. And he was fair, he was not a homer. And Eddie, having played the game and being so thoughtful about it, came up with excellent insights. He still is a fun guy. It was a blessing to work with them.

EDDIE WESTFALL: I love Stan. He's a dear friend - I don't see enough of him. We had an interesting start though. When I was a Bruin and Stan was writing his books and doing articles and so on - 'Bobby Orr and the Big, Bad Bruins' and all that - he never once was ever in our dressing room. And never once talked to any of us. He had young people in each city that would do the questioning and send the stuff back to him. We knew he had these people around, and some of us weren't too happy about…he was never detrimental to me, but to some of my teammates he was. We always figured he was a big Ranger fan, so it was easy not to like him. [Laughs] So we would invite him all the time and send messages all the time - "Come into the dressing room and interview the players, if you want to write about us." But he never would.

So when I came to the Islanders as a player, I said to Stan, "Look, I know you have to do it because it's your job and so on.

Please understand that I don't want to undermine or deface my teammates from Boston. You go ahead and do your job, you can ask me anything you want, and I'll do my best with it." And lo and behold, when we had that understanding, he respected that and I liked that. And I respected him for what he was doing in hockey. Then when I retired as a player, now we were working together, so it was really fun. He has a history of hockey - not only physically in his home, but in his mind. He is probably the best hockey historian that I know. And as I say, our friendship grew out of that, and I enjoyed working with him and enjoyed his family - they were a joy.

JIGGS McDONALD: At one point, you could walk all the way around the back of the seats in what they call "the lower bowl" [of the Coliseum] - that was before they built in premium seating, where they have TV monitors built into a table in front of you. I think they provided food and beverage at that time, as well. That was before the press box moved from our side of the building up to the rafters where it is now. When that was completed, we begged to go up there, in order to get a better overall view. We were kind of limited with what we could see of the ice. At the time, I think we were told that if we went up there, the cameras had to go up there as well, and they would sell that area - put seats in. This is when the building was full every night, of course. We said, "No. The cameras can't really go up there, because they're going to be shooting just the top of heads." Eventually, it was negotiated between SportsChannel and Mr. Pickett and the Islanders that we would go upstairs, and the game coverage cameras could stay down.

GARY "BABA BOOEY" DELL'ABATE: I interned for the Islanders the second championship season…what I really did was I interned for SportsChannel. So part of my job was to go to every home game - I had a little press pass - and I had a whole routine I did. I'd get there at about four in the afternoon. I would go in the truck and check if anyone needed copy for anything, get their copies. And then I would take the pagers that they gave to the referees, and I would walk around the ice, to make sure the pagers worked - that they had fresh batteries in them. I had to go on the ice every home game, why I never took a picture, I still don't know. I should have brought my camera. Nowadays, I'd be taking movies with my iPhone. I'd do that, and then my job was to leave the pagers on the referees' table in their room. I was a gopher, running back and forth between trucks.

I didn't work directly for Stan, but I did a lot of stuff for Stan. One of the jobs I did do for Stan every time was Stan used to have a set, and the way his set looked was it was alternating jerseys of the Islanders and whatever team it was [they were playing against]. Once the Islanders' manager knew me after a couple of games, he would give me three of the jerseys on hangers. Then I would go to the opposing guy, and go, "Hey, I need three jerseys on hangers," and they would always look at me, and several times they said to me, "If I don't get these jerseys back, *I'm going to hunt you down and fucking kill you.*" So I would go and hang them on the wall alternating - an Islanders jersey, a Flyers jersey, an Islanders jersey, a Flyers jersey. And that was the set that Stan used. I played Score-O with Wayne Gretzky that year. I hung in the room and watched the game with Ed Hospodar. Remember Ed Hospodar? "The Boxcar" they used to call him, because he used to rail everyone into the boards. I probably met a ton more players I don't even remember. I also remember seeing Herb Brooks that year, too.

STAN FISCHLER: Yeah, I talked to [Dell'abate] about it. It was kind of neat that he remembered. He didn't do it for long, but he was there when I had my classic interview with Gretzky, because I had been critical of Gretzky. But Gretzky came on, Gary was helpful - it was a landmark interview in my career. [Dell'abate] was a fun guy, a great guy.

GARY "BABA BOOEY" DELL'ABATE: My proudest job was I think Eddie drank coffee and Jiggs drank Diet Pepsi. And one of my jobs was to unfurl the SportsChannel banner in that little corner, where they did their in-between-period stand-ups…and get them their beverages.

STAN FISCHLER: Denis Potvin was always a great interview, because he was always skeptical, and then once he got going, he was just tremendous. They had a bunch of terrific guys to talk to - a lot of articulate guys. Bossy was very thoughtful, Trottier was thoughtful, Bobby Bourne was one of the best ever. It was like when Roger Kahn did 'The Boys of Summer' about the Brooklyn Dodgers, and the press agent, who was a friend of mine, Irving Rudd, he did a paraphrase of Charles Dickens, he said, "There was not a rotter in the lot." You had some tough personalities - Billy Smith could be very difficult, because he was so focused. Bossy could be. But as a group, they were the best ever.

JIGGS McDONALD: There wasn't really a tough interview, other than Boss. And again, you had to be prepared, because Mike, very intelligent, and wasn't going to just give you mundane and short answers. He had the game figured out and what he wanted to say. I think probably Clark and Johnny Tonelli were always a good interview. The one guy that stands out was Kelly Hrudey. Goaltenders usually don't like to talk on game day - and this is of course after the Stanley Cup years - but Kelly loved to come down the hall and do an interview with you on game day. It didn't matter to him at all. Very easygoing. Kenny Morrow, dry. Had to work on getting Kenny to give you a good three or four minute interview. But when you went back and listened to what he had to say, very intelligent, very well spoken and to the point. But if you wanted to just fill four minutes, Clarke could do it in a hurry. He was a gem.

EDDIE WESTFALL: I suppose early on, *I* was the toughest [interview], as far as I wasn't that good at it! Your tendency is to go to the guys that would be a good interview. You try to set the interview up so that they're comfortable. The hardest part was that you always knew what the answer was before you asked the question. When you've been a participant in playing the game, and then you go and interview somebody, you almost know the answer *before* you ask them.

JIGGS McDONALD: Game day, it would start with…at that time, we didn't have as much satellite TV or the availability of games in the other markets to watch. If the Rangers were playing, or quite often, you could get a Flyers game - but either watch or listen to the game the previous evening, so you're up to date. Practice in the morning, the morning skate - both teams. I don't know that we talked to as many players as they do now. We would talk more with the visiting writers and broadcasters, and get stories, get the lines - who was playing with who, how the power play was working, who was on the power play, who they thought would be in goal, who was in the dog house, who wasn't getting as much ice time as they would like to have. You just talked about all the different things going on between the two teams, and throughout the league, as well.

The afternoon would be spent - in my case - going over statistics and numbers. Being able to memorize. At the time, there weren't 30 teams like we have now, but memorizing names and numbers, and trying to relate that into the make up of the lines, so if you saw #10, you knew that #14 and #12 should be with him as well. Just preparation.

I would leave home probably around 4:45/5:00. Some days, it might even be earlier than that. We would have our production meeting, graphics were built. At that time, I don't think we did as much in the way of graphics as they do today, because of the equipment. You might pre-tape an interview to run between periods or certainly in the pre-game show. At that point, we were working in the seats right in the crowd of the Coliseum - we didn't have the big press box upstairs. A 7:30 game, we were probably in the booth between 6:30 and 6:45. And then let the game unfold, let it go.

EDDIE WESTFALL: Working with them was absolutely the best. They had two different roles - the role that Stan plays is a lot different than the one Jiggs plays. But they were just absolutely the best. Stan still is, and Jiggs has always been the ultimate professional.

CHAPTER 47:

THE COLISEUM

The home of the Islanders since the very beginning has been the one and only Nassau Veterans Memorial Coliseum, in Uniondale, New York.

BRYAN TROTTIER: The greatest building in the world. To me, Nassau Coliseum was home for 15 years. I thought it was a beacon, an absolute beacon. There was no better ice, I thought Roberto was the best ice maker in the whole wide world. He made the ice for the Islanders, and he was like a teammate. We had perfect ice all the time, perfect lighting, perfect noise in the building. It was like a perfect building.

STAN FISCHLER: One thing about the Coliseum - right up until today - is the rink in terms of viewing hockey is the best rink there is. It's got the best sidelines, you're right on top of the action. Everything about it is just phenomenal. And the crowd is close - they're very close to the players. It's not the biggest rink, and because of the fact it just goes straight up, it made it more like one of the classic rinks, like Maple Leaf Gardens and the Montreal Forum.

JIGGS McDONALD: There wasn't a louder arena, there wasn't a group of fans with more loyalty to their team. Yeah, depending who you played - on a night it was Islanders/Rangers, it would swing either way. Whoever had the lead, it seemed. But coming down to playoff time, that building was rocking. You talk about support for your team - guys feeding off that, the adrenaline in the building. They can talk about Montreal, they can talk about Maple Leaf Gardens back when. Nothing compared to the Nassau Coliseum.

That building...and this is something we see these days - the cookie cutter design of the new arenas. "Austere" if you will. Yeah, they're big and they've got all kinds of point of sale things, and bars and food courts. The personality just isn't in these buildings. Chicago, for instance - United Center can't compare to Chicago Stadium. Air Canada Centre can't begin to compare to Maple Leaf Gardens. The TD Bank thing in Boston [TD Garden] doesn't begin to compare to Boston Garden.

Yeah, Nassau Coliseum has to go - it would be a shame to see it go, but it has to in order to keep pace with what drives the franchise, and that's point of purchase and all the amenities all these new buildings offer. You need that revenue stream. But going back to the '80s, wow - loud and just a great place to be.

CLARK GILLIES: Back in the 1980's, that was not such a bad place to play - amenity-wise. But the Coliseum is a great venue. Once it's full and everybody's in their seats watching a game, there's not a bad seat in the house. It just lacks a lot of the extra stuff.

BILLY HARRIS: New York fans are very vocal, but the thing about Nassau Coliseum was it was outdated when it was built! There were no private boxes, it was just too small. It was a nice arena, but probably the nicest thing about it was I came back for Clarkie's retirement, when they put his jersey up there on the wall or whatever, and it was the same guys parking cars, the same guys working - they all remembered me. All the ushers. It was like a big family in the '70s. We'd go out to the pubs an they'd all come with us. They had access to the players, we all hung out with everybody.

AL ARBOUR: That atmosphere in there was just outstanding. Great to see the people and great to see the fans. The only thing is the rink is perfect, but the outside aisles, there's not room enough on the outside. But once they got inside, forget it - they'd start cheering.

CLAIRE ARBOUR: I had the same seats all those years - I got to know all the people. Then, they were the same people every game. At the beginning - not at the end. It was kind of sad what happened there - there was hardly anyone at the games. But boy, we arrived there in 1973, and we were there 26 years. It was a long time. Anyways, I had the same seats, and I never missed a game. Towards the end, when Al didn't coach for a little while, and when he went back to it, I didn't miss any of those games. But when he wasn't coaching anymore, it was hard to go to the games. But anyways, the Coliseum was home away from home. That was for sure.

BOB BOURNE: I think the old building is pretty sad right now. But I'll tell you what - in those days, we sure loved playing there.

MIKE McEWEN: That's always electric, no matter what building you're in [the atmosphere of a playoff or Stanley Cup Finals game at the Coliseum]. It was one of my favorite buildings to play in - I don't know why. It's a matter of the ice, the way the boards are angled, and the lighting. I always liked playing in the Coliseum. The fan base, it was good when we were winning. I don't know how it is when they're losing. When I was there with the Rangers, I know sometimes the building would be full, and other times, it wouldn't be.

GARY "BABA BOOEY" DELL'ABATE: Like nothing I'd ever seen before. I hadn't been to a sporting event like that. I'd never been to a playoff game in baseball or football - not that there were any to go to in that period of time anyway if you were a Jets or Mets fan. It was the first time that I'd ever been in that environment. It was unbelievable. The place would just shake. It was exciting. It was our time.

BILL TORREY: In spite about all the things that are said about it now, Nassau Coliseum, the sightlines for the average fan were terrific. It was a great building for hockey. It didn't have suites, it didn't have this or that, or a lot of other things. But as far as for a real hockey fan to go and sit and watch a hockey game, it was a great building. And it had great atmosphere, lots of noise. Eventually, we began to start to fit some suites in there. But no, it was a perfect place to go and watch a hockey game. Good parking, easy in - the roadways in and out were terrific. It was really good.

JIMMY DEVELLANO: Terrific. It was a brand new building. We opened the first season with 8,000 season tickets, which was pretty good for an expansion team. It had parking all around it, and it was -

for its time - a good NHL building. Nothing wrong with it. I'm a little different than most people, I think the best way for the Islanders to get a new building is to fill the one they've got. I think the worst part of the Islanders in getting a new building is that it's only half full. I think that's the worst thing. I'm convinced that if the Nassau Coliseum was sold out night after night, they'd have no trouble getting a new building. I really believe that's the biggest problem they have.

KEN MORROW: It's a great old building. The closest I've seen it to what it was when we were playing was when our team was in the playoffs against Toronto [in 2002]. That series against Toronto, I was back for a couple of those home games, and it was as loud as I've ever heard that building. The atmosphere was there. That's the way it was when we played. It was packed, you had the people with the sparklers on the one end. I think we all got spoiled - the players got spoiled and the fans got spoiled. We expected to see a packed house and a loud crowd all the time, and they expected to see our team win. [Laughs] We had a good thing going for a long time there.

EDDIE WESTFALL: Wonderful. A great, exciting…it's only as exciting as the fans and the team, together. That building *rocked.* And there was no place that you could squeeze another person in it from 1975 to 1985. That Islander franchise for those ten years was as good as any other franchise in the league - if not better. It was humming. That 85 by 200 is still the same 85 by 200. Now, do the fans deserve a place? Yes. But the problem that they have is people may buy a seat once or twice to look at the building. Now, if this new, young team that the Islanders are trying to put together, if they get it going like we did in '75, no one's going to care about the building - they're going to show up again. They'll fill up the boxes and fill up those seats. And then when you're doing that, who's going to argue with getting a new building, however you're going to get it? It's the old "cart before the horse" thing.

Yeah, there's lots of things, look at what they're doing with Madison Square Garden - a three-year program. Who cares how much it is, if it's going to make it more comfortable and better for the fans, that's what you have to do. So there's some temporary things they can obviously do, but I can see where Mr. Wang [Charles Wang, modern day Islanders owner] doesn't want to put money into it, because he doesn't have a contract until 2015 I think, when the Spectacor Management Group's contract is up, and then he can bid on it or whatever. But until that changes, for him to put money into it, it's only going to be an advantage to Spectacor. So, I can see his point. And having the fans or the Nassau County people build it, it's just the wrong atmosphere. The highest taxed county in the country, and you're going to try and add more taxes?

There's no question, the building has got so many wonderful memories. But so did the Boston Garden, and they tore it down and it's a parking lot now. So it can be replaced. I just think it's timing.

GLENN "CHICO" RESCH: Still love the Coliseum, and know one day they're going to build a new one. People are trashing it, and they shouldn't, because it's not the building - build a team, you'll fill that place, it will get rocking once more, and then that will bring in money to build a new arena. Yeah, eventually you're going to have to do it. But it's not that arena holding back the team. As a matter of fact, that could still be a big asset to them, and they're getting close. So hopefully it'll happen.

PAT FLATLEY: The Coliseum, everybody talks about it. Just stop talking about it, let whatever happens happen. But if that arena is full today, it's still "the Coliseum." Nothing wrong with it.

BOB NYSTROM: That building, it's outlived its glory, and they need a new one. But in those days, it was *rockin'*.

CLARK GILLIES: My ultimate dream is to be at the game - whatever the new building is called - when the Islanders win the Stanley Cup. You will see a grown man cry that day, I will tell you that. If and when that happens during my lifetime - I hope it does - it's going to be special. But this building, as much as I love it, as much as it has great memories in that building, it's got to go, and we've got to get something new there.

CHAPTER 48:

THE FANS

What did the Islanders' fans bring to the equation?

EDDIE WESTFALL: What did the fans bring? *Everything.* They poured themselves out. They really did. For every fan in the building, in those '75-'85 years, there must have been 20 out in the streets. When you think of today, these kids that play for the Islanders now, I don't think anybody knows who they are no matter where they go. And of course, the helmets and all that. Even when we weren't winning big time yet, people recognized who you were. They lose out on that in some ways too, because they're not involved - all of the players when we were playing in that era, we were all involved in different things in the community. The players were recognized. So I think the fans, they were hungry, and by the time '75 had come around, we were feeding that hunger. And they were enjoying it.

BOB NYSTROM: We started off being the ugly duckling to a certain extent. Our relationship with the fans I think is different than anyone in the league, because we were so close with our fans. We were an upstart team, so we had to meet-and-great, and that just brought us so close to the people. We used to watch whole sections walk in, and know just about everybody in that section. We'd be saying, "Oh, there's Jerry and Phyllis. There's Eddie and Susan." It was just absolutely amazing how many people we knew that were season ticket holders.

LORNE HENNING: We had pretty passionate fans. It was loud and they were very supportive. You can't beat New York fans. It was almost like a family. We spent the summer there and did charity ball games. It was almost like you knew everybody in the stands.

JP PARISÉ: It was unbelievable. It was loud, the fans were great. For me, it was just a pleasant welcome, because by this time, the Met Center had become dull and [the North Stars] were not winning a whole bunch. So all of a sudden, you go there and the atmosphere was just unbelievable. And the fans got a liking to us, and we were just young kids - I wasn't a young kid - but it was just tremendous. They had fan clubs - I never had a fan club in my life until I got there! It was all part of it.

BRYAN TROTTIER: From the standpoint of inspiration, motivation, and support, it felt like we were a big part of the identity of Long Island. We felt like we were a big part of the community of Long Island. We felt like we belonged. And the Islander fans of that era certainly made us feel all of that. It didn't matter if we were at the building, in the community doing charity events or fundraisers - always the same sense of appreciation. I think they appreciated the kind of blue-collar-ness of the team. They appreciated the fact that we were young and they embraced us for a while. They made us feel like a part of Long Island, because we were all coming from different parts of Canada, Europe, and the US. They wanted us to make Long Island home, and I think the guys played a little bit harder because of it. The atmosphere in the building certainly raised the level of our play on many nights. We played as hard for our fans as we did ourselves. We wanted our kids to go to school the next day and feel pretty proud of who we are, too. Win, lose, or draw, my kids loved being born there and going to school there, and feeling good about it all. I can't say one negative thing about our fans and the people of Long Island. I think they're great, great people.

DUANE SUTTER: Away from the rink, they were very open-armed to us. It was a huge thrill to live in a great place like Long Island, and to be welcomed with open arms pretty much wherever you went. They were loud and they were a very supportive group - the whole Island really reached out, and basically adopted us. Just to take your families around the little cities and towns we lived in - it was really special off the ice.

CLARK GILLIES: We had the best fans in the world - we were sold out every game. We'd give them something to watch. Many years, you'd go back and look at our home record, we'd win 35 out of 40, 33 out of 40, and a couple of ties along the way. We didn't lose too much back in those days. So we gave them something to watch every night on the physical side, goal scoring. We were a pretty complete team back in those days. It was really an advantage for the fans to come. They supported us, and hopefully, we gave them something for their money.

CLAIRE ARBOUR: They are the neatest people. When Al did that 1,500th game [on November 3, 2007], that was Ted Nolan's desire, and Al went back. At first, he was like, "Oh gosh, I haven't coached in 15 years." We went back there, and I could not believe the fans that used to come all the time, showed up at that game. It was the most touching thing. What an absolute classy move to do. Joanne Holewa - the dear secretary, who's the neatest person on earth, she's still with the Islanders - she said, "You could see it. First, a 'What am I doing here?' kind of look. All of a sudden, he had his leg up - it was just like old times." But the players were so gracious. It was fun that they won and all that [the Islanders beat the Penguins, 3-2]. And then our grandchildren were there - they had never seen their grandfather behind the bench or anything. And little Michael, he was six years old. So he was in his mother's arms, and he had watched hockey on TV. And there they were on the ice, and the players being so nice to them - giving them sticks and everything. And he said, "I can't believe it...*this is real life!*" And there they were. It was a lot of fun. But all the fans that used to come on a regular basis - a lot of them were there that night. That was a very touching night.

JIMMY DEVELLANO: From about our third year right to the end of my time - year ten - all I remember were sellouts, night after night. It was a tough ticket. It got good in a hurry.

BILL TORREY: For a fan, when your team is winning, there's nothing like it. And for a very, very long period of time, we had a really good run. And not only that, but what made it special was they were there when we were terrible. And they saw this team grow. It's almost like your children - you see them born, and then you see them grow up and become something. That's exactly what the Islanders were.

AL ARBOUR: They brought everything to the team. The Islanders fans were great people. They supported us very well - through thick and thin. They were always backing us up.

DAVE LANGEVIN: It was great. It was home. Just the fans, it's not the building, it's the fans. They had the heartaches, too - they had a lot of crummy teams. They had to hear about the Rangers. I'm sure the fans probably got it worse than us. I just think that winning those Cups was our gratitude as players for them, for sticking through. I wasn't there from the beginning, but it was pretty bad. You see the team progress and get better. After games, walking outside and signing autographs. I know they don't do that any more, but we used to come in before the game and sign cards. And people would be giving us high fives. You'd see the same people there for five years, while we were going for the run. A lot of people still to this day, the greatest time they had was when we were winning those Stanley Cups. You'd go out to restaurants and people would say hi. It was one of the best times of my life. It would be nice to relive it somehow. You never know - maybe I'll be coaching somewhere.

PAT FLATLEY: The fans were so amazing. They're educated fans. They appreciate little things, they cheer little battles. So as a player, it's meaningful - you don't have to go score a goal to necessarily get the appreciation of the crowd. The Coliseum was always special to me because of the fans.

MIKE McEWEN: We got booed a couple of times when we were winning four Stanley Cups! A few times, the power play was going bad or we just weren't doing good. I was like, *"Come on...you're kidding me?"* It was good, I liked playing in the building and I liked the fan base. To me, "fans" are short for "fanatics" - not all of them. I hate to say, but it's almost like generic. To me, it was almost like a generic building. At the time, you go into Vancouver - now it's different - but it was like a morgue in Vancouver. You never heard nothing. Even on an exciting game, it was just kind of clapping and a little bit of ohs and ahs. But it was very quiet.

Fans are part of what you play for. When the building's full, it's nice to play…well, it's kind of a double-edge sword. It's nice to get out there and see a full building and play, and hear the crowd and everything else is exciting. Everybody gets to look at your job and criticize and praise whatever you're doing. I don't know, I played on so many teams - fan base, the Rangers weren't bad. The Islanders obviously were very good when we were winning the Stanley Cups. Obviously a great fan base and a lot of interest. It was great. As a professional player, you understand the fans are there, but there's a lot of playing for your teammates and yourself. I appreciated the fans and all that, but I didn't get into that aspect too much.

BOB BOURNE: I think what happens when you play on a team or in a place for so long, you get to know a lot of the fans. You'd see them all after. I was just down there for an autograph signing three weeks ago, and there are people that walk up that I remember very well. They made you feel special. Very loud, very intense. And New Yorkers know their hockey - that's the greatest thing. A lot of times, you'd go into [a city] and they don't know hockey that well. But not on Long Island. They've got a great fan base there. I think that team is moving in the right direction, and hopefully, the fans will come back out again.

KEN MORROW: It's hard to separate the fans. Just the whole time for me, again, my timing was great. I came to the team right when they went on this great run - five straight years in the Finals. Let me say, life was good out on Long Island. It wasn't just the fans - it was everything. The Islanders were the pride and joy of Long Island. Everything was going well - the team was winning. We made great friends that we still consider great friends, neighbors. And my two daughters were born there. So Long Island was home to us. We loved it out there.

BILL TORREY: Billy Joel sang the anthem before our games, before he was big. The McEnroes all came - father and kids. Particularly in the playoffs, there was always somebody. Everybody wanted to go. Hey, we even had to buy out John Denver, because NBC switched the playing date of a game, and we had a conflict - we had to buy his concert out, so we could play the game! And he came and watched the game.

EDDIE WESTFALL: Someone told me - and I can't confirm it - Billy Joel was an Islander fan. And back in those days when I was the captain, apparently, someone said that he asked for and got my sweater and wore it at a concert at the Coliseum. Now, I can't confirm that, but I was told that. And who would dream that up? [Laughs] The father [of the McEnroes] lived up in Oyster Bay Cove, I think. I remember, because when that Avianca plane went down in Oyster Bay Cove some years ago [1990], it was right by his home. That's how I found out that he was living there. The guy that played 'Sweeney Todd' [Len Cariou], he sang the national anthem at the Islanders games. He's from Winnipeg and a Broadway performer and star - he was Sweeney Todd. He used to be out [at games] every now and then.

MIKE McEWEN: I met [Billy Joel's] tour agent through a mutual friend, and got to know him and his wife. His wife at the time was his business manager, Elizabeth. If you know the song "Big Shot," that was about Elizabeth. She was my manager for my third year with the Rangers. She put together that "Oh La La Sasson" commercial [with the Rangers]. When I got traded, I never heard from her again - I left New York, and that was that. I knew him and kind of got friendly with him, but I knew his tour agent. When [the Rangers] were playing the Montreal Canadiens in the Stanley Cup Finals, Billy came and sang the National Anthem. He was kind of amazed with hockey. He'd watch it and go, "It's hard to believe they're skating out there. They're so sure-footed." I've got to figure he was an Islanders fan - he did the Rangers thing, but he grew up on Long Island. I'd imagine with the Islanders winning the Stanley Cups, he was kind of loving that.

GLENN "CHICO" RESCH: Love those hockey fans. They always say the best fans are in Montreal and Toronto. And I'm thinking, "Perhaps." But no area has three teams who when they're winning, are as enthusiastic and loyal and appreciative as the New York fans. That's the thing people don't realize - *three teams.* We've just got to come up with a name for it - "Hockey Town USA." New York has to have a hockey name!

GARY "BABA BOOEY" DELL'ABATE: I think that a lot of people felt like, "This is *our* team." The thing that was interesting about the Islanders - the Pittsburgh Steelers have a legacy, the New York Yankees have a legacy. The Islanders didn't have a legacy. So while they were becoming a team, they were becoming our team at the same time. I think that was something there. I don't know where they all came from, but here they are on a team in a jersey that no one had seen before eight years ago. Everybody sort of grew up together.

BOB NYSTROM: The best moment that I've ever experienced [with fans at the Coliseum] was in the sixth game of the Stanley Cup against Philadelphia. The Flyers had gotten just an incredible ovation from their fans, and not to be outdone, the Islanders fans, someone had put out pieces of paper and said, "We're not going to be outdone by them." I swear to god, I almost broke out into tears when I came out in warm up. It was thunderous and deafening. The fans were *phenomenal.*

BRUCE BENNETT: It's kind of interesting how fans change through the years. When a team starts out and they're not very good, the fans have low expectations. I think they enjoy the game more. Maybe it's less stressful for them, because they go into it, and "Hey, if we win, that's fabulous." Then what happens is fans, when they start getting used to the winning days, they get a little jaded, upset, angry, and boo the team when they're not playing that well and don't win as expected. What was interesting was Long Island was really always known as "the bedroom community for New York." People would basically come home to sleep, and then get on the train and go into New York City. Obviously, they had the Rangers. Then when the Islanders came along, it started to build an identity that Long Islanders could cling to and could identify with. A bunch of ragtag kids from all over the world - mostly Canada, but a bunch of Swedish players on those teams. It helped give Long Island its own identity, which is kind of an odd thing. They were the underdog, and people like to relate to the underdog. Long Islanders did because they were the underdog for New York City. Maybe it would have been better if they weren't the New York Islanders, if they were *the Long Islanders.*

CHAPTER 49:

THE GREAT ONE

Was Wayne Gretzky the greatest player the Islanders faced?

BOB LORIMER: Gretzky is an unbelievable talent. Great vision, and I think that was the differentiator with Gretzky, the fact that he had such great vision. It's not that he was faster than anybody else, he wasn't bigger than anybody else, and he didn't have a harder shot. But he had such great vision - that's what made him such a great player. But as far as raw skill level, Mario Lemieux is the best player that I ever played against. Because he was a big guy, made the game look so easy, great hands, and a great finisher. Mario, if he had a chance, never missed.

But Gretzky's vision is what set him apart. In the latter part of my career, I spent more games than I wanted in the press box. And when you watch the game from up there, it's very easy, because the game slows down, and also, you can see how plays develop and how lanes open up for passing. It's like Gretzky's eyes were at the top of the rink of the press box, and he was physically on the ice. With the speed of the game on the ice, and the way bodies are flying, you can't see the lanes open up. But his vision was unbelievable - it's like his eyes were up there, and his body was on the ice.

BRUCE BENNETT: There's no one like Wayne Gretzky. Let me preface this by saying I just came back from Wayne Gretzky Fantasy Camp, which I shoot every year, and he presented me with a jersey. These campers pay $13,000 a pop to come to Gretzky Camp, and I was given a jersey…and I paid nothing! [Laughs] I go back to photographing Wayne since he was 17 years old. What they always talk about is Wayne "setting up in his office" - his position behind the net, how he would see the entire ice surface. He would see which players would be in the clear to accept a pass. In the same way that Wayne controlled the game from behind the net from his office, I see him having the control of a room in the same way.

CLARK GILLIES: We have to give Wayne his due, he was pretty special. He had a great supporting cast though. He had all the offensive talent in the world around him - between Kurri, Coffey, Anderson, and Messier. But he made a lot of great players a lot better. He was very, very special. We had a basic system when we played him - we'd put one guy really close to him, and just cover all his releases. Cover Kurri, cover Coffey, cover Messier, and we didn't give him a lot of "outs." I think a lot of teams got drawn to Wayne Gretzky, and if there's two guys on him, one of his other guys is going to be open. But Wayne is a tremendous player. You don't score those many points and set those many records without being absolutely phenomenal.

DAVE LANGEVIN: One on one against Wayne was not a problem, because he wasn't a big player. But the thing was he knew where everybody was on the ice. He just had a feel for the ice. He knew what to do. He made everybody better out there. When you score that many goals, you're in a certain situation. He knows when to score or when to pass. The greatest player ever? I think if it's overall statistics and the most impact player in modern history, I'd say that would probably be Wayne. But then, we had some great players on our team. We had Mike Bossy and Bryan Trottier. See, the thing is, Trots and Boss would never have won a Stanley Cup if they weren't together. And I don't think Wayne would have won a Stanley Cup without Mark Messier.

If you're looking as an individual, you'd have to say just by stats, he was a very exciting person to watch. Whereas Bossy and Trottier, they weren't very flashy, but when Mike Bossy had the puck, you got excited, because you figured he was going to score. When certain guys get the puck, you just know that every time they have it, they have an opportunity to score. Modern day - Sidney Crosby. I think it takes more than one year, a couple years to be considered. I mean, he's got it all, but hopefully that concussion thing is over for [Crosby]. I didn't play against Trots or Boss - except in the

Canada Cups, when they were for Team Canada, but they had a lot of players there. But yeah, I'd have to say Wayne could be in the one or top two.

STAN FISCHLER: Absolutely *not* the greatest of all time. First of all, he was a one-dimensional player. He was an offensive scorer/playmaker. He didn't know how to body check. He never body checked. He didn't fight his own battles - he had Semenko, Lumley, and all these other guys to do the dirty work for him. And he was loaded with stars - Messier to me was a better hockey player than Gretzky, all around. Gordie Howe, to me, is the greatest of all time, because he could do everything. He was the best fighter in the league, he was the best scorer in the league, he was the best playmaker in the league - he could do everything. Howe is at the top. People think hockey started in 1990. I've got news for you - the NHL started in 1917. How could anybody overlook a guy like Eddie Shore? So when you talk about great players, Eddie Shore would put Gretzky in his pocket! Gretzky was a wonderful hockey player, and he had the smarts to give himself a name, "The Great One." So automatically, people think he's the greatest. It's nonsense.

MIKE McEWEN: No, not at all [in response to if Gretzky was the greatest hockey player of all time]. He changed the offensive game of hockey. He is the one that invented "the quiet zones" and "cycling" and everything else. He revolutionized the game offensively - that, along with the Europeans coming in. Offensively, yeah, probably the best player to ever play the game. But defensively, no. From what I understand, a great competitor and all of that, a good team guy and everything else. I never got to know him. Nobody hit him - he was tough to hit. I know he had a thing that if anybody got within two or three feet of him, he was like a ghost. You'd have him lined up, you were ready to check him, and he'd just disappear. Probably the best skater in a ten foot box you ever saw. Able to squirm and do stuff.

But one time, he came down on me, and it was a three on three or a two on two. He came down and faked wide, and tried to cut into the middle. He was right in front of me, and it was really kind of a nothing move. I just stepped up, and basically pancaked him - I hit him in the chest and he went on his back. *Hard.* What I remember was the crowd reaction. I'm looking at him while he's on the ice, and

I hear the crowd go, "Oh no, no, no, no, no." It wasn't like, "Booo!" It was like, "Oh no, no, no, no, no. *Don't do that.*" I'm looking at him, and then the next thing I know, I don't know where I am. Semenko came over and gave me a forearm shiver. It took me about a second or two to figure out where I was. There were four or five Islanders guys around me, and Semenko goes, "Don't hit him again." I don't think I ever saw him ever get hit hard…well, probably I did, but he just had this "radar." You weren't going to get close to him. I was kind of shocked - he was two feet away from me, going half speed, and then he stepped up. But it was the crowd reaction that got me. I guess they saw Semenko coming over.

BOB BOURNE: I don't think he was the greatest, but he was certainly in the top five. I'd compare Bryan Trottier to him any day. But now, Wayne was at that forefront, where there was a bit of an evolution in hockey and it became a little more wide open, and he had some great players to play with. I mean, he was unbelievable. He had eyes in the back of his head. That's the thing that bothered you the most playing against him - you'd think you'd have him, and then all of a sudden, you didn't have him. For me, I felt honored that I played in a time that I got to play against him all those years. Playing against the best is always a challenge. There are a lot of times that he was hard to play against, because you couldn't get at him. He was a very smart player. When I look back, I got a chance to play against Bobby Orr, who to me, is the best player that ever lived. But Wayne is certainly right up there.

JIMMY DEVELLANO: You can't dispute he was the best, most dominant player of the era. I mean, he would always put up double the points that anyone else put up. But during the Islander run, Gretzky didn't really become "a super superstar" until they won that first Cup, and stopped the Islanders' "Drive for Five." Then he became the best player in the game, for sure.

AL ARBOUR: Edmonton would say so [that Gretzky was the greatest player of the era]. I think he was great after we lost. I don't think he was that great until he won the Cup. He was a very good player though - there's no question about it.

BILL TORREY: First of all, he played on a very good team. One of the greatest teams ever. They could skate, they ushered in a more offensive style of game, because it fit their skills. You compare Gretzky to Trottier, Gretzky - number wise - dominates. But when it came to the physical part of the game, Gretz couldn't hold a candle to Trots. But Wayne Gretzky was just an unbelievably skilled, gifted athlete. His vision, his creativity. He did things with a puck that quite frankly nobody hardly ever did. But we got two out of three from him, so more power to him! And he was complimented, just like Bossy and Trots were complimented by Bob Nystrom, Clark Gillies, Wayne Merrick, and Billy Carroll, who made winning all possible.

GORD LANE: I don't think I would say he was the best player. I'd have to throw that at Messier. I think the deal with Gretzky was he had uncanny instincts. He was not the biggest player, he was not the fastest player, he was not the strongest player. But he understood the game extremely well. He had that "sixth sense." And hockey, as you know, like with almost any sport, it's your sense for the game. And I think that's what made him the player that he was. But if I was going to start a franchise from scratch, I would probably pick Messier.

BILLY HARRIS: In my era, yeah, he would probably have to be [the best hockey player]. There's no denying that. I've since got to know him fairly well. He's a pretty good guy. He just made everybody around him so much better. You'd think you got him lined up, and then all of a sudden…he used to look in the glass and see if you were coming. He told me that, and I couldn't believe it - he would look in the glass and see who was behind him! You'd think you had him lined up, and he's such a small guy, you didn't want to hurt him, so you'd sort of ease up on him a little bit. And then the next thing you know, he'd make you look like an idiot. He just had that ability to get out of the way. He was a skinny, little guy, but he could shoot the puck. He was a deceptive skater. He was a lot quicker than a lot of people gave him credit for. But just amazing how he could see the ice. His record speaks for itself.

GLENN "CHICO" RESCH: He was the best. Orr could have been if Orr didn't get hurt. He just had that extra intangible and all that goes with greatness - that was Wayne Gretzky. I remember when I was with the New Jersey Devils, the first two games of a road trip [for the Oilers] would be Rangers and Islanders, and I'd think, "Good, maybe he'll be a little worn down by the time he plays us." No! The guy just never ever let his play slip. Now, I know there were times he had greater games than others, but to me, you couldn't put him in a difficult situation. Every player has something about them that if you boxed them into this scenario, they're probably going to turn the puck over, or they're going to make a less than extra special play. But with Wayne, his ability to pass out of trouble...he couldn't go through everybody, but even at that time or even today because it's a more wide open game, there were like "toll booths" seemingly all over the ice. Somebody hooking you or whatever, trying to grab on to you. And that guy could pass in two spots, in spots that you were just amazed.

And honestly, as a goalie watching it all unfold play after play, it wasn't so much his ability to score. Someone said to me, "If there was a breakaway, who would you want and who wouldn't you want?" And I said, "The player I'd want is Wayne Gretzky, because he wasn't very good on breakaways, and everybody would think, 'Wow, you stopped Wayne Gretzky.' And Wayne admitted that. And the guy you wouldn't want was Mario Lemieux, because he was lights out on a breakaway." So the one little glitch that Wayne had was breakaways, only because the goalie now could be so intensely focused on him, whatever he did, you just knew it was him and you. But when it was a team play, it was like Wayne using everything available to him. Every asset that he had or every resource that was out there - slipping the puck from behind the net, over the net. Passing through a three-inch opening. Guys going down, laying down. "Saucer passing" it.

Trust me, there was nobody better. Stan Fischler will tell you it was Gordie Howe, but in terms of consistent greatness, nobody but Wayne. And he was a great gentleman and a great ambassador. I would say that's the only place where Wayne Gretzky is tied, with Bobby Orr. Bobby Orr was "the Wayne Gretzky" of the early '70s, but he got beat up so bad. But in terms of class and doing what was always right for the league and for the fans, Wayne had it all. I got to play against them all - Howe, Orr, Gretzky, and Lemieux. And you know what? I put a few of them in the Hall of Fame with some of the goals I let up! [Laughs] I'm not in the Hall of Fame, but I'm a Hall of Fame *maker*.

BRYAN TROTTIER: Certainly one of the best. Unfortunately for me, Wayne and I didn't get on the ice - head-to-head - a lot. But it was always exciting when we did. I enjoyed those kind of battles, whether it was the Sittlers, Perreaults, Gretzkys, or Lemieuxs, it was always really exciting to get on the ice one-on-one. You always felt "one-on-one" when you were taking face-offs or got tied up along the boards or behind the net. And at the end of the night, whose team won. I always enjoyed those situations. But Wayne was a phenomenal hockey player. He had a unique style, deceptive speed. He was slippery like an eel - you couldn't get a lick on the kid. He had a vision and skill set that took him to another level.

PAT FLATLEY: Him and Lemieux [were the best players Flatley played against]. People say to me, "When Gretzky played, you weren't allowed to hit him." And I would call that a complete fabrication and lie, really. Because we had a lot of Hall of Famers on our team, and let me tell you, everybody on our team was trying to get a piece of Gretzky. But he's got a sixth sense, and you can't contain him. You can't get a beat on him and you can't hit him. The reason you can't hit him is because he's too smart. He gets out of the way. [Laughs] You go to him, and he finds that guy that is open. In hockey, there are moments in time that are very fluid, and there's a split second where a guy's stick is open, and most players in that split second don't hit the guy's tape. That's why the games aren't 20-19. If everybody was Gretzky, that's what the score would be, because he does find those opportunities. That was his gift - he had a special sense.

DUANE SUTTER: I think Gretz competed in his own way. Some fans may have thought that he didn't, but as an opposing player, there was "big time compete" in him. He had an uncanny ability to know where the puck was going ahead of other players, and that's what made him so good. He just had that "seventh sense."

GARY "BABA BOOEY" DELL'ABATE: The two Gretzky stories I have is one time he was [at Nassau Coliseum], and the Islanders used to have this game called Score-O that they'd play between periods, where you put a board up against the net, and there was an opening that was like a micrometer on each side, to let the puck go through. If you shot the puck from center ice and you got it through, you won a car. I remember Gretzky walking around, wearing one-piece flannel underwear - like you see old timers wear. He was probably a year older than me, and he was bored shitless. He was a kid. I remember him saying, "Hey, grab that board there." And I remember holding the board for him, while he kept trying to win Score-O.

But the other thing that I remember was that Fischler had written an article for the Hockey News, and the article was "If you could pick one player to start a team with, from anybody in the NHL now, who would you pick?" And Gretzky was great, but he wasn't "The Great One" yet. Quite honestly, Trottier was pretty damn good. So Stan's article was basically he would pick Trottier over Gretzky. He sort of pointed out a couple of Gretzky's shortcomings. Boy, talk about a bad review you'd like to take back, eh? So what happened was once in a while when Stan Fischler wasn't around, I would help out, and it was one of those days when the game was over, Stan will pick the star of the game. And Stan would always give you a choice - choice one, choice two, and choice three [of people he wanted to interview].

So I went in and I sort of knew about this thing that was going on with Fischler. Stan may have talked about it earlier that night, "I hear Gretzky's mad at me," or whatever. So I went into the locker room, and I said, "Excuse me Mr. Gretzky, Stan Fischler would like to interview you because you're the star of the game." And Gretzky goes, "Fuck him! That asshole, he says that I'm not any good, and he wrote that shitty article? Blah blah blah." So I moved on looking for whoever number two was - a little mortified - and he goes, "Hey kid, hold on a second. Tell him I'll be there in a minute." I remember he came on, and Stan said, "So Wayne, you had a really great game, blah blah blah." And Wayne goes, "Hey, let's not talk about that Stan. *Let's talk about how you said I'm not that good and how Trottier's better!*" It was really funny, uncomfortable, and ballsy. And I thought very interesting - it made me think Gretzky's a funny guy.

STAN FISCHLER: Gretzky playing for Edmonton and me doing Islanders games, right off the bat, there was sort of a rivalry there. But he's basically a very, very nice guy. He's a good person. But when he came to the Rangers [Gretzky played for the Rangers from 1996-1999], if one could say we had a feud, I wouldn't call it really a feud, but certainly, there was some "sizzle" between us. And I asked him to come on between periods at the Coliseum - there was a lot of tension, and I'm sure reluctance. But he came on, and was very fair about it. My first question to him was, "You've taken a lot of shots from me. Here's your chance to come back." And he said, "Listen, criticism is part of your business, and I accept it." He was very, very fair. And he's a great guy. That doesn't mean he's immune from criticism.

BRUCE BENNETT: He's an unbelievable human being to be around. I kind of equated him at one point to a couple of shoots that I had done with Presidents of the United States, when teams would go in to be honored for winning the Stanley Cup. When a US President comes into a room, the whole room is changed. And with Wayne Gretzky, when he comes into a room, the entire dynamics of the room changes.

JIGGS McDONALD: Yes, several times [Jiggs interviewed Wayne] - more so after the '80s. I mentioned on the outset, being from the Brantford area, or at least north of Brantford, there's a relationship between Ayr and where he grew up - where his father grew up, more so than Brantford. Very early on, when I first introduced myself [to Gretzky], I mentioned a little drive-in restaurant that existed at that time - no longer there - and he said, "You know that place?!" And we got along great from then on. He sought me out in Phoenix a couple of years ago when he was still coaching [the Phoenix Coyotes]. He saw me in the seats at the morning skate, and he sent the PR guy to get me and come through his office. He's a good human being - just a great guy. With all the ability in the world, all the talent. I had the opportunity to do the game when he broke Gordie's record - that goes back to SportsChannel America days. His ability, he was probably three, four plays ahead of what was actually happening on the ice. He could move the puck.

What he brought to the game - and so many people have tried to emulate - was the ability to play from the back of the net. Not so much to score goals, but to sense what could happen, how to get a guy in position to feed him the puck from behind the net, and also, get a defenseman or the goaltender out of position and carom the puck off of somebody into the net. He brought an asset to the game, or a whole different dimension, as to what could happen from behind the net. And especially when they gave a little bit more room back there in his later years. He was so creative.

When he first came along, I read all these things about this kid from Brantford and the peewee tournament in Quebec, and what he was doing in bantam hockey and midget and so on. Way ahead of his years. "Spindly kid, not big enough." "Yeah, OK. *Catch me if you can.*" Wow, what a player. But that said, if you were to ask me the best hockey player I've ever seen, I'd have to go with Bobby Orr. Bobby combined everything - the offensive end of the game, the defensive end of the game, skating, smarts, personality. "1A" and "1B" - he and Wayne.

KEN MORROW: He was the best hockey player of that time. Kind of categorized with Bryan Trottier, the best two-way center. But Wayne Gretzky was blowing people away with the scoring, and they were winning championships through the later '80s. Playing against him was just a matter of trying to contain him, really. You try to limit the damage. He had a great supporting cast there. So for me as a defenseman, it was always try not to give him time to do his magic, and trying to get on him. We had some success on him. It was "a five man job" - it wasn't just the defense. You knew he was going to get the puck to somebody, so you had to take away all his options. So it meant the forwards had to cover their guys, and we had to try and not give him as much time to make things happen. We had some success against him, and I'm sure he lit us up sometimes.

LORNE HENNING: When the Oilers came in, they had a phenomenal team, but he was the guy who was driving it. For his vision, setting people up - he had a lot of complementary players, but he was the guy that was the face of the franchise. I don't know…you could argue Gordie Howe, Bobby Orr, and Gretzky. Those are probably the three guys. But in our era, the things that he had done and accomplished, it was pretty amazing stuff. He's a great player for sure, and he was competitive - he hated to lose. Even when he was coaching, he hated to lose. That's what drove him. The great ones are competitive. And he's a good guy - he's an ambassador for the game, so that helps.

BOB NYSTROM: I would have to say he was [the greatest player Nystrom ever played against], but there were a couple of close seconds. I think from a player's standpoint, Mark Messier, Mario Lemieux. Wayne had a pretty good supporting cast, and I think that some of these other guys, like Mario, I don't think he did. We had a pretty good rivalry against Edmonton, also. I think that they maybe learned a little from us. But they had a hell of a team. From a talent standpoint, they may have had one of the best teams ever. But it just took them a little while to grow up.

CLARK GILLIES: There were a lot of great players in the '80s, and Gretzky has overshadowed most of them. It was not just Mike Bossy [that Gretzky overshadowed]. Thank god Gretzky couldn't score goals like Mike Bossy, or else he'd have a few more arrows in his quiver because he *really* would have been dangerous. But they're both great players in their own right. Wayne, when you score 212 points [in the 1981-82 season], you have to be doing something right! [Laughs] Because it wasn't easy to do - he scored 200 when most of the other great players were scoring 100.

JIMMY DEVELLANO: There's always somebody - now it's Sidney Crosby. Hey, that's the way it is. There's always somebody that comes up. It doesn't diminish our Islander guys.

CHAPTER 50:

THE GREATEST OF ALL-TIME?

Are the Islanders of the early 1980's the greatest hockey team of all time?

JIMMY DEVELLANO: There's no US-based team that has ever won four in a row. We did it in our eight, nine, tenth, and eleventh years of our existence. No US-based team has ever won three in a row, how do you like those apples? Quite a few of us have done it twice in the US - I did it with the Red Wings back-to-back in '97/'98. I couldn't win a third and fourth one together. I did win a third and fourth Cup, but they were scattered.

JIGGS McDONALD: Absolutely. You can take those [Islanders] teams, put them up against teams from any era - including today's era - and they would find a way to beat you. They could adapt, they could adjust midstream. If you want to get into a track meet, an all out skate, we'll beat you at it. If you want a slugfest, we're ready - we've got Garry Howatt, we've got Bobby Ny, we've got Clark.

PAT FLATLEY: I think they were, because one, their character. And the fact that they could play any style you wanted. Philly wanted to play tough? OK, no problem. You want to go to Washington and play a finesse game? OK, no problem. They can beat you any way you choose to get beaten. They'll adapt. And that's the thing about great teams - great teams adapt to whatever is put in front of them. There is nothing they would view as a problem - everything is adaptable. And that's what the Islanders would be. Their intensity, their character, and their adaptability.

BOB NYSTROM: We could really play any style of game, and I think that we played a system that was…when we won the fourth Cup and we shut Edmonton down, I think they got six goals - that is probably the biggest tribute of all. To win the number of series that we won was also pretty amazing. So I would have to say that we rank up there with the best.

CLARK GILLIES: I'd say we absolutely have to be put in that category. One simple reason is you go back and there is no other franchise in the history of this league that ever won 19 straight playoff series in a row. And we lost to a very good team in the 20th series, to lose the fifth Cup. So you can talk about a lot of different franchises, but there isn't one out there that has done what we did. So, does that make us the greatest? Hey listen, arguably, yes.

DUANE SUTTER: No question. Again, 19 consecutive playoff series, four consecutive Stanley Cup wins. Two records that will never be matched.

JIMMY DEVELLANO: The other record that the Islanders obtained that I don't think will ever be broken is that they won 19 straight playoff series. I repeat that, *19 straight*. The four Cups times four rounds is 16, and then their "Drive for Five" they lost to Edmonton in the Finals. 16 and 3 is 19. I've been in Detroit 30 years, the best we could do was nine straight series. And we've had a good team. So it just points out how good it was.

KEN MORROW: No doubt. I don't know how you compare teams from different eras. I guess there's no perfect way to do that. But no doubt our record speaks for itself. The one that I'm probably most proud of is the 19 straight playoff series. That's a record that will never be broken - I'll go on record as saying that right now. It will *never* be broken.

STAN FISCHLER: You could make a legitimate argument for the Islanders as the greatest team of all time. Why? The Canadiens are the only team that ever won five straight Cups. But the Canadiens only had to go through two teams each year. So when they won five Cups, they went through ten consecutive teams, ten consecutive playoffs. The Islanders went through 19 - almost twice as many. And with a break or two, it could have been even more. So right off the bat, you've got a reason why the Islanders are the greatest of all time. They had the best money goalie in Billy Smith. They had the best mix, in terms of playing the game any way you wanted to play it. The Oilers could never play it defensive. Now, the Canadiens of the '70s, when they won four in a row, is another terrific team. It depends on your values. I would put the Islanders right up there, one/two, with the Canadiens that won five straight.

JEAN POTVIN: No doubt. It's not for me to say, but I think they have to rank in the top two, three. I really do. I have a lot of respect for the Montreal Canadiens team of 1955 through 1960, who won five in a row. But they only won *ten* series. There were only six teams in the league. And back then, Montreal was by far the dominating franchise in all of hockey. The Toronto Maple Leafs were next. Montreal had such a huge farm system, that they probably owned half the hockey players in the minors!

But I think the Oilers are probably a team that people would [consider]. They played a slightly different game than we did. I think they had more speed. They also had a lot of talent. I mean, both teams are like dynasties, and rightfully so. I think we turned out to be better than the four time Stanley Cup-winning Montreal Canadiens of the late '70s. I would say right now, if someone was to ask me, I'd say it's between us and the Oilers.

And that's why I think the '70s and '80s were the best years ever for hockey. The reason I say that is because at first, you had the big, bad Bruins with Bobby Orr, when he was at his prime. The guy was amazing. Then you had two great Philadelphia Flyers teams, then the Montreal teams, then us, then the Oilers. I mean, that's the '70s and '80s - you can't get better than that.

GORD LANE: When you look at all the possibilities that could go wrong - injuries and whatever else - there was always somebody [who could fill in]. When we won that first Stanley Cup, Wayne Merrick was centering that third line, and he nicked up his thigh. Lorne was just thrown in, and he sets up Nystrom with the winning goal.

MIKE McEWEN: Everybody was just smart. We had a saying on that team, *"Everyone's a leader."* I mean obviously, our big four - Potvin, Trottier, Bossy, Smith - led us. Our first line was one of the top three lines. Our second line could have played with any first line in the league. And our third line could have played with any second and some first lines in the league. So everybody contributed, everybody was important, and we knew that. It was fun to be a part of.

AL ARBOUR: We had the players, and they were a great team - there's no question about it. Montreal had good teams, Edmonton had good teams, but we had a good team, too. We should be right on top. Wherever rated, we should be right on top.

BILL TORREY: All I can say is in our time, we were a very special team. Have we gotten as much recognition as say, Gretzky? No. Even the Rangers, who have won one Stanley Cup in how many years - it's always somebody else first. And Montreal, growing up in Montreal, are you kidding me? They were so good those teams in their era. Somebody will ask me, "Is this guy better than that guy?" I say, "Just take teams in every ten year period and say who's the best." You can't compare it - Montreal had certain advantages, and they maximized them. They had years where they could draft any French Canadian before any of the other teams could draft! And that was such a special gift - they had to stop doing it, or otherwise the Canadiens would win every year.

There are things that make each different. The Canadiens were phenomenally gifted - Doug Harvey, Bert Olmstead, and Rocket. That was a phenomenal team. But they weren't as big as our team. Who knows who was better? All I know is our record for a certain period of time was as good as any, and in some respects, better. Montreal won five, and we tried like hell and just missed. But Montreal didn't have to play in world tournaments and all the stuff that our players had to do. I mean, our guys - for five years - hardly ever had a summer vacation! Montreal, when they won their Cups, they played two rounds and they were over and done with in May, and didn't start again until October. But Edmonton, when they were in high gear, they were something really to see. They were really a great, great bunch. And Gretz, god bless him, what he's done for our game. He's popularized it in the United States, and he's been a perfect gentleman through it all.

BOB LORIMER: Different eras dictate different types of teams. But we have to be in the discussion. It's hard to compare yourselves to who's better with the dominant Edmonton teams, because of the skill level they had, and the number of Hall of Fame players they had on that team, and their ability to score. And also the Canadiens, who won five Stanley Cups in a row. One year I think they lost nine games, or something unbelievable [eight loses in 1976-77]. It's pretty hard to beat those teams as being dominant teams. But we've got to be in the discussion. Four Stanley Cups - we were able to win it physically, with skill. That was important back in those days, because you were challenged physically. If teams couldn't beat you skill-wise, they'd challenge you physically. So you had to have both elements on your team.

BRYAN TROTTIER: I think we're just proud of our achievements. I don't think we can gloat, I don't think we can boast. We can take pride in what we achieved. I think we take pride in how we played and how we achieved it. We take pride in where we were, what we came from, what we'd become. It's a really cool reflection on all of us. I can't accept all the credit - I take my fair share, but I'm certainly going to point fingers to all my teammates, management, the greatness of Long Island. There are a lot of things that were special about that group and special about that time for all of us. It was a great time for hockey. No one handed us the Cup - we had to earn it. And when we earned it, we had to defend it. There was nothing easy about it. We set some records, we achieved some really great friendships and terrific bonds because of it. I cherish those years tremendously.

I don't compare us to any team, unless somebody asks me to. I always think of us as being our own team, at our own time. There's more similarities between championship teams than there are differences. You need great goaltending, skilled players, depth, foot soldiers, you've got to stay healthy. And all those things happened for us - like they happened for Montreal, like they happened for Edmonton. You need the luck of the bounce at the right time, you've got to take advantage of your breaks. There are more similarities for me than there are differences, and I just think it was a special time for our group. It was our time. And we took complete advantage of it. Management let us be creative, and at the same time, we had a really great system that all of us believed in. There were probably little bumps in the road, but we overcame a lot of them. For that, everybody deserves a lot of credit, because championships aren't easy. They're hard, and if they weren't hard, everybody would do it. That's what everybody loves about championships.

When I reflect on all these championships, it's really kind of fun, because I look back and I say to myself, "I came out not so bad. There are lots of guys that have a lot more bumps and bruises than I do. But I played hard through it and I gave my fullest." And because of that, I can feel good about what I did. And I can look at my teammates, and say, "I feel good about what they did for me, to feel like a champion, too." The appreciation factor. There are a lot of things that I'm even more appreciative of, even now. And I was extremely appreciative at the time. You can't thank the guys enough. That "championship feeling" kind of washes over you every once in a while. But there's a new champion every year, and they get to strut. We strutted for our four years, and I got to strut for a couple more in Pittsburgh after that [1991 and 1992], and one more as a coach [2001, with the Colorado Avalanche]. So I say to myself, "Over a 30-year career in the game, to walk away with seven rings and feeling like a champion is a pretty good percentage." I'm thankful to a lot of guys. But I have to grab a hold of the rope, too - you make sure no one's looking at you, saying, "You're the weak link here." Everybody wants to be the strongest link.

JIMMY DEVELLANO: There was an eight year period where only two teams won the Cup. Montreal won four, and then the Islanders rolled off four. Even the great Edmonton teams with Gretzky couldn't win four in a row - they didn't win three in a row. They did win five Cups [but not consecutive] - the same with Detroit, they won back-to-back in '97/'98, then we won in 2002 and 2008, and then we had a heartbreaking [loss]. We should have had one more Cup, which would have been our fifth Cup in '09. Pittsburgh beat us in game seven, 2-1 in our building, to win the Cup. Otherwise, we would have again done back-to-back. But anyways, that's sports.

BILLY HARRIS: A lot of people ask me, "Where you pissed off after they won it?" And I say, "No, no - not after the first year. After the second, third, and fourth year, yeah, *I was getting a little pissed off."* [Laughs]

EDDIE WESTFALL: Yes, they deserve being recognized. Given yes, Montreal did it four times, and they also did it five times - those are givens. But that wasn't the '80s. That team, they deserve to be recognized forever as being one of the great teams. It looked like the Bruins of old - every time you turned around, they were breaking another record. They would have been a really tough team to play against - that's what I used to say then. "They're having so much fun. They're the hardest team to play against."

MIKE McEWEN: I read a book, they did "The Greatest Twelve Sports Teams of All-Time," and they had OU in there in the '50s, and they had the Islanders in there. And they had the Canadiens in there in the late '50s when they won five, I think they had the Canadiens from the late '70s, too. All I know was sitting in that room, there was a real chemistry and a real feeling that, "If we go out on the ice, *we can dominate."* That's kind of unbelievable in pro sports, that you can say that. It wasn't a hope or anything, it was like, "Everybody do your job. That's what we're going to do." This was just sort of a fact. And if we didn't dominate and if we did lose, we knew why. And we'd go out and correct it the next game. The atmosphere in the room and the guys off the ice - a lot of great character guys. Guys that came to play and were willing to pay the price to do whatever it takes.

GLENN "CHICO" RESCH: The Canadiens won four in a row, and the Islanders won four. So now you're narrowing it down to two, because remember, the Penguins were good but only won two, and could have won another, but didn't. The Oilers didn't win four in a row, they had a little glitch there, however you want to read that. But both the Canadiens and the Islanders never ever underachieved in those four years. When every game counted, they didn't underachieve. To me, probably their greatest Cup - in terms of winning the first, yeah, but we were the best team then - when they beat the Oilers in their last Cup, the Oilers were a pretty darn young, hungry team, and they could have beaten them. You've got to break down the roster and roles. The Montreal Canadiens late '70s, Islanders early '80s, and then it is completely, completely impossible to say one team is better than the other. I won't say the Islanders were better than the Canadiens, but I will say that there was no team better. Maybe there was a team tied with them, but there was no team better.

RON WASKE: It was the just the combination of talent, work ethic, camaraderie. They really cared about each other. And that was a common thread through the ten years that I was involved with them. We all came together, we enjoyed each other, and it reflected on their play on the ice.

DAVE LANGEVIN: The greatest team ever? It's hard to know. Montreal had some great teams. At Edmonton's best and our best, I think we were better, just because I think defense would win over goal scoring. Montreal, they had that wild card, where they could get every French-Canadian player for a while. They had some great teams, they had some great defensemen. "Ever" is a pretty big word. Being one of the top teams ever, I would have to say yes. Being *the* best, there's no way of measuring.

BOB BOURNE: Montreal in those days I thought was the best team there ever was, when their defense had three Hall of Famers on it, and three guys that could have been. But I think our team would stack up against any team, and all the better teams that we played against - Edmonton, Montreal, and all those Rangers guys would have to tell you we were one of the best teams. Certainly, I would put us in the top five.

GLENN "CHICO" RESCH: If you had a four playoff fantasy of the greatest teams ever put together, you would have to take the Canadiens of the late '70s, the Islanders of the '80s, the Oilers of the '80s, and even though they only won two cups, that Penguins team [of the early '90s], when they had Mario Lemieux, Ronnie Francis, and Bryan Trottier as their centerman, that was a pretty good team, too. You have to put those four teams in the top, and then the arguments can be made for who's the best. Of course, you never come to a unanimous conclusion on that one.

BOB NYSTROM: It's kind of like we just wanted to keep it, so we never thought of winning two or winning three as a major accomplishment - we just wanted to keep it. It's probably not until after a guy's career is over that you're laying in bed and you're saying to yourself, "Wow. *We really accomplished something.* To win the number of series that we won and to win four Stanley Cups is just absolutely incredible." I don't think it's ever going to be done again. I think it was a tribute to our coach, to our team. The greatest group of guys. Just phenomenal. We can be away from each other for five years, and we'll walk in the door, and it's just like we're there every day.

BOB BOURNE: I thanked my lucky stars every day, because I got drafted by Kansas City - I could have been in New Jersey or in Denver. I really did thank my lucky stars. I remember I was a free agent - I think it was in '82 - and Bill Torrey and I sat down, and I probably took less money than I could have got somewhere else. But you're playing with some special people.

JEAN POTVIN: It was a real privilege playing for that organization. Really super, nice people - from Bill Torrey to Al Arbour, Jimmy D on down. You know what's amazing is a couple of years ago, they had the reunion for the players who had been on all four Cups, and I think there was a total of 16 players. That's remarkable. You'll never, ever see that again, because of free agency the way it is today.

JIMMY DEVELLANO: Now, the thing that saved the Islanders - there's always bad news behind everything - was there was no free agency then. The players couldn't really go anywhere. Today, running Detroit or any other team, you'd never keep a team like that together. You wouldn't be able to afford it. Somebody would poach Trottier away from you or Potvin, because you couldn't afford to pay them all. So, those days are over.

CLARK GILLIES: I talk to people about what it was like on that team, and how good that team was. That team was so good that that team wouldn't be together in this day and age! You couldn't keep them together, [due to] free agency. You're talking about 16 guys that played on all four Stanley Cups. It's ludicrous to think that anything remotely close to that could happen [today]. Again, we were that good, and we believed we were that good, and everybody knew we were that good. So it was just a matter of us playing to our ability, and we weren't going to be beat.

EDDIE WESTFALL: There was a great line, did I ever tell you about the line that Clark Gillies said? We used to go - we still do - to these charity functions, and he and I would be there together. And of course, there isn't a microphone that Clark Gillies would ever pass. [Laughs] He'd be up there pontificating, and he'd say, "You'd think about the Islanders and the four Stanley Cups and our 'Drive for Five.' Just think, if Westfall would have retired two years earlier, we would have had *six!"* Thanks Clarkie. [Laughs]

BRUCE BENNETT: Through all the years that I've photographed this sport, the Islanders and the Oilers, I think about those two teams having the balance more so than any other teams.

GARY "BABA BOOEY" DELL'ABATE: For me, yeah, because the other great team, the Canadiens before that, I didn't really know hockey that well, when you go back to the Canadiens of the '50s. And the Oilers that came right after the Islanders. I'm sure they were a great team, but this is where I become an asshole New Yorker - they were in Edmonton, *who gives a shit?*

CLARK GILLIES: Unfortunately, we don't see each other as much as we'd like to, but I hope everyone's doing well, obviously. Shit, this is the 40th anniversary of the Islanders franchise, that makes it 31 years since the first Cup. But knock on wood, we're all still around - Coach Arbour, Bill Torrey, the training staff, and all the guys. We haven't lost anybody yet.

STAN FISCHLER: The bottom line is no other team has won 19 straight playoff series. And that is why they can be called "The greatest team of all time."

CHAPTER 51:

TODAY

What are the folks interviewed for this book up to today?

KEN MORROW: The director of pro scouting [for the Islanders]. I've been fortunate enough after playing my whole career with them, I coached for three years - two years away from the Islanders and then one year back with them. And then I've been scouting with the Islanders since '92-'93. My title is "Director of Pro Scouting," and I've been doing it for 18 years. Again, I'm just thankful to have been with the same organization and the loyalty that they've shown me, and I think I've shown them as well. I still enjoy it - it's great being involved in the game. I want to see the team get up to where we should be.

BOB NYSTROM: I've been at the same company for 21 years now [Kinloch Consulting - www.kinlochcg.com]. Right after I retired, I went into the employee benefit business, and we basically provide health insurance or group coverages to corporations here on Long Island and nationally. I just have really enjoyed this and have been with the same group of people for a fairly long time.

DUANE SUTTER: I'm the Director of Player Personnel for the Calgary Flames. This is my third season with them.

GLENN "CHICO" RESCH: I've been doing Devils TV for fourteen years [for the MSG Network]. I've been color commentating, working with Mike Emrick. That in and of itself was a real blessing, because working alongside Doc was like working with the best in the business, who was very demanding of himself. Doc really taught me how to be an announcer. It's been a good run. Let's see, from '74 to '81 I'm in New York, then '81 to '82 I leave for one year, then from '82 to '87 I'm in New Jersey and Philly, so I've spent most of my adult life in the New York area. It's kind of like a home. I remember when I first went to New York when I was a kid, just looking at everything. The tall buildings. All of us from the prairies couldn't believe we were in New York. It just seemed so magnificently diverse, and you're never going to figure things out. Now, what's nice for me is it kind of seems like a bit of a small town feel. And people are still so good to me. I don't know how it happened, but I am as much forever a New Yorker/New Jersey [resident] as I am anywhere else.

GARY "BABA BOOEY" DELL'ABATE: I'm the producer for 'The Howard Stern Show' for 28 years, and I had a best-selling book out last year [2010's 'They Call Me Baba Booey']. Running the show is the bulk of my time.

STAN FISCHLER: I work for the MSG Network, I'm a reporter for them on hockey, and I do a lot of blogging. I do a weekly column called the Maven's Raven. I just did an interview with John Tortorella and I wrote part one of a two part story. I do a lot of hockey writing. I publish my own insiders newsletter - it's in its 18th year - called the Fischler Report, and it comes out 52 weeks a year. A very special clientele - people like Gary Bettman and GMs subscribe to it. And I write hockey freelance stories for assorted magazines.

BOB BOURNE: Right now I have a hockey fantasy camp here in Kelowna [Hockey Greats Fantasy Camp - www.nhlhockey greats.com/site/], which we work on pretty much all year round. We've begun a new foundation, called the Bourne Family & Friends Foundation [www.nhlhockeygreats.com/site/2011-12-21-04-10-55/bb -foundation.html], and trying to raise some money for people with disabilities. My son has spina bifida and has been in a wheelchair all his life, so we're just trying to raise some money and make these people's lives a little bit better.

MIKE McEWEN: I'm doing youth hockey at Oklahoma City [Oklahoma City Youth Hockey Association - okcyouthhockey.com].

I run a beginner program. I coach travel teams, give private lessons, do summer hockey camps. I know every kid and parent in Oklahoma City that plays hockey. I've been doing that for twelve years. I kind of wanted to be a teacher when I was growing up. I don't think they'd let me in the public school system with the language I use. [Laughs] But just having fun with kids. Parents, it's kind of a misnomer with sports - 90% of them are pretty much there for the right reasons, to give their kid a good sporting experience. The 10% are, *whatever.* It's fun and keeps me busy.

DAVE LANGEVIN: I'm a real estate appraiser - I do Wells Fargo appraisals. I coach a high school team [Edina Hornets] in Minnesota with Curt Giles, and we won a State Tournament a couple of years ago. We've got our own little dynasty going on here - we got a few players drafted. It's a lot of fun. And a grandparent, like most of the players.

LORNE HENNING: I'm in Vancouver. I've been working with the Canucks the last seven years - the Assistant GM for the Canucks.

JIMMY DEVELLANO: I'm the senior vice president of the Detroit Red Wings. I'm entering my 30th year with the Red Wings. I'm also starting my eleventh year as the senior vice president of the Central Division Major League Baseball champion Detroit Tigers. And I don't know whether you know what the common thread is - same owner owns both teams [Mike Ilitch], that's the reason that's the way it is. 'The Road to Hockeytown: Jimmy Devellano's Forty Years in the NHL' [is Jimmy's book that was released in 2008], published by Wiley Publishing. It really is the story of my 45 years in the NHL - how I was a boy, how I grew up in Toronto, how I got my first scouting job with the St. Louis Blues, how I met their young coach, Scotty Bowman, who was 33 at the time, how I met the captain of the team, Al Arbour, and how I become associated with Bowman and Arbour in St. Louis.

And how years later, they would intertwine in my life - one with the Islanders, Al Arbour, and then I would bring Scotty in many years later to coach Detroit. And then I go into a little story about how I got canned by the St. Louis Blues in a personality conflict with my boss, and how I get to meet Bill Torrey, who is running an expansion team, and he hires me with the Islanders. And then I go into great detail on the first ten years of the Islanders. Facts, figures, the two ownerships, the coaching changes at the beginning, all the players. And then I talk about my two years in Indianapolis running the Islanders' number one farm team, and then getting the job in Detroit with the Red Wings. And I go into unbelievable detail about my 30 years in Detroit - culminating in the four Cups. It's all there - 'The Road to Hockeytown.'

AL ARBOUR: I'm doing nothing, and I enjoy it! [Laughs]

CLAIRE ARBOUR: We're two retired people, and it seems all we do is run to doctors! We're aging here in Florida. I miss being up there with the kids and doing what we used to do. But you learn to accept where you are and make the best of where you are. It's very pretty here, so I can't complain. We're going to go to New Jersey at our daughter's for Christmas, and the whole family will gather. So that will be nice. It's easier to gather up there then for them to come to here.

BILL TORREY: I'm sitting here in the arena that we built in 1996. I am the alternate governor for the Florida Panthers. At the owner's request two years ago, they asked me to find a general manager to help turn this team around, and I live about an hour away from this rink. I found Dale Tallon, and I think he is doing an outstanding job in rebuilding this franchise. I see him and talk to him almost every day. I help him in whatever way my experience can help him. And I come to the games. I've got grandkids now that are playing hockey, so hockey is part of my life. To me, it's the greatest game.

JEAN POTVIN: I'm a senior vice president with Morgan Keegan [www.morgankeegan.com]. I sell the institutional sales, so I sell their research. In a nutshell, we have 30 analysts, and each analyst covers companies in different sectors, like probably 15 to 20 companies in transportation. It could be in technology, it could be health care, it could be energy. So I sell that research - I cover Canada for Morgan Keegan, which is predominately Montreal and Toronto. So it's SVP, institutional sales. It's Wall Street.

BILLY HARRIS: I've been in the bar business, and nightclubs in Manhattan Beach and Columbus, Ohio. I started this thing as just a summer hobby thing eight years ago, and now...I manufacture soybean wax candles [Muskoka Candle Company - www.muskokacandleco.com]. They're green, they don't pollute - they're not a paraffin wax. That's the big thing about them, they're environmentally friendly and they're all scented. But we started making them for the tourist area up where I live on the lake. And now I've got over a hundred stores I supply, and we do the odd trade show/gift show. But started out just as a little thing - I thought I'd be going back to Columbus in the wintertime, and the restaurant went under. The strike killed us - I had a big restaurant/bar in the arena where the Blue Jackets play. So it was nice, getting back into the hockey world again, and seeing the guys when they'd come in the restaurant. But then this thing started, and it just started getting bigger and bigger.

CLARK GILLIES: I'm sales and marketing for a company by the name of Hilton Capital Management [www.hiltoncapitalmanagement. com], over in Garden City. We're a money manager. I go out and try and market products and just bring assets into the firm for them to manage.

BOB LORIMER: I work with Fiera Capital [www.fieracapital.com] - we're an institutional money manager in Toronto. I've been doing that for the last 20/25 years.

GORD LANE: I own a general contracting business in Maryland [Lane Building Services - lanebuildingservices.com]. I do commercial and residential work.

EDDIE WESTFALL: I'm sitting here at my office at the bank. I've been a banker for 22 years. I hope my boss isn't looking over my shoulder! [Laughs] Hockey's always been a part-time job. I've always had full-time jobs, and this is one I've had for 22 years, going back to '89. I do customer relations for State Bank of Long Island [www.valleynationalbank.com] - a wonderful local bank. When I started, the bank had one branch. Today, we have 17. It's grown nicely and it's a well-run bank.

JP PARISÉ: It is so nice, I waited for decades and decades to be retired. Now, I have no pressure - I do what I want, when I want to. [Laughs] And of course, I follow my sons - Zach plays for the Devils [in 2012, Zach signed with the Minnesota Wild], and then my other son [Jordan] is a goaltender and is currently playing in Germany. There's always one of them playing, so I watch a lot of hockey.

NELSON DOUBLEDAY, JR: I'm retired from everything. I'm having a fun life.

JIGGS McDONALD: I'm supposedly retired. But I come back - I fill in for Howie Rose. Howie had a vacation or the way his contract now is written he is contracted for 70 games. So games he opts to miss for vacation purposes or games that conflict with the Mets [Rose does radio work for the Mets], I manage probably ten games a season for the Islanders. Spend the winters in Florida, the summers in Ontario. Love my grandchildren - wish I had them before I had my two daughters…no. [Laughs] They're just the greatest. Don't see enough of them. Just generally enjoy life.

BRUCE BENNETT: I'm the director of photography for Hockey Imagery for Getty Images. My role includes shooting every major NHL event each season, deciding what games around the NHL will be covered, along with which photographers will cover them. On a nightly basis when I'm out shooting, those images are up on gettyimages.com, and that's open to everyone. And my own site, with portfolios through all the years is brucebennettstudios.com.

BRYAN TROTTIER: Lots of stuff - it seems like the phone never stops ringing, and for that, I'm always grateful. From the standpoint of family, all the kids are doing well and I've got grandkids. Love them all to death. Just enjoying all the kids and all their activities. My son is a doctor in Minnesota, my daughter's married to a Navy SEAL - they're living down in Florida. I've got a fresh, brand new granddaughter. My daughter's senior year in NYU, she's had some great internships in the City. And we have a ten-year-old left at home, and he's our hockey goalie. He's a sports-minded young man. We're enjoying all that in the family.

As far as work is concerned, just doing a ton of events. Speaking engagements, charitable fundraisers, and old timers hockey. A lot of alumni events here in Pittsburgh, because we live here and we do a lot of stuff with the Pens. I try to make myself available to the NHL and the Hall of Fame for their events. No stress. I do a lot of school visits, a lot of community visits - especially the Native Reserves in Canada. Really enjoy that a lot. We get to work with a lot of youngsters in development. Spent four years working with the Islanders working with their young kids, and proud to see a lot of those faces on the Islanders today. Especially the fact that a lot of them are core players.

Trying to develop teenagers, college level kids, and junior hockey level kids into becoming young pros, and giving them some skill sets - on the ice and off the ice. Probably going to push that a little bit more and market that stronger. So that will be a fun thing to do - that's in my blood, I can't get rid of that. It's kind of like coaching kids, and as a 55-year-old-man, I've got a lot left in me to help youngsters achieve their dream to play in the NHL, or get to the highest level they can possibly play. Really enjoying the life of where I'm at. Don't like burying people, but it seems like that's where I'm at in life. That part's not fun. But at the same time, there's a lot of birth, and it seems to happen every day.

JIM PICKARD: I am retired and I live in Tampa, Florida. And life is good.

RON WASKE: Right now, I'm sitting on my lanai in Fort Myers, Florida, looking out over the pond and golf course, and waiting to walk out with Jiggs McDonald and play golf this morning with my wife.

PAT FLATLEY: I'm in the commercial real estate business, in Canada. I have four kids and coaching them all [in hockey]. I've coached a lot of kids over the years. I phoned Al after my first year of coaching nine-year-olds, and I almost had about three strokes that year, just getting so frustrated. [Laughs] I phoned Al, and said, "Al, I think I know why you had all those heart attacks!" *Coaching's tough.*

EDDIE WESTFALL: Mike Bossy works for the Islanders and works with trying to get corporate customers involved with the team [Bossy's title is "Vice President, Corporate Partnerships"]. Don't know [regarding what Billy Smith is currently up to]. I have no idea. My guess would be that he's retired. He used to be a goalie coach around different teams. I haven't heard, talked to, or even had any of the guys I see around Long Island that mention what Billy Smith does or doesn't do.

Denis Potvin left Florida - he was the color analyst for the Florida Panthers. And now he moved back to where he came from - outside Ottawa. I understand he's doing the Ottawa Senators' TV work, as a color analyst. Butch Goring is the color analyst for the Islanders broadcasts for the MSG Network.

Pat LaFontaine runs a foundation [Companions in Courage - www.cic16.org]. They create these rooms - these are kids that are quite sick, and they can communicate with the different hospitals and different kids that have problems. The families and so on. They can communicate with each other through a network of hospitals that Pat LaFontaine has been very good at organizing and putting up the money and making these rooms. It started out in New York State, but it may have expanded beyond that now.

Don't know anything about John Tonelli. The last I heard, he was in a title company. I don't know whether he still is. They do research or properties bought and sold - I haven't seen or talked to him in years.

GLENN "CHICO" RESCH: It was absolutely the best of times to be an Islander on Long Island. It was just magic, electric, and fun, and people were excited. It was the best time you could have ever had as a hockey player, and obviously, the guys who were there for four years experienced it. And guys like me, who were just there for one and three quarters, we were just as thankful, because you don't get those opportunities very often.